Italian Baking Secrets

Also by Father Giuseppe Orsini

COOKING RICE WITH AN ITALIAN ACCENT!

And Writing as Father Joseph Orsini

ITALIAN FAMILY COOKING: UNLOCKING A TREASURY OF RECIPES AND STORIES

FATHER ORSINI'S ITALIAN KITCHEN

Italian Baking Secrets

Father Giuseppe Orsini

THOMAS DUNNE BOOKS
ST. MARTIN'S PRESS ❧ NEW YORK

THOMAS DUNNE BOOKS.
An imprint of St. Martin's Press.

www.thomasdunnebooks.com
www.stmartins.com

Library of Congress Cataloging-in-Publication Data

Orsini, Joseph E.
    Italian baking secrets / Father Giuseppe Orsini.
        p. cm.
    ISBN-13: 978-0-312-35820-4
    ISBN-10: 0-312-35820-2
    1. Baking. 2. Cookery, Italian. I. Title.

TX765.O68 2007
641.8'150945—dc22

                                        2006051186

First Edition: April 2007

10   9   8   7   6   5   4   3   2   1

Contents

Acknowledgments

Ruth Cavin, my editor, and Toni Plummer, my assistant editor.

Thomas Dunne, my friend and publisher.

Joseph Rinaldi and Peter Horan, my friends and publicists.

To Calabria and Sicily, the fertile soil of my family roots.

*To my nieces Carmel O. Ferrante, Jo-Anne Martin, and Inez C. Orsini,
who generously shared their recipes for this book.*

*To all of my friends and family in Italy, who gave me
their special recipes for this book.*

*I must mention Vincenzo Calderone, the only master Italian baker in Bayonne,
who gave me many secret tips about Italian baking that I could pass on to my readers.*

*Finally and foremost, to my God, who inspires me always
to share his truth through my books.*

Italian Baking Secrets

A Brief History of Bread

There are no existing legends or documents that tell us when man began making bread to use in his diet. We know that in prehistory, cultivation of various grains began over eight thousand years before Christ. Most probably, the first grain used to make bread was barley. The use of millet, a more nutritious grain for breads, came next. In Africa and the hot-dry regions of southern Asia, the use of millet was widespread until the end of the Neolithic period. Rye and spelt were used in the Bronze Age as evidenced by the presence of these grains in the caves of that era. The cultivation of wheat was widespread in Western Europe around the fourth century B.C. This indicates that wheat bread is among the most ancient of foodstuffs.

The first step toward bread making began when people began to grind wheat and other grains between two flat rocks. This coarse flour was mixed with water and eaten as cold cereal. When fire was discovered, the grains were toasted to make them tastier and more digestible. When this flour was mixed with water, the dough was cooked on hot flat stones. Thus, the first flat breads came into use. The ancient Egyptians invented the first ovens to bake their flat breads.

The next revolutionary step in bread making was the discovery of yeast. Scientists and archaeologists cannot fix the date when natural fermentation was first found; they guess that someone threw a handful of dough into a dark and warm corner of a cave, forgot about it, and found it days later bubbling with life and smelling sour. This brave unknown person baked the dough anyway, and so the first loaf of leavened bread came into existence. The ancient Egyptians were the first to learn, through experiments, how to control fermentation and became the first bakers of leavened bread in the ancient world.

During the period of Greek civilization, leavened bread baking reached new heights. The ancient Greek bread bakers made fifty different types of loaves. The Romans' conquest of Greece brought bread into the Roman Empire. Bread became the "staff of life" as evidenced in the building of public flour mills and ovens throughout the Roman Empire. It was the Romans who invented flour mills, where grains were ground in between giant slabs of granite, and thus produced finer grades of flour.

It was near the end of the Roman Empire, when the emperors decreed free bread and entertainment for Roman citizens. "Panem et Circenses," bread and circuses, were an effort to maintain a semblance of Roman law among the increasing disorder of the declining Roman Empire.

However, the glorious Empire fell when invaded by the barbarian tribes of France and Germany. This was the beginning of the Middle Ages of European history, when the monks in their monasteries not only preserved great classic literature but the art and science of bread making. The monks began wine making later in history.

Food history is as important to study as an integral element of the history of mankind as are wars, philosophies, theologies, and social movements. Without food there would be no history at all.

Bread in Italy

B read" in Italy is rough country loaves with thick chewy crusts and flat disks of *focaccia* seasoned with the wild herbs of the fields. Their tastes and shapes are fragrant reminders of a tradition of baking that is older than the Roman monuments and Romanesque cathedrals that we travel to Europe to see. These breads are expressions of an earthy culture that still talks about its most fundamental experiences in terms of bread. In Italy, a down-to-earth man with a real heart of gold is described as *buono come il pane*—good, like bread. When Americans talk about being direct and straightforward, we say we're calling a spade a spade, but Italians say *pane al pane e vino al vino,* "calling bread bread and wine wine." Bread gives us real glimpses into the complex and fascinating history of all the regions of the country. Italy wasn't even even united until a little over a hundred years ago, so many of the roots have remained a little more exposed than might be true elsewhere. All the rivalries and bloody battles between neighboring cities and regions brought the inhabitants an intense pride. So just as each village and city had its own bell tower looking over its own fraction of countryside, ready to call citizens to arms and alert them to danger, their breads expressed a passionate attachment to local customs and ingredients.

Bread is so fundamental to everyday eating that the Italians are forever using the word *companatico,* an all-purpose term for what one eats with bread. "What's for lunch?" *Pane e companatico*—bread and something that goes with it. And bread is such a basic part of life that while there are no cookbooks devoted to baking bread at home, many recipes begin "Take 500 grams of bread dough that you've bought from your baker." *Pizzas, focacce,* enriched breads, and holiday breads often begin just that way.

Each day in Italy, more than thirty-five thousand bakers rise early to knead their dough and shape their loaves, and of that number 90 percent are artisan bakers, working on a small scale and dedicated to keeping a family and regional tradition alive. They are preserving the past by making it a living part of the present, but they are also showing the baker's dazzling imagination, producing "new wave" breads that turn the luscious provender of the vines and fields into tantalizing loaves.

They have taken the olive paste of Liguria, made from the first crushing of salty, aromatic olives grown near the sea, and incorporated it into a bread. They have taken pesto and sweet peppers and tomatoes dried by the sun under a dappled screen of latticework arbors: use the humble potato and the most expensive aged cheeses; they have taken dark grains that once belonged to a peasant culture and given them new companions and shapes to make a range of breads that appeal to the Italian passion for *fantasy,* in the most inventive and tantalizing tastes imaginable.

Life without bread is inconceivable in Italy, and yet if I had decided to write this book twenty years ago, it would have been an elegy, a bittersweet testament to breads of another time. In the 1950s and 1960s, massive companies took over the bread baking of Italy, turning out airy white loaves like the spongy, cottony slices Americans know from our own supermarket shelves, and threatening to homogenize a tradition of breads, pastries, cookies, and pizzas that were once the culinary equivalent of Italy's numerous dialects. Gone were the indigenous specialties. The tastes and flavors of the past were interred by high-speed rollers that milled grain to a bland, highly refined flour without texture or nutrients, and by huge machines that mixed and kneaded faster than the human eye could see—by automation that removed the human touch from the most basic of all human food. Suddenly, giant Italian companies were making deals with American consortia to produce biscuits and crackers by the millions to be eaten instead of bread. They were replacing grissini, the archetypal artisan-made bread stick, with pale little batons all the same color and width and length, extruded from the dies of a machine. Gone were the knobby thick bread sticks whose length was determined by the span of the baker's arms. Blandness suddenly ruled, leaving the centuries-old tradition conquered, as one writer puts it, "by the imperialism of city bread."

But just as the monks kept culture and bread alive during a dark time in the country's history, there were a few bakers who refused to follow the new ways. To them—those who safeguarded tradition and perpetuated the taste of the countryside—this book owes its inspiration and its recipes.

In Florence, a pastry and bread baker has given life again to the Tuscan specialties that were once a part of country life and tradition. He put the tastes of this extraordinary landscape into oil-drizzled *schiacciate* and *pizzette* with elegant slices of vegetables and fine powderings of herbs, into festival specialties such as sweet rosemary-scented buns and breads bursting with fat golden *zibibbo* raisins.

A Roman baker made one hundred kilos of pizza a day in his wood-burning ovens in Rome, and rendered the rustic loaves of tiny towns such as Genzano and large cities such as Terni, and created a *coccodrillo* (crocodile) bread that people in Rome travel far across the city to buy.

A Venetian baker has worked in Venice since he was a very young boy. His skill with pastry was phenomenal and his flights of imagination created the *ossa de mordere,* the focaccia laced with zabaglione cream, and the bolzanese in this book. In Venice, too, another baker with forty years of baking experience showed how breads and rolls were made before machines had such a large part in the cutting and shaping of dough. And specialty bakers in Venice all showed me secrets of bread and pastry baking. A baker in Genoa made the true focaccia of the region crammed with the pungent tasty olives of Liguria and the fresh herbs of the hillsides.

Truckloads of breads from Altamura fan out across the countryside to Milan and Turin in the north and to tiny villages deep on the heel of the boot. I have shaped and dimpled pizza dough in Naples, watched bakers in Palermo making calzones and cassatas, and eaten their brioches filled with ice cream, as all the Palermitani do for breakfast. In Palermo, I learned about *mafalda* and *sfinciuni,* the bread and pizza specialties of the city, and wouldn't leave without tasting everything in the "Spinato" bakery. These and many more are the sources of the recipes and folklore of Italian bread, and they are the bakers who day after day make the breads and sweets that bring these tastes to the fortunate Italians who eat them at breakfast and dinner, over coffee and aperitifs in the trattorie and restaurants, coffee bars and piazze, where the people of Italy live out their lives.

The revival of bread and a new pride in its myriad forms has led real aficionados to wonder why different breads aren't served with each course, in the same spirit as wine.

If wine is made by transforming grapes, yeast, and water, and bread is made by the alchemical fusion of flour, water, yeast, and salt, why not confirm its regional authenticity with some special highly respected authority such as a D.O.C. classification. D.O.C. means "determination of origin controlled," as is done with wines.

Seeing really good bakers at work can be eye opening. When they roll out the dough, their touch can be as delicate as a lover's caress, and when they knead, their authority can almost command the dough to respond. They can take an inert and colorless piece of dough and with their fingers give it form, elasticity, and vitality.

The pale white dust that sifts over everything, and the sounds of the slapping and banging of the dough as it hits the table right out of the mixer, the thunk of the canvas carrier being snapped into the oven and then retracted—the smells, and the sights—all make the bakery a special world of its own.

Knowing the story and tastes of the regional breads that come out of these ovens is like taking a trip through the Italian countryside. Savoring and honoring them is like preserving the stone villages on the hillsides or their churches and frescoes, for saving the taste of the past keeps it alive in the present. The bakers who are committed to rediscovering the past and creating new ways of eating in the present do honor to the oldest of man's foods and to authentic Italian tradition, for bread is one of the most persuasive images of man's struggle to survive. No wonder baking is called *l'arte bianco,* the white art, for the mystical life-giving magic of yeast creates nourishment that sustains a people and keeps alive memories connecting the collective past to the world of today.

Bread is merely flour, water, yeast, and salt as the world is merely earth, water, fire, and air. These four elemental ingredients—grain from the fields, water from rivers and mountain streams, leavening from the wild yeasts of the air, and salt from the sea—have been combined since Roman days to make the breads of Italy. In a country where the family is the primary source of physical and emotional sustenance, bread celebrates the richest and simplest pleasures of daily living. It is the single inevitable presence at the table during all three meals of the day, for no Italian would contemplate a meal without bread.

Bread is such a basic part of life in Italy that every restaurant automatically sets it on the table and imposes a cover charge (*coperto*) to cover its cost. Almost every street in Italy's large and middle-sized cities seems to have at least one *panificio* (bakery) and *pasticceria* (pastry shop), and even tiny towns without bread ovens have a grocery store where bread is delivered warm in the mornings from nearby bakeries. It is calculated that Italians eat almost half a pound of bread a day, the highest consumption in all of Europe, a statistic that translates to 4.5 billion pounds of bread a year.

Even the academic body that serves to maintain the purity of the Italian language is called Academia della Crusca—the Academy of Bran—for it sees itself as sifting the wheat from the chaff. Its symbol is an agricultural flour sifter.

Walk past a bakery and you'll often see displays of grains set in the window so people can learn about what they are eating. Go inside and you'll notice that every bread is labeled not only with its name but also with every ingredient, as well as the price per kilo. Bread is so basic to a sense of well-being that local governments regulate the prices of the traditional breads of the commune, keeping it affordable for anyone with but a few euros in their pockets. The saltless bread of Tuscany, which is very cheap in Florence and Siena, can be sold for any price outside regional limits, though most of the people of, say, Milan and Rome have no cravings for or childhood ties to saltless bread. Anyone from the countryside around Chianti, however, or from the little hill towns that have sat in this landscape since the Etruscans first sited them, will tell you that saltless bread is part of a heritage that stretches back long before Dante.

A Tuscan would no more choose to eat a Roman *pagnotta* or a Milanese *michetta* than he would expect to find Wiener schnitzel on his dinner plate. So how could it come as a surprise that each region boasts variations on its breads and ingredients and makes its local tastes into breads that define a small geographical area?

How could it be otherwise in a country that has a dial-a-message service for regional recipes? Each day, the recording gives a new recipe for a dish from each of the regions of Italy. And how could it be otherwise in a country scarred in medieval times by cities that chose to fight ferociously with their closest neighbors to prove their supremacy, their dedication to local alliances finally leading them to stamp their own identity not only on the landscape but on the foods as well? This rich, complex, and combative heritage influences Italian baking and is embellished by the reality that everyone from the Saracens to the Austrians conquered different regions and left their culinary signature behind. The porous and crunchy-crusted Pugliese bread of the south is a legacy of the brown country loaf brought by the Ruks who long ago walked the streets of Apulia, and the famous michetta roll of Milan was born of the Kaiser Semmel of Vienna, which was brought to Milan by the Austrian cavalry in the late 1800s.

In the country at large, there are more names for the shapes of bread than Eskimos have words for snow. This is a very fragmentary list:

Azzimo (unleavened), *casareccio* (homemade), *ciabatta* (slipper), *ciambetta* (wreath), *corolla* (crown), *manini* (little hands), *mattone* (brick), *pagnotta* (round loaf), *panino* (roll), *piadina* (flat disk), *quattrocorni* (four horns), *ruota* (wheel), *schiacciate* (flattened), *sfliantio* (long, thin thread), *stella* (star), *tegola* (tile), *treccia* (braid). Italian bakers say there may be somewhere between one thousand and two thousand different breads in the national repertory, although "only" a few hundred are commonly available, and while there are numerous typical regional breads—*biove* from Piedmont, *ciopa* from Venice, *crocetta* from Ferrara, *minichette* from Milan, and saltless loaves from Tuscany—each type may have slight variations attributable to individual bakers. The taste of bread is so much a product not only of local ingredients, of the humidity of the air, and the quality of the water, but of the fingers and hands of the baker, that people know immediately when a local baker has died, because the bread suddenly tastes different.

Secrets and techniques for making bread have been handed down from baker to baker through the years, and they belong to an oral tradition like folk tales and peasant wisdom. Apprentices learn by watching and asking and doing, since this is a tradition that relies not on specific recipes but on formulas that are expressed in proportions. I once asked a baker how he made the chewy, crunchy crusted bread of his region and he told me "Use 2 percent yeast, 2 percent flour." I knew exactly what he meant, but his answer left a few loose ends for me. How long did he mix the ingredients? Did the dough rise twice or three times its original size to produce the special texture? Was the water cool or warm? The bakers' formulas are merely guidelines; knowledgeable baking depends on touch, taste, sight, smell, and experience, knowing when to add a little water or when to work the dough a little longer. Clearly, the flexible formula leaves room for the baker's individuality, his personal touches, and flashes of imagination that put his stamp on the bread and make it his own. These recipes do not exist anywhere in written form. Unlike the French, who make numerous regional breads and sweets according to quantified recipes and a codified tradition, Italian bakers are forever experimenting and dreaming up new interpretations. If forty bakers at Lake Como are making ciabatta, you can be sure there will be forty slightly different tastes.

These breads of Italy have their fragrance, their color, and their flavor, but most also have their raison d'être. Most Italian breads are soft, but the tradition of hard breads is rooted with a people who needed their basic nourishment to keep for a long time. Sardinian shepherds carry wafer-thin *carasau* bread, big flat crackly disks also called *carta di musica* (sheet music bread), for its parchment color and fine veining of horizontal lines. The *frisedde* of Puglia, the *gallete* of seagoing sailors, and the *ciambelle valtelline* of the cold north, where snow isolates regions for weeks at a time, are all hard breads made to last for months. When eaten, they are dipped into water or broth, or moistened with slices of tomato, flavored with oil, salt, pepper, and herbs such as oregano that grow wild in the countryside, then perhaps topped with slices of cheese like the Venetian *pani biscotti,* biscuits that are rather like hardtack, were a perfect provision for sailors or even businessmen who went to sea for months at a time. They were made, as their name implies, by being twice cooked (*biscotto*) to draw off almost all the moisture and produce a very light, long-lasting biscuit that couldn't possibly mold or go bad. It is said that both Marco Polo and Christopher Columbus relied on biscotti on their long voyages.

There are many rituals and elements of etiquette connected with bread. In Tuscany and Puglia, big rounds of crusty rustic loaves are always held in the crook of the elbow and sliced toward the chest. Knowing how to cut bread is as important to an Italian man as learning how to carve meat is to an American.

In Italy, bread is an object of respect, a sign of the grace of providence, which is treated with almost sacramental reverence. Mothers teach their children that no one is allowed to waste a crumb of bread. Should a single bit accidentally fall to the floor, it must be picked up, immediately cleaned off, and eaten. It is said that anyone wasting bread will be condemned to a purgatory for as many years as there were crumbs and will be compelled to collect each little bit upon the eyelids, one at a time. A loaf of bread placed upside down on a table will bring bad luck. No one should even leave a knife plunged into the crust of bread because it is like the flesh of the Lord, and the person responsible will never again partake of grace. Bakers always make the sign of the cross over the oven and often make it in the dough itself before baking, as many peasants do before taking a first bite of a freshly baked loaf. Bread is so powerful that even the smell of it is believed to have healing power.

Some forms of bread have roots in prehistory, and are charged to this day with symbolic significance. Round *pan di morte* bread of the dead appears in late October, and cookies called *ossa di morte* and *fave di morte* are eaten in honor of the dead on the Day of the Dead on November 2, All Souls' Day. On those days families participate in ceremonies meant to show the dead that they have not been forgotten and continue to share in the life of the family. The tibia-shaped *ossa di morte* cookies are eaten all over Italy, from Lombardy to Sicily, and are known regionally as *ossa da moredere, oss de mord, ossi da morto, oss tinchetti.* Outsiders may find these little nougats a bit strange as Paul Valerie did on a trip to Italy in 1834, when he made it very clear that he didn't care for "this horrible confection," to which he attributed the ancient reputation of the Umbrians for ferocity. He had a point—Umbrian history is nothing short of hair-raising before the seventeenth century—but the bone-shaped cookies seem a bit more abstract than the serpent-shaped cakes of Perugia and Umbria, which are bristling with primitive associations; they are phallic symbols.

In Calabria for the feast day of San Rocco (whose specialty is protecting against contagious diseases), bakers shape *panpepati,* which are similar to spicy Italian gingerbread cakes, into ex-votos that represent various parts of the body. A parade of local pilgrims winds through the city streets on its way to a statue of the saint, where they offer these baked arms, legs, heads, and various organs decorated with the imagination of the local bakers. They are collected the next day in a huge basket and sold at auction to support the singers and comics, puppeteers, actors, band players, and makers of fireworks whose arts furnish the ceremonies for the saint's day.

In three of the most rustic regions of Italy, Puglia, Basilicata, and Calabria, where the poor generally eat only the darker, lesser grains, wheat bread is given only to the dying ("he has arrived at the bread" is the local proverb) and to women about to give birth.

In some remote mountain communities in the Alto Adige, the Val d'Aosta, and the Trentino, far in the north of Italy, superstitions surround the choice of days that are most propitious for the baking of bread. It is universally agreed that bread must never be made on days when the furrows of the earth are open for the sowing of the wheat, for then the bread would mold. Some say that the moon must be rising, others say that it should be in its last quarter, but there is no question that the worst time for making bread is at the first sign of the new moon, which would surely bewitch the loaves. Some folk wisdom maintains that bread must be baked in the early morning, for it swells in the oven in harmony with the ascension of the sun. In the same spirit, breads in their round shapes are seen as being like the sun, which appears anew every day to keep away darkness and make the earth grow grains.

Braided breads, which surfaced in the late Middle Ages, are also richly symbolic. In ancient days, women were expected to join their dead husbands in their tombs, but over time human sacrifice was replaced by the symbolic sacrifice of the woman's braided hair. When women were finally allowed to keep their hair, the symbol was replaced by a loaf of bread plaited like a braid, which was given to the poor instead of being placed in the grave.

Some breads are literally meant to carry the blessings of home and church. Traditional rolls made only for Calabrians who are leaving their native countryside are stamped with an image of the Madonna and then blessed by a priest before they are entrusted to the departing family.

Breads created to celebrate New Year's Day, Easter, or marriage ceremonies are hard to tell apart because all three deal with beginnings, which must be nourished with the most affirmative symbols. Votive breads in south and central Italy take the form of wheat sheaves, clusters of swollen grapes, and doll-like figures called *pupazze*. All three have overtones of fertility and religion. The pupazze made for Easter always have a red egg tucked under each arm. Red is the color of fertility, and an egg represents renewal in both pagan and church terms. These breads celebrate birth and rebirth and new beginnings in physical, emotional, and religious connotations and they celebrate as well the sensuality inherent in the stalks of wheat that are plaited and plowed in the warmth of mother earth.

The simple aromatic breads of the countryside are more than the flavors and smells of ancient culture. They are rife with sexual symbolism. The *banana* and *barlino* from the Emilia Romagna region and various Venetian breads are rolled into unmistakably phallic shapes or curved with a round *ciambelle* with a hole in the center. The high swollen shapes of softer *pagnotta pasquale* (Easter bread) are as round as breasts or pregnant bellies. Some breads, such as the *coppiette* of Ferrara, are barely disguised images of coupling, which were once made to propitiate the forces of nature and encourage the fertility of the fields. Bakers in some small towns in Lazio still make breads in the form of women with three cone-shaped breasts, recalling Diana of Ephesus who had one hundred breasts and represented the mythic ferocity of fertility.

The sweets and breads of Sicily are especially rich with sexual imagery. Little almond treats called "breasts of the virgin" (*mammelle di vergine*) are shaped just as you might imagine and are surprisingly prized most by the nuns who created them. Don Fabrizio in Lampedusa's *The Leopard* asks for the "virgin cakes" at a huge sumptuous party in Sicily. As he looks at them on his plate, he sees a profane caricature of Saint Agatha, and exclaims, "Why didn't the Holy Office forbid these cakes when it had the chance? Saint Agatha's sliced-off breasts sold by convents, devoured at dances! Well, well!" To this day, phallic babas and plump round brioche cakes come with a squish of cream and the crown of a single fat berry. Succulent images of sexuality line the glass cases of bakeries all over Palermo.

Italy is a landscape of hundreds of small protected valleys enclosed within mountain chains and dramatic seacoasts. Its valleys and soft open plains are etched with pale ribbons of rivers and stone walls and punctuated with silvery olive trees, rows of grapevines, and ancient stone villas. Even today, much of it looks as it did in the Renaissance paintings from which we still preserve our image of the country. In this countryside, the historical roots of bread are no less significant than the geography that produced the regional tradition and the peasant culture that gave it its flavor.

The Romans learned to bake from the Greeks, who followed the victorious Roman armies back to Rome in 170 B.C. and revolutionized the practice of bread baking that had belonged to housewives for centuries. The Greeks were great bakers who made more than fifty kinds of bread, milling their grain to very fine flour. They actually worshiped bread, which was intimately tied to religious rituals that centered on Demeter, goddess of grain and abundance. Demeter originally made the earth dry and infertile while she searched for her daughter Persephone, who had been kidnapped by Pluto and taken to the underworld. She pleaded with Zeus for the girl's release, but only after she refused to allow grain to grow was the god forced to restore Persephone to her mother for half the year, the period corresponding to the sowing, ripening, and threshing of the fields. The famous Eleusinian mysteries, which revolve around Demeter, celebrate the force of feminine fertility that is profoundly tied to the fertility of the earth. In Sicily to this day, an annual holiday in honor of Demeter and Persephone includes offerings of sesame-and-honey focacce shaped like women's sexual organs. They are intended to make the goddess laugh and to distract her from the sadness brought on by her daughter's disappearance.

Before they ever tasted or made bread, the Romans ate *puls*, a kind of mush of grains boiled in water, a predecessor of polenta. It was made of millet or, more commonly, spelt, a grain called *farro* in Latin, which comes from the root for *farina*, which is the Italian word for flour. By 147 B.C., the Greek slaves who tended the ovens in Roman bakeries had taught the Romans their trade, and those Romans had become so important that they were given social status and rank and had formed a professional corporation that had very strict rules about the quality and ingredients used in making bread. Bakery owners were generally freed slaves—the second mayor of Pompeii was one—but once a man became a baker, he could never change work, and his sons and sons-in-law after him were obliged to follow the trade as well.

Bread baking reached its greatest moment around 25 B.C. in the time of Emperor Augustus, when there were 329 public bakeries in Rome alone. The bakers leavened bread by using a bit of dough from the baking of the day before or by adding beer yeast, which they had learned about from the Gauls and Germans. They made saltless sponges, called *biga*—as they are today—by fermenting wheat flour with grape must, sprouted barley, or bran soaked in white wine. They also made enriched breads with milk, eggs, oil, honey from Greece and Asia Minor, anise, poppy seeds, nuts, cheese, and sesame seeds. They even developed some baking forms, such as the long, thin sandwich bread mold still in use today.

The big central bread market in Rome boasts round breads; breads notched into eight sections, which are easy to break off into individual pieces; breads shaped like keys, cubes, or braids; breads that look like mushrooms; and breads that look like wreaths. Each social class had its own bread—senators' bread, knights' bread, citizens' bread, people's and peasants' bread. White bread was already a status symbol, even though some writers note that darker, coarser loaves were healthier and gave sustenance to hard-working peasants and farmers. The rich used *siligo*, the finest wheat flour, which was so white that the women of Rome powdered their faces with it. Pliny noted that in some places bread was named after the dishes eaten with it, such as "oyster bread," in others from its special delicacy, as "cake bread," and those called "hasty bread," from the short time spent making it. Even the method of baking gave the bread a title, such as "oven bread," or "tin loaf," or "baking pan" bread.

In those days, breads were made with wheat, millet, and rye. Bran was usually baked into loaves that were tossed to the dogs; oats were fed to cattle. A clever Roman baker dreamed up a labor-saving mechanical kneader that was powered by a horse or donkey trudging in circles, churning the water, flour, and leavening inside a big basin, the KitchenAid mixer of its day. Whereas flour was originally made by crushing grain with a mortar and pestle, then sifting it through a fine cloth, it was now ground between two hourglass-shaped stones that were rotated by mules. The word for the grinding action was *a pistor*, a term still used today in Venice to define a baker; elsewhere in Italy, a baker is called a *fornnaio* or *panettiere*, from the words for oven and bread.

Bakers' brick and stone ovens insulated hot air in a hollow square space set within an arched opening; wood from tree branches provided the heat, and there was even a container for water so that humidity would make crisp crusts. The Romans celebrated June 9 as the festival of Fornax, goddess of the ovens, by decorating oven mouths with flowers and hanging wreaths from the necks of the mules that turned the mills.

Wheat and bread shaped the destiny of Rome and were intimately tied to its rise and fall. In early Roman days, all land belonged to the state, except for small parcels of acreage given to soldiers returning home from the wars. The state protected the farmers, but as its ambitions grew, its need for more capital led to the decision to lease the land to the rich. These wealthy landlords, who forced small farmers to abandon their fields, were able to combine parcels of land into vast estates. Rather than grow wheat, they turned their farmland into pasture, which was more profitable. Wheat growing was virtually abandoned, and the small farmers were forced to the city, where they melted into the growing mass of the dispossessed and unemployed. Ceasar, Augustus, and Nero provided free grain to keep the restive unemployed from rebelling, hoping that bread and circuses would distract them, but each ruler was forced to import ever greater amounts. The constant search for more and more grain was partially responsible for the expansion of the Roman empire. While Trajan established the first bakers' school in A.D. 100, the architect Vitruvius discovered hydraulic milling, which could produce much more flour from the same amounts of grains. Rome continued to swallow up territory until the empire stretched from Britain to the deserts of Africa and grew too large to be controlled by a single ruler. When the empire was divided between east and west, Rome lost control of the vast wheat fields of Egypt and Africa, which fed its population. The end of the wheat supply coincided almost precisely with the fall of the empire. Barbarian tribes plunged across the borders and virtually dismembered the state. The once rich-arable land that had been given over to pasture reverted to swamp. Bread, as the Romans knew it, disappeared from Rome and the farther reaches of Italy. For a while, whatever bread existed was baked at home and was contrived of roots, beans, acorns, and minor grains.

Surprisingly, Byzantine general Belisarius built mills at the end of the Tiber, and produced enough grain to fill the needs of sixth-century Rome. But it was at the monasteries that fields were cultivated and bread first baked again, under the watchful eyes of the monks. To get on with their work and studies, these monks needed every labor- and time-saving device they could find. The powerful hydraulic milling machines they put to work again were major forces behind the rebirth of bread making. It became more important after 800, when Charlemagne came to power. Mills multiplied and eating became more than keeping body and soul together. In the years that followed, rich lords with great castles and estates took control of much of the countryside. The peasants used what grains were left to make their daily bread. People collected in cities once again—in self-defense as much as anything else, since they needed security against those nobles who were decimating the landscape with their power struggles. As urbanization proceeded, bakers organized guilds as they had in Roman times.

The breads of the Middle Ages were as stratified as Roman bread. There was bread for the Pope, bread for knights and pages, bread for the cavalry, bread for priests, and bread for soldiers, as well as the little loaves of rye and wheat meant for everyday eating. Bread was so basic to daily nourishment and survival that during many battles a bread baker always rode off with the soldiers, bringing his iron oven and his grain to bake *gallete* and loaves for the army.

These late medieval centuries were the years of a new spirit of independence, when regional identities were being forged. Just as each area had its own currency and customs (imagine having to clear customs several times on a trip between Milan and Florence, and you begin to get the picture), each region had its own ingredients, and its own attitudes about bakers and bread. Verona and Padua had baking corporations before 1200, which made them avant-garde for the times. In Venice, where bakers had already been at work in the first years of the eleventh century, there were strict laws about quality control. If bread was discovered to be short weighted, it was distributed to the poor; if the quality was below standard, it was crumbled into pieces and tossed off the Rialto Bridge. By 1280, artisan bakers in

Florence had already collected in professional guilds and were baking breads and sweets in the city's 146 ovens. Although Florence's church-influenced sumptuary laws prohibited serving more than one dish per course, some bakers got around the problem by layering all kinds of meats and vegetables in a single dish, wrapping them in pastry, and cooking them all under the embers. What they pulled out of the fire were meat and vegetable tarts, born as a strategy of having one's cake, so to speak, and eating it, too.

Things were entirely different in Rome, where bread making, like everything else, had fallen into a deplorable state after the popes left for Avignon. When they returned in 1378, there were only thirty thousand people in the city. The popes knew that they had to do something to revive urban life, so they imported a number of foreigners, including German bakers. We know that bread was the basic food of the city, either by itself or with a *companatico* (something to eat with bread), because carefully kept records show that bakers used 85 to 90 percent of the grain that came into the city. Pasta was barely eaten at all and bread baked at home by individuals was extremely rare. White breads were made and sold only in special separate luxury shops. Dark loaves accounted for the vast majority of what was baked and eaten.

And what of Milan, the city that now symbolized urban sophistication? Milan didn't have a single independent baker in the Middle Ages because the bakers were all under the thumb of the powerful ruling Visconti family until the end of the sixteenth century. Which isn't to say that bread didn't have a powerful position. To the contrary, the only people in the city who could be elected to the medieval parliament of Milan had to produce their own bread and wine, which says a lot about who the producers were as well as the position of bread. Please understand that we're not talking about white bread here, the Milanese ate millet bread called pan *de mei*, the ancestor of today's corn loaves, or they ate breads that were either totally dark or made of mixed greens.

Progress was substantially set back by the plagues of the fourteenth century. The Black Death marched across the cities of Italy, decimating as much as 40 percent of their populations and bringing with it famine and hunger for many Italians, and bread became a mere memory. The high cost of wheat compelled some bakers to come up with whatever substitutions they had at hand. Many of them found themselves mixing rye, corn, and millet or grinding acorns, using hard wheat instead of soft, or even baking with elm leaves and roots mixed in. Some bakers resorted to mixing in clay from the earth to make their loaves look whiter. Many of the best bakers gave up their ovens. To cope with the shortage, the pope effectively municipalized bread by opening numerous bread ovens in Rome. Still, as late as the eighteenth century, the poor were rioting around the famous fountains in the Piazza Navona with placards lettered "Let these cobblestones turn into bread."

Although cooks in Renaissance Italy devised sophisticated techniques of bread baking, the Italians lost their supremacy as bakers to the Viennese, who opened their first coffeehouses in 1782, offering phenomenal sweets and pastries that made Vienna the capital of elegant baking. New high-speed roller mills turned out cheap and plentiful white flour, the basic material not only for these sweets but for bread.

The French shared honors with the Viennese in the field of baking. While white bread had once been reserved for the rich, the soldiers of Napoleon's army introduced it to the masses as they made their way across the continent. French bread became synonymous with bread. When Napoleon sold Venice to the Austrians in 1797, the Hapsburgs brought with them an army of inhabitants whose gastronomic traditions were enthusiastically accepted. They made the *kipfel,* a croissant-like pastry that is still a great favorite at breakfast, and a century later the Austrian cavalry brought the *michetta*, the quintessential roll of Milan. The contribution of other cultures made an impact in Italy as well. America contributed her ingredients: the tomato, which eventually made a perfect marriage with Neapolitan pizza: the potato, the pimento, vanilla, and chocolate transformed the pastries of Turin; and the corn that was milled and then baked into delicate round cakes and heartier breads. Much earlier gifts from the Saracens—citrus fruits, grappa, and distilled spirits—and the Arab contributions of anise, nuts, almond paste, spices, and sugar gave special inflections to the cooking of Sicily and the south. The culinary signatures of invaders, conquerors, and explorers are all part of the heritage that remains today.

It wasn't until the beginning of the twentieth century that Pellegrino Artusi, a Florentine, rekindled Italian culinary pride by writing a cookbook that preserved genuine Italian cooking and gave respect to the regional tradition of the middle-class food in the north. The book is chatty and amusing, and a fair number of its recipes are based on bread.

It could be said that an undercurrent common to these centuries was a class struggle between the *bocche di pane*, bread eaters who had white breads on their tables, and *bocche da biada*, literally "fodder eaters," peasants and members of the rural and urban poor who ate only dark breads made of whatever grains and beans the land offered up. In Italy, bread has always been a symbol of quality of life, and the quality of bread has always been a statement of social distinction. The privileged ate white bread even in Roman times.

Until the last decade, dark breads have been identified with deprivation and hunger in the collective memory of Italy. The identification was particularly intense during the years when scarcities forced people to rely on *pane selvaggi*, breads made of whatever seeds and grains could be harvested from the countryside. (For centuries, scarcity has been the mother of invention in Italian baking. A baker in Venice reports that as recently as World War II, he mixed sawdust with whatever grain he had, and used water straight from the sea to compensate for a scarcity of salt.)

Today it is rare to find many people baking at home. When there's a bakery on every block or in every neighborhood there's scarcely a need to, but there are still pockets where the old ways prevail, among both the poor and the more privileged. In these places, almost always in the countryside, bread is baked in wood-burning ovens every few days by women who keep a nugget of natural yeast from one baking to the next. In the south, women share the yeast, passing it from household to household. Where once there were numerous communal ovens where women of the community took turns baking the breads, their hours assigned on the basis of seniority, today there are very few. These women know the temperature of the interior of the brick oven as it changes during the day, know where the hot spots are, and where to put the breads so they will bake correctly. In the heyday of communal ovens, when there were numerous loaves being baked together, women would score their doughs with a special identifying mark on the top.

The old and honorable bakery tradition, with its roots that reach deep into the Roman past, changed with the advent of high-speed machinery, but things really took a turn for the worse in the 1950s and 1960s when huge machines were introduced that mixed and kneaded practically at the speed of light and produced cottony breads and bland grissini. To many people they were a denial of the art of the Italian baker, which was nourished by an agrarian past and by a passionate attachment to local ingredients and customs.

The counterrevolution of the past several years is again changing the face of baking. It is not that industrial methods have been banished but that the conformity and lack of imagination connected with them are being challenged by artisan bakers. These men (and a tiny number of women) have touched a profoundly sensitive nerve in Italians who remember the true tastes of breads, pizzas, focacce, and sweets. They are restoring the real taste to bread, and bringing back a tradition that offers the best of genuine fragrancy that has given pleasure to Italians for centuries.

Baking Basics

In these recipes I have tried to re-create the breads and pastries, the focacce, biscotti, and cakes that I have lingered over in Italian cities, towns, and those tiny entities of geography that are called fraz, for *frazione* (fraction), because they contain only a handful of buildings and really are splinters of the larger nearby community. These recipes are a means to bring the tastes of the Italian countryside to the American table and evoke memories of a way of life in which bread and the food it accompanies are shared among friends and family. As many of the recipes come from small towns that are off the beaten track or are baked for special holidays or to commemorate ancient regional practices, only travelers who have strayed from the usual hotel and restaurant route will have found them. No matter: Try the breads and pastries this way first, then go to the country and sample them in context.

I have tried to keep these baked goods tasting as they do in Italy. I haven't sweetened the breads or added ingredients that would please the American palate, though I have reduced the amount of sugar in a few of the desserts and cookies; the Italian sweet tooth didn't get its fame undeservedly. Occasionally, I have made an ingredient or two optional; the Italian passion for candied fruit is not reciprocated in the United States, so I have used candied orange peel as a substitute from time to time and required candied fruit only when a recipe truly couldn't do without it. When I have made an ingredient optional, I have often noted how the Italians would use it. I have specified the best-quality ingredients, using butter where some bakeries use vegetable fats or oils. (If your preferences run to vegetable oils, canola, and/or corn oil, you can certainly use them, especially in the breads.) In light of the current national preoccupation with reducing our intake of animal fats, you may prefer to use olive oil in place of lard, although it is lard that gives some of these breads and focacce their special taste and texture. I do suggest that Americans try to use whatever Italian ingredients are available.

The recipes in this book are all Italian. They began in huge quantities—20 kilos of flour is not an uncommon starting point, but they have been scaled down, reworked or tested so that they can be made in an ordinary American kitchen, using American ingredients that most closely approximate their Italian counterparts. I've given weight as well as volume for measures of all dry ingredients because it is a much more accurate way of measuring—4 cups of flour can vary by as much as 100 grams, depending on how the flour is scooped and packed into the measuring cup. I much prefer weighing flour; but for the sake of simplicity, I have given all measurements for active dry yeast in teaspoons, using 2½ teaspoons per packet (7 grams) as a general rule of thumb. Many of these recipes, especially those calling for a starter, use much less yeast than traditional American recipes, and as a result bring out the mellow, nutty flavor of the grain. Italian bakers never use sugar to activate yeast, but I do. But where sugar is called for, it is part of the recipe's ingredients. Italian bakers have used mixers since a baker designed the first automatic kneading machine in ancient Rome, and things have only grown bigger and faster since that time. I have given instructions for making the breads with an electric mixer such as KitchenAid or Kenwood. (Please don't even think of using a handheld mixer; it doesn't have the power to engage these bread doughs, and all you'll get for your trouble is a burned-out motor.)

You will find descriptions of the various ingredients and equipment called for in the full range of these recipes, and a review of the basic steps of bread baking and pastry making. Please read these sections carefully, and refer to them whenever you need a bit of clarification. The one ingredient and technique not specifically listed in this chapter is *patience.* Rome wasn't built in a day and some of its breads need a little time to let their character mature. Should your plans change after you've embarked on bread baking, and your presence be required somewhere other than the kitchen, just leave the dough in a cool spot or in the refrigerator. Please don't let bread baking dictate your day.

The Ingredients

The regional breads of Italy are made only with flour, water, yeast, and common salt, because that is the law of the land. "Special bread," another category entirely, may be enriched with milk, oil, or lard and flavored with the dazzling products of the countryside, including myriad types of olives, vegetables, and grains from the earth, spices, herbs, fruits, raisins, nuts, and various essences and aromas. But it is the basic four ingredients that become the traditional rustic bread of the country, and to trace their flavors from Lugano in the north to Sicily off the toe of the boot is to make an odyssey in history and taste. It is how they are measured and mixed, and in what proportions, how they are left to rise and be shaped, that determine their ultimate texture and taste, for these are the variables that give each bread its individual personality.

Flour/Farina

Flour in Italy. Bakers in Italy think it's impossible to find flour in America that isn't wonderful. *Manitoba* is a code word for fine flour, since the powerful wheats of the American and Canadian prairies absorb considerably more water and produce large and more expansive dough than the common Italian grain. Bakers spoke of it with admiration and a tone of distant longing, for the Italian earth, which remains so hospitable to grapes and olives, has been so consistently exploited that today it produces weak grains that lack the strength and flavor of the grain of the past. Some Italian flours may have as much gluten as ours, but they are unable to absorb the water and then free it when the baking process requires. Many Italian bakers give a boost to their dough by mixing in some of the higher-gluten, stronger American flour they admire, to approximate our all-purpose flours.

Flour in Italy comes commonly from the species *Triticum aestivum*, which is divided into two major varieties—soft wheat and hard wheat (*grano tenero*)—and from which almost all bread is made. Durum hard grain (*grano duro*), or *Triticum durum*, a different species, is the hardest wheat grown, and is usually milled into semolina. It is a golden grain that has a higher protein and gluten content and is used almost exclusively for pasta production. The creamy, silky golden durum flour makes wonderful bread, used alone or in combination with unbleached or all-purpose flour, but it does need to be mixed and kneaded for a longer time. The Italian baker has five grades of *grano tenero* to choose from, although they are classified not by strength and protein content like ours but by how much of the husk and whole grain have been sifted away. The whitest flour has the least fiber; the lower the number, the more refined and whiter the flour, so that of the five categories, "00" is the whitest and silkiest flour, "0" a bit darker and less fine, since it contains about 70 percent of the grain, "1" even darker, "2" darker and coarser, which almost entirely disappeared from Italy. *Integrale*, or whole wheat, contains the whole wheat, berry husk, wheat germ, and varies only depending on how it is milled. If you were intent on reproducing Italian "00" flour, you could mix about one part pastry flour with nine parts unbleached all-purpose flour, but, ironically, the white flours have the least nutrition of all the refined flours. Bran is taken out in an industrial process and used frequently for feeding animals. For all the talk of the prevalence of healthy nutrients and vitamins in whole grain, it's very expensive, since the refining process is so costly. Unfortunately, it doesn't follow that healthier whole wheat flours are cheaper, because most mills have adapted the Mediterranean diet, which uses white flour; only about 2 percent of Italian breads are made with whole wheat. The health revolution is only beginning. And in one of the stranger twists in the contemporary story of flour, I have heard of millers who simply take refined white flour, stir in a quantity of bran, and pronounce it whole wheat.

In the United States, we are used to thinking of flour in terms of its strength, which is measured by the amount of gluten-forming protein, although there is enormous variation in flours from region to region. The hard winter wheat produces strong bread flour with a high 13 to 15 percent gluten-forming content, and it must be kneaded longer and harder than other flours. Soft wheat, grown in the hot months between spring and autumn, when it is harvested, is much lower in gluten, usually 4 to 9 percent, and it is generally used for cake and pastry flours.

Most recipes in this book can be made with all-purpose flour, which is a blend of the two, although at 11 or 12 grams of protein per cup, which is how we determine the percentage of gluten, it is slightly stronger than its Italian counterpart. If you can find stone-ground flour that hasn't lost its natural qualities from a speeded-up milling process, I'd encourage you to use it. I generally use unbleached flour, which is confusingly misnamed, as the aging process, a characteristic it shares with Italian flours, bleaches it. No chemicals, however, give it its color. Our flours are enriched with thiamine, riboflavin, niacin, and iron and have a small amount of added malt. (Italians add malt as a grain extract to their doughs to encourage their rising and the golden bloom of their crusts, and they also use a tiny addition of ascorbic acid, a form of vitamin C, intended to mature the dough.)

Many of the major brands of all-purpose flour note on the package that the flour has been pre-sifted. Actually, once a bag of flour has left the miller, been trucked to a grocery store, put on the shelf, and then brought home with you, it couldn't possibly still be sifted. Just treat it like unsifted flour and, if possible, weigh it on a scale to measure it correctly. Never sift flour for bread but always sift it for pastries and cookies. If you weigh your ingredients, sift the flour after measuring; if you use measure, sift before measuring.

Go to any supermarket these days and you can find not only the basic flours—all-purpose, unbleached, high-gluten bread flour, whole wheat, and rye—but you'll probably find semolina, too, although it may be in the pasta section. It is sometimes a bit trickier to find a few of the more exotic flours, such as pastry, graham, or durum, but even they may appear in small packages, or in the big bins of loose ingredients in today's supermarkets and groceries that hark back to the general stores of the last century.

All the bread baking going on in this country has impelled large flour companies like Pillsbury and Gold Medal to market their own high-gluten bread flour with 13 to 14 percent protein content. Very few recipes in this book call for its use. Please do not substitute it for all-purpose flour, even if you are tempted by the promise of its more expansive dough, because it is much too powerful for traditional Italian breads. In addition to these most basic flours, other grains include:

CORN FLOUR

Corn first appeared in Europe when Christopher Columbus brought some back from America, but the first boatload didn't reach Italy until the eighteenth century. And then, against all evidence, it was called *grano turco* (Turkish grain), on the theory that such a strange import must come from an exotic eastern locale such as Turkey. Corn became the grain of the poor, for whom polenta, to this day, replaces bread in some areas, but it was used particularly widely in Lombardy, where it grows in profusion and is made into wheels of fairly dense, but delicious, corn bread. Corn flour is essentially a finely ground version of golden cornmeal, and it can be stone ground, so that it retains a bit of its grittiness, or water ground, for its silkier texture. Since it has no gluten, it must be combined with wheat flour, unless it is being used for an unleavened bread like *pan meinon.*

CORNMEAL

Cornmeal is used for baking and for dusting baking stones. When it is an ingredient in a bread or cake, I recommend the traditional gritty texture. Do not buy the degerminated variety for baking, because you'll get a lot of starch without any food value. Be sure to store the stone-ground variety in the refrigerator, so that the oils in it don't go rancid.

DURUM FLOUR

Durum flour is a creamy, silky fine golden flour milled from durum wheat, which is different from the hard wheat that is used for almost all bread making. It grows in very cold climates, such as Montana and Manitoba, as well as the great Tavoliere plain in Puglia, on the heel of the boot in southern Italy. Durum flour is the hardest kind of wheat. It is very high in gluten and, contrary to general opinion, makes wonderful bread, either alone or in combination with all-purpose flour.

GRAHAM FLOUR

Graham flour is actually whole wheat flour from which the bran and wheat germ have been extracted, finely powdered, and then reincorporated. It is named for Sylvester Graham, a militant nineteenth-century reformer from Boston who crusaded against the lack of nutritional value in white flour and was such an ardent advocate of the entire wheat grain that his name has become synonymous, in some parts of Italy at least, with whole wheat. You wouldn't expect to find such flour in Italy, but it has become rather stylish recently and it makes wonderfully rich, nutty-tasting bread that has a decidedly lighter and flakier texture than whole wheat.

PASTRY FLOUR

Pastry flour is made from soft wheat that produces a flour lower in gluten than all-purpose flour. It is perfect for baking pastries, tarts, and cakes. Although mixtures vary from brand to brand, pastry flour tends to have 8 or 9 percent protein, or gluten, content while cake flour has 7 percent. If you are unable to find pastry flour, you can approximate it by mixing 60 percent cake flour, such as Soft-as-Silk brand, with 40 percent unbleached all-purpose flour.

RICE FLOUR

Rice produces a fine silky flour that has less gluten but more starch than wheat flour. Regular rice flour is made only of the interior part of the rice, while brown rice flour comes from the entire grain, including the bran and the germ, and it lends its nutty rich taste and smooth, if somewhat dense, texture to multigrain breads. These are having a small boom in some parts of Italy, where a strong interest in health and nutrition has become a real concern. *Cinque* and *sette cereali* breads (five and seven grain) are where these special grains are most in evidence.

RYE FLOUR

The truest indigenous rye tradition in Italy comes from Lombardy's far northern valley of the Valtellina, which is wedged tightly up against the beginning of the Alps, and from Alagna Valsesia at the foot of Monte Rosa on the Swiss border. The rye is dark and the flour contains the bran of the grain. Rye breads were common in Italy in the Middle Ages and today are found extensively in the Trentino and Alto Adige, which were part of the South Tirol until the end of World War I, so that they essentially represent an Austrian tradition. A little grappa is still added to the rye bread of Venice in memory of days when slices of rye were flavored with aquavit. Rye has a low percentage of gluten, so it is combined with wheat in various proportions to help it rise effectively. Always make a rye starter to give a boost to the fermentation process and to add a lovely sour taste. Rye makes a dough sticky, so it is usually easier to handle if you use a dough scraper as an extension of your hand in the kneading process. When kneading dark rye in a mixer, keep it on low speed so that the delicate gluten strands don't break.

SEMOLINA FLOUR

Semolina flour is made from the amber-colored granular grain that comes from grinding the heart of the durum wheat berry. If you read most imported pasta packages, you'll notice that they list *semolina di grano duro* as the major ingredient; this hard high-gluten wheat flour is the basis of the best industrially made pastas, as it cooks firmly and absorbs less water than softer flour products.

In Italy, semolina is ground especially for bread making, but here it is hard to find and never quite as silky as its Italian counterpart. If you can find the fine-grain semolina, wonderful; otherwise, you'll have to grind the slightly gritty semolina with some unbleached white flour in your blender. Or you can use pale golden durum flour, which comes closest to the Italian equivalent.

SEMOLINA

Coarse, grainy cream-colored particles of semolina, milled from the hearts of durum wheat berries, are perfect for dusting your baking stone or sheet. The starch will keep your bread dough from sticking. Don't, however, substitute semolina granules for semolina flour; they simply won't make bread.

Starters

Before yeast was manufactured industrially, bakers' choices of leavening were rather limited. Many used a piece of dough left over from the previous day to ferment a new dough. A number of the best bakers do essentially the same thing today, using *biga* (see below). *Biga* is a simple saltless mixture of flour, water, and a minute amount of commercial yeast left to ferment at cool room temperature for 5 to 16 hours. It is essentially the same as a fermented day-old chunk of saltless Tuscan bread dough, left to triple and bubble with vigorous activity (don't worry if it then collapses) before it is added to the ingredients of the new dough. This is then left to rise again before it is shaped in some of the recipes that follow. For unfermented sponge, yeast is mixed with water and a small amount of flour and allowed to stand for an hour or two (so called because of the spongy texture of the resulting dough). The remaining flour and all of the flavorings are then kneaded in. Yeast breads made by the sponge method or with the added tang of the fermented *biga* have a special dimension of texture and flavor. These forms of leavening that create new life are known as *la madre,* "the mother" in northern Italy, and as *il babo,* "the father" in Tuscany and further south.

BIGA

Because the first *biga* must come from somewhere, you may make it following these instructions. This *biga* is remarkable. It freezes very well and needs only about 3 hours at room temperature until it is bubbly and active again. It can be refrigerated for about a week; after that, it gets a big strong. When using it in recipes, it is best to weigh it, rather than measure it, for it expands at room temperature. Some Italian bakers advise 10 to 11 hours for the first rise and then another 3 hours after adding more flour and water, but others are very happy with the 24 hours it takes for dough to become truly yesterday's dough. If you like sour bread, allow your *biga* to rest for 24 to 72 hours. The important point about starter dough is that it is very close to natural yeast, and the breads made with it develop a wonderful taste because their risings are long and bring out the flavor of the grain. Another benefit is that the loaves remain fresher and taste sweeter than those made with large amounts of commercial yeast.

1 teaspoon active dry yeast or ⅓ cake (3 to 5 grams) fresh yeast	1 cup plus 2 tablespoons water, at room temperature
1 cup warm water	3 cups (500 grams) unbleached all-purpose flour

Stir the yeast into the one cup of warm water and let stand until creamy, about 10 minutes. Stir in the remaining 1 cup plus 2 tablespoons of water and then the flour, 1 cup at a time. Using a mixer, mix with the paddle at the lowest speed for 2 minutes. *Rising.* Remove to a lightly oiled bowl, cover with plastic wrap, and let rise at a cool temperature for 6 to 24 hours. The starter will triple in volume and still be wet and sticky when ready.

Yeast

Yeast is considered the soul of the bread, the source of life, and its character. A bread made without it ends up as flat as the *piadina* of Emilia, a thin disk that looks very much like a Mexican tortilla. Virtually every bread in this book is made with an infusion of yeast.

Yeast is a living product suspended in a dormant state until it is reactivated by being completely dissolved in water. Although Italian bakers chunk half-kilo bars of fresh compressed yeast into dough, we Americans can use much smaller cubes of creamy fresh yeast which come foil wrapped in two sizes—the smaller weighing about ½ ounce (18 grams) and the larger 2 ounces (70 grams)—or active dry yeast, fawn-colored granules packed in small (7 grams) sealed envelopes. Since fresh yeast is perishable and keeps only about a week under refrigeration, I find that I use active dry yeast almost exclusively. It is much easier to store and can be kept at cool room temperature; it stays fresh in the refrigerator for as long as three years. It's important to know that active dry yeast is about twice as potent in relation to its weight as fresh, so that an envelope of the former is the equivalent of a small cube of the latter. If you were going to buy individual packets, I would recommend El Molina, Fleischmann's, or Red Star. The new high-speed yeasts work in a miraculously short time, but speed is achieved at the noticeable expense of flavor. Better yet, if you do much baking, I strongly recommend buying yeast in bulk. Not only does it come without preservatives but also the money you save is absolutely astonishing, a pound bought in bulk for $1.20 can cost $14 in individual packets.

Now yeast is successfully standardized, but I still always proof it to verify its freshness. Simply dissolve the yeast in warm water along with a pinch of sugar and wait about 10 minutes to see that it foams.

Water

Water is the one ingredient in bread baking that we can take for granted, since we can simply turn the tap and draw out what we want. Or so I thought until several Italian bakers looked somewhat dubious when I talked about making their breads in America. It wasn't the flour they were concerned about but the water. "Too many chemicals," said one. "Too much chlorine," said another. "The water's too hard," volunteered a third. Hard water can be a real problem, even in Italy, where bakers sometimes use a filter, and you can do the same if you get really involved in making these breads. Some breads are said to owe their ineffable taste to the water of their towns, and obviously we can hardly hope to duplicate the flavor of water fresh from cool mountain springs, although I admit that I have made some of these regional breads with bottled waters of their area. True, it's an expensive way to search out the authentic taste of one of the most basic foods in the world. Still, would I recommend it? If your water is heavily chlorinated or full of chemicals, I'd certainly tell you to give it a try. Or at the least to boil and cool your water before baking.

Salt

Salt in Italy is in two forms: first, the coarser sea salt that is used in the kitchen and second, the fine grains that appear only at the table. The fatter grains, which still taste a bit of the sea, are considerably cheaper there and are what Italian bakers always use in their breads. The best sea salt comes from Europe, and still has all its natural nutrients. In America, the FDA requires that all the magnesium and trace minerals be washed off table salt; many companies go further and use an additive that allows it to pour freely, for salt is naturally moist and tends to clump. Still, I hesitate slightly to tell you to use imported finely ground sea salt, because it's so expensive. After all, this is bread, which has nourished the poor for centuries; it is a basic food as it exists, and is made of the most earthy ingredients. But, let's face it, the salt of Italy is pulled right from the sea and hasn't been washed free of its nutrients, so it's a question of how much you value the natural qualities and taste of real sea salt. Please understand that I am talking about fine sea salt crystals, not the coarse ones that I use to sprinkle the top of *panmarino* bread, or big crystals of kosher salt. I personally use fine sea salt from the Mediterranean, which can be bought at health food and gourmet stores. It tastes saltier than any other salt, while kosher salt tastes the mildest. Two teaspoons of kosher salt are equal in weight and taste to 1 teaspoon of fine sea salt.

Salt was a state monopoly in Italy, a national product of such importance that in the old days you could tell whether a region was doing well simply by the price of its salt, rather as we can judge countries today on the price of their oil. In Italy, salt has only recently appeared on supermarket and grocery shelves, after centuries of being available solely at the *tabacchi* where other state-regulated items, such as stamps and tobacco, are sold.

Salt not only gives flavor to bread and adds to the elasticity of the gluten but it retards the action of the yeast, so that many bakers add it to the dough only at the very end of the mixing process. If, for some reason, you forgot to add the salt, don't worry; you can dissolve it in a little water and mix it in slowly even after the dough has come together. If the amount of salt seems somewhat high, remember that Italians never put butter on their bread and Americans, who almost always do, predominantly use salted butter.

Additional Ingredients Especially for Bread

Luigi Barzini was once asked to contribute an introduction to an Italian cookbook. In it he wrote that "every recipe should begin by advising readers to buy a small estate in Tuscany so they can produce their own cheese, olives and oil, and raise their own chickens for eggs." The editors deleted the leading section, "because," they said, "it was not practical and readers would be discouraged."

Barzini was perhaps a bit extreme in his approach, although it is hard to disagree with his sentiments, given the Italian reverence for food. It is a rare conversation that doesn't sooner or later turn to the subject of eating, so maybe it is an exaggeration to conclude that the DNA of Italians must include a special gene predisposing them to care passionately about the quality of their food. Italians won't tolerate indifferent ingredients or dishes. They continue to rely on natural products, and enough people live on the land or maintain a closeness to nature for many products even now to live up to the high expectations created by centuries of good taste. Colors and flavors are clear and clean: bright green basil, darker glossy rosemary, fat red tomatoes, golden and scarlet peppers, rich green olive oil that comes from the first pressing of the fruit. The yolks of Italian eggs are almost orange-gold because the chickens are fed daily rations of corn. The tastes are as clear and clean as the colors, and they embody an attitude about life that is as Italian as the Fra Angelico frescoes and the Renaissance plazzi that we identify as the cultural patrimony of the country.

ANCHOVIES

Acciughe

Anchovies are tasty tiny fish that are a wonderful source of flavor. They are preserved in olive oil (filleted, and in small, convenient tins or jars) or in salt. The anchovies packed in salt in large 1- or 2-pound tins have more taste, but since they are not filleted, you should clean them under running water and slip out their central backbone, a simple procedure. Tubes of anchovy paste can be used as a substitute and while a fresh paste tastes better, there is a lot to be said for the convenience of having mashed anchovies on hand.

CAPERS

Capperi

Capers are the small unripe buds of the plant that grow wild, anchoring itself in the fissures and cracks of stone walls and cliffs around the entire Mediterranean. They climb the ruins in Sicily and can be seen on walls of ancient buildings in small Italian towns. Capers come in two sizes: plump and large, and the smaller variety, called nonpareils, which are considered finer. Both sizes are sold in vinegar brines and may need to be rinsed before they're used. If you manage to find capers preserved in salt in an Italian market, be sure to rinse them before proceeding.

I drain capers by putting them in a strainer over a bowl. I save the liquid and return it to the caper jar; after I've measured out the capers that I need, I put the unused ones back in the jar along with the reserved brine.

CHEESES

Formaggi

Regional cheeses are often served with regional breads.

CACIOCAVALLO. This hard cooked cheese from southern Italy and Sicily has a smooth and firm pale yellow interior. It is made by warming the curd so that it can be stretched and kneaded into its idiosyncratic shape resembling an elongated flask with a small knob on top. The knob has a purpose: It allows the cheese to be tied in pairs, as if to be slung over the back of a horse (caciocavallo means "cheese on horseback"). The most mature caciocavallo, aged for six months to a year, is meant for grating. It is piquant and tangy and adds pungency to southern pizzas and calzones. If you can't find fresh caciocavallo, mild provolone is an excellent substitute.

CRESCENZA. A fresh semi-, medium-fat rindless cheese that comes from the countryside around Milan, crescenza is made with fresh cow's milk. White or very pale golden cream in color, it is especially gentle and delicate. Crescenza means "growth," and the cheese is so named because when left in a warm place, it begins to expand, as if it were dough rising.

FONTINA. One of the most distinctive cheeses in Italy. Named for the Mont Fontin near Aosta, it is an Alpine cheese synonymous with the Val d'Aosta of Piedmont. It should only be made of milk from that region, which produces a rich, aged, firm cheese that is golden in color and very lightly dotted with holes inside, rather like a Gruyère. Its slightly nutty, buttery taste is so delicious that fontina is considered at least as much a table cheese as one for cooking. There are a variety of Italian fontinas, but the finest has on its brown-gold rind the purple ink trademark of the producer, the Fontina Corporation.

GORGONZOLA. A rich semisoft blue cheese made from the milk of the cows of Lombardy, gorgonzola was once aged in caves that were home to the mold that invaded its creamy interior and gave it its distinctive blue veins and wonderful taste and smell. Today, quantities of gorgonzola are made in factories by injecting the cheese with bacteria to encourage the growth of its blue veins; the aging process is speeded up but the taste is still glorious. You can choose from two kinds of gorgonzola: *gorgonzola dolce,* as sweet and buttery as blue cheese can be, or *gorgonzola piccante*, which has a more pungent flavor and aroma. Be sure the cheese you buy is fresh and moist. If you can't find Italian gorgonzola, you may substitute Maytag blue cheese, as long as it is still creamy and fresh.

GRANA. Grana is the grating cheese made in a number of northern Italian locations. The cow's milk differs from place to place and the aging fluctuates between one and two years.

GROVIERA. This cheese is similar in all ways to French Gruyère except that it began life in Italy and has an Italian name. Gruyère is a perfect alternative.

MASCARPONE. This is a fresh thick cheese made from sweet cream, although it sometimes tastes as if it were whipped cream made of fine cheese. What we get in America has been pasteurized so that it isn't as fluffy or delicate as the fresh Italian product, but it is still a lovely dessert cheese that can be flavored and tucked between layers of cake for *tiramisù*. In its place you can use the freshest possible cream cheese made without stabilizers or preservatives, or you could beat ½ pound of ricotta with a cup of whipping cream until the mixture is very, very smooth. Both would be more than adequate replacements for the highly perishable snowy white cheese. Depending on whose story you believe, mascarpone may be named for the Lombard dialect word for ricotta, *marcherpe*, or for the response of the high Spanish official in the seventeenth century who tasted the cheese and exclaimed, *"Mas que bueno!"*—"Better than good!"

MOZZARELLA. Is the classic pizza cheese because it melts to such a lovely creamy consistency. Italian mozzarella is ideally made from the milk of the buffalo that still roam the marshy plain of Campania outside Naples. More and more frequently, however, the familiar egg-shaped ovals or spheres are made with some, if not all, cow's milk. Both varieties are flown to America, so should you decide to buy them, be sure they are fresh, creamy, and still sitting in their own milky brine. The real product bears almost no relationship to the rubbery ball that Americans know as mozzarella, which is made of skim milk and must be grated to be used. If you are fortunate enough to live in a city where a cheese maker produces whole milk mozzarella, leap at the opportunity to use it. Otherwise, you may either make do with the American equivalent or use Bel Paese as a fine substitute.

PARMIGIANO-REGGIANO. This is undoubtedly the most famous of all Italian cheeses. It belongs to a group of hard grating cheeses (*grana*) of which there are many produced in northern Italy. Like fine French *appellation controleè* wines and D.O.C. wines in Italy, Parmigiano-Reggiano is produced only in strictly controlled areas under very specific conditions.

Production begins with the high-quality milk of summer on April 1 and ends on November 11 and can only take place in the provinces of Parma, Reggio Emilia, and Modena, in Mantua on the right bank of the River Po, and Bologna on the left bank of the river Reno. The cheese is made entirely by hand in a centuries-old artisan tradition and is left to age for a minimum of two years. What is produced at the end of this long process is a straw-colored cheese with an extremely attractive flavor that is clean and somewhat salty. It is slightly crumbly in texture. You can know that you are buying the real thing if the rind is etched with the words "Parmigiano-Reggiano" around the entire circumference. Lesser Parmesans include *grana padana*, which simply means that the cheese comes from the plain of Lombardy. Italian Parmesan is bland; Argentinean Parmesan has some bite to it. Both are infinitely preferable to pre-grated American Parmesan, which has no real taste at all. Buy a whole chunk of Parmesan and grate just before using it, so that the taste and perfume of the Parmesan truly become part of the bread or pizza you are making.

PECORINO. What Parmesan cheese is to the north, pecorino is to the south of Italy, where it has the most widespread popularity of all hard grating cheeses. Though there are a variety of pecorini, all are made from sheep's milk (*pecora* means sheep) and all are sharp-tasting medium-fat cheeses. They look similar to Parmesan with their compact gold-colored interiors. The difference comes on the tongue; pecorino is saltier, tangier, and sharper tasting, clearly meant only for grating and not for eating at the table. The best pecorino to use for these recipes is Pecorino Romano, the most widely imported of all pecorini, although you may try an aged pecorino sardo as well. Buy the cheese in a chunk and grate it only when you are ready to use it. You will notice that recipes sometimes call for a mixture of the piquant pecorino and the milder parmigiano, and sometimes for pecorino alone.

PROVOLONE. Even people who know very little about Italian cheese seem to recognize the long bulbous provolone, which is divided into sections by the strings that hold it. It also comes in less picturesque shapes, and can be conical or round, in sizes ranging from as small as two pounds to gigantic. When well aged, it is always a hard cow's milk cheese with a smooth golden-yellow rind. Both the sweet, mild provolone dolce and the more mature piquant variety are specialties of the south of Italy and can be used interchangeably with caciocavallo.

STRACCHINO. A rindless fresh cheese from the plain of Lombardy, stracchino is made from two milkings: The fresh milk of the morning is mixed with that from the night before. It gets its name from the dialect word for "tired," because the best cheese is said to have come from the evening milking, after the cows have grazed all day in good alpine pastures and have returned home exhausted. Stracchino is creamy in both color and texture and has a slight tang when it is fully mature.

TALLEGIO. This is another pale golden whole cow's milk cheese from Lombardy, rich and semisoft. It is compact, smooth, and buttery, although it gets a delicate aromatic flavor as the cheese ages and grows stronger. Tallegio, stracchino, and crescenza may be used interchangeably. If your taste buds remember these cheeses from Italy, where they are farmhouse cheeses of wonderful smooth and creamy texture, you may detect a bit of difference when you sample them in America, because the U.S. government requires that all cheeses under sixty days old must be pasteurized to be imported into this country.

HERBS
Erbe

Today most local markets carry fresh herbs. Or you can buy a window box or planter to grow your own. I don't mind sounding like a fanatic: The taste that fresh herbs gives to dough and pizzas is so fragrant and lovely that it's a shame to miss their aromatic seasoning. Dried rosemary and oregano are fine in any of these recipes, but dried basil isn't even a distant relation of its fresh self and there's no hope of making pesto with it.

BASIL/*BASILCO*. The aroma of fresh basil is so enticing that I think it must imprint itself on our sense memories forever. It is what makes pesto so fragrant, what gives the wonderful taste of summer to tomatoes and mozzarella, to zucchini and other vegetables. The green leafy herb doesn't grow all year long, but can be preserved in any of three ways. Pick the leaves and pat them clean with a damp paper towel; you can pack them in plastic bags for the freezer or layer them in coarse salt in Mason jars, or cover them with olive oil. The olive oil method is particularly successful in retaining the bright green color of the leaves.

There is a number of prepared pestos on the market, and if you choose to buy one, be sure it is still green from fresh basil and is made from authentic Italian cheese, fine olive oil, and pine nuts *(pignoli)*.

OREGANO/*ORIGANO*. This good, hardy herb grows wild in Italy and is a sturdy perennial that grows in America without demanding anything other than a bit of land, sun, and water. It is characteristic of southern Italian cooking and appears frequently dusting the tops of pizzas. It is considerably milder in its fresh state. Use it accordingly.

PARSLEY/*PREZZEMOLO*. Italian parsley is dark green and flat-leaved and has a much more tantalizing flavor than the curly leaved variety Americans know. If you look in Italian markets or specialty shops, you'll see that it is appearing more frequently among herbs. In its absence, substitute regular parsley.

ROSEMARY/*ROSMARINO*. Rosemary grows wild in many parts of Italy, in thickets and hedges and dense low ground cover. The glossy dark leaves look rather like pine needles and have a strong taste. They will take root easily in most gardens and pots. Rosemary is so often used with roasts and chickens in Italy that the butcher frequently includes free branches with your order, since it has been taken for granted that the herb belongs in your roasting pan. Fresh rosemary is preferable to dried, but should you use dried, be sure to use smaller quantities, since the taste is concentrated. When adding fresh rosemary to bread, cut the leaves with a sharp knife to release their fragrance and strong flavor.

LARD
Strutto

Italy is a country full of pork—hence all the salamis, sausages, prosciutto, and *pancetta*. Good pork lard, cheap and plentiful, gives a smooth, moist, creamy texture to dough and is commonly used in any number of breads, pizzas, focacce, and grissini. In diet-conscious America, where high-cholesterol animal fat is frowned upon, good lard is difficult to find. There is inexpensive lard on some grocery shelves. Keep it in the refrigerator or freezer. If you have to substitute for lard, olive oil makes an acceptable alternative in non-sweet bread dough. I think Crisco or other vegetable fat leaves a cottony taste and coating on the tongue, so I would never use it.

LIQUEURS AND WINES
Liquori e vini

GRAPPA. An aquavit, the distillation of the residue of pressed grapes, grappa can have a strong, fiery bite and be a little rough around the edges unless it has been adequately aged. Grappas are now easily found in this country. Most liquor stores carry them.

MARASCHINO. This is a favorite of Italian bakers, who use it in remarkable quantities. It is distilled from *marasca* cherries, but is neither sweet nor viscous.

MARSALA. A fortified Sicilian wine that is essentially the Italian equivalent of Madeira in French cooking. Marsala was originated in 1773 by an Englishman who wanted to improve the staying power of good Sicilian wine. Use Marsala Superiore or Fine, not the egg (al'Uovo) or cream variety. It comes sweet or dry. Use the sweet for baking cakes or pastries. The dry wine is not for baking, but for cooking veal or chicken cutlets. The best is still made in Sicily by the Florio company. It is available in most liquor stores.

SAMBUCA. The liqueur of Civitavecchia, the port of the city of Rome, sambuca is made from aniseed and sugar and has a distinct licorice flavor.

MALT EXTRACT
Malto

Italian bakers use malt as a yeast food to improve the dough in a variety of ways: It encourages the growth of the loaf, retains moisture in the dough, and is definitely responsible for a lovely golden crust. Malt extract is a grain product in syrup form, usually made of barley, or of barley and corn mashed and malted, and it should be used in such tiny amounts that its taste is almost entirely hidden. It can be found in supermarkets and health food stores. Be sure to get the type that is not flavored with hops.

DRIED WILD MUSHROOMS
Funghi Secchi

PORCINI MUSHROOMS. These wild mushrooms, which are the same as French *cèpes*, are the most highly prized mushrooms in Italy, where they still grow in abundance. During the season, markets are full of huge-capped fresh mushrooms, but they can be found all year long in a dried version. Their rich earthy taste flavors dishes with a pungent fragrance of the woods. They are traditionally added to numerous risottos, pastas, and main dishes, but I think adding them to bread is an imaginative new use of one of Italy's most fragrant ingredients. Dried porcini mushrooms are expensive, although a little goes a long way. They are always soaked in warm water for at least half an hour, and the soaking liquid should be strained and saved, since it is so flavorful. Be sure to ask for Italian porcini mushrooms.

NUTS
Noci

ALMONDS, WALNUTS, HAZELNUTS. *Mandorle, noci,* and *nocciole* constitute the great triumvirate of nuts frequently used in sweet breads and desserts. Italian bakeries get them already toasted, but you will have to toast your own by spreading them on a baking sheet at 350°F for about 10 minutes.

Almonds may be purchased whole or slivered, with skins or blanched. If you need to blanch your own almonds, drop them into boiling water and after about 2 minutes remove them with a slotted spoon or skimmer. Lay them on a tea towel and let them cool briefly. Then just squeeze each one between your fingers and let it pop out of its skin.

Hazelnuts have much tighter skins than almonds and it takes a bit more work to remove them. Lay the hazelnuts in a single layer on a baking sheet and bake them at 350°F for about 10 minutes until the skins crack, shrivel, and flake. Remove from the oven, wrap in a tea towel, and let them steam and cool off for about 5 minutes. While they are still in the towel, rub them vigorously together with your fingers; while this won't get all the nuts to shed their skins, it will be a good start. Then you'll need to take the nuts individually and rub them between your fingers to encourage them to shed the rest of the still-clinging skin. Unless the nuts are being used for decorative purposes and must look perfect, feel free to use nuts with some skin still apparent.

The lazy way to remove hazelnut skins is to put the toasted nuts into a food processor with plastic blades in place and pulse. This ingenious solution does work, but the drawback is that you lose a third of the nuts.

PINE NUTS. Tiny *pignoli* come from the seeds of pinecones and must be individually shelled and extracted, which explains their great cost. Their rich, creamy flavor is unique and they are folded into any number of sweet breads and fillings as well as desserts. They are also the traditional nut in pesto, although walnuts may be substituted. Pine nuts used to be served regularly in Liguria during Lent, when clever people skirted the prohibitions of ecclesiastical authorities by adding them to give taste and substance to otherwise rather thin dishes. Italian bakeries have their pine nuts already toasted; you will need to toast your own, where noted, in a 350°F oven for 10 minutes. They are expensive, no matter how you buy them.

OLIVES
Olive

Were there but world enough and time, we could talk of olives almost indefinitely. Olives in Italy are a world unto themselves, for 90 percent of the world's olives are cultivated on the Mediterranean shores and many of the most prized come from central Italy. Olives for eating or cooking are either picked green or are tree-ripened until they are mahogany or purple-black in color. They may be cured in salt oil, or brine. Those most commonly used in these recipes are:

GAETA OLIVES. Grown in the Campania region around Naples, these are succulent reddish-purple olives with a wonderfully salty, mildly bitter flavor, somewhat like Kalamata olives from Greece.

LIGURIAN OLIVES. These come from the Italian Riviera, the region that wraps around Genoa like a boomerang and extends from the border of southern France to the northernmost edge of Tuscany. Benedictine monks first introduced olives to the area, but now many hillsides are silvery gray with olive trees that are nourished by fertile earth, warm sun, and saltwater from the Mediterranean, whose moisture is drawn in by the roots of trees. Black *Ponentine* olives are tiny and mild, while fat, flavorful *Ardoino* are saltier and more pungent; both are purplish black and are perfect for using in pizza or bread. Pitting them takes a bit of time. Tiny black Niçoise olives from Provence are an excellent substitute, since they are the same type of olive, cured slightly differently.

SICILIAN-STYLE OLIVES. Crisp, big, fleshy green olives that are cured in brine, these are somewhat salty tasting. The easiest variety to find come from California and are cured in the Sicilian style. They are perfect for use in green olive bread, although I have used cracked green Greek olives with splendid results. Please don't use canned California green or black ripe olives; they simply haven't enough taste. They are so mild, I would say, as to lack all flavor when baked into bread. What makes the Sicilian-style olive different is that it ferments in a salt brine cured up to six months. Its pungent, salty taste and crisp texture give the bread the strong personality of a full-flavored, well-aged olive.

OLIVE OIL

Olio d'oliva

Bread, focacce, and pizza dough flavored with olive oil are richer and longer lasting than regular rustic breads. Use a well-made cold-pressed olive oil, but that doesn't mean you need fruity, expensive oil that you purchased at a double-digit figure. The flavor should be mild and delicate, not heavy. The oil gives lightness, springiness, and moisture to the dough and makes it supple and easy to work with. Since oil is a preservative, some of the focacce and bread made with it tends to last several days. Don't forget to brush the crusts of pizzas hot out of the oven with a glaze of oil.

OLIVE PASTE

Polpa d'oliva

Olive pastes, such as the wonderful Olivada San Remo imported from Liguria, are rich and strong salty mixtures made of pulverized olives that are preserved in extra virgin olive oil and flavored with herbs. They make wonderful *crostini*, especially on Tuscan bread, which is the perfect foil for the salty mixture. Bread dough that incorporates olive paste can be treated like focaccia dough by spreading it in a focaccia and baking it according to focaccia instructions. And Genoese focaccia can be topped with a liberal washing of olive paste. Olive paste is known in Italy as *caviale nero*, black caviar.

PANCETTA

Pancetta is unsmoked Italian bacon that has been preserved in salt, seasoned with pepper, and rolled up like fat salami. Good pancetta is a nice balance of creamy fat and lean meat with a salty taste and a peppery crunch. It should be easy to find in Italian markets or delicatessens. If you can't find any, don't use smoked bacon; instead, substitute salt pork to which you have added some pepper.

PROSCIUTTO

In Italy, *prosciutto* simply means ham. If you want cooked ham, ask for *prosciutto cotto*; to obtain raw air-dried cured with salt and black pepper, specify *prosciutto crudo*. Since Italian prosciutto is only beginning to be imported into this country, you may need to find a high-quality American product, such as Citterio brand. Don't buy thinly sliced prosciutto in plastic packages; if you have the chance to go to a delicatessen or specialty shop, buy it there, you'll simply get a better value and better taste.

RAISINS

Uva Passa

Raisins are concentrated grapes. The Romans were such connoisseurs that they made distinctions between grapes to be eaten at table, grapes to be made into wine, and grapes that would be dried for raisins, usually the biggest and sweetest white grapes. Several types of raisins are used in Italy, for which counterparts are readily available here.

MALAGA. These raisins from Pantelleria, the island off Sicily, are a big seedless variety that tastes almost as rich as a fig. Muscats can be substituted.

SULTANINA. These seedless blond raisins from Turkey and Sicily have a wonderful sugary taste. For a substitute, use either a golden or dark seedless raisin.

UVETTE. Very sweet tiny raisins, always used in plum cake, these are much like our currants.

ZIBIBBO. These big, fat raisins are both amber and chestnut colored, are sometimes as much as an inch long, and have just enough seeds inside to be slightly crunchy. The best American equivalent is a golden raisin.

Our American golden seedless raisins have achieved their color by being bleached in sulfur dioxide; the trick is to never soak them in hot water, which will bring out the strongly sulfur flavor. Plump raisins in cool water or in something stronger, such as rum or Marsala.

SESAME SEEDS

Sesamo

These pale little seeds that give the slightest hint of a peanut taste are often used in Sicily. Buy them in bulk in ethnic markets or health-food stores and you will be staggered at how much money you save in contrast to what you spend buying them in little spice jars. Store them in the refrigerator in a tightly closed jar to keep their oils from becoming rancid. To bring out their nutty flavor, you can roast them in a dry iron skillet over medium heat for 5 minutes.

SPICES

Spezie

Many of the imaginatively spiced breads you can now buy all over Italy sound like wonderful creations of an innovative new breed of baker, but the breads of the Roman Empire were flavored with just such unusual combinations. The bakers of ancient Rome made loaves with fennel seeds, anise, raisin juices, and poppy seeds, and even a perfumed variety with maidenhair.

By the time of Augustus, when a real bread-baking industry was thriving, there were three hundred bakeries in Rome alone, white bread had taken on a class distinction as a status symbol, and there existed a long and astonishing list of breads available. Breads had even been divided into special functions: There was a bread for keeping a beautiful complexion, a bread for sailors to eat on the high seas, a bread meant to be eaten with oysters, and even a bread for dogs, made mostly of bran.

Spices were familiar components in these years of the early empire. Then in 410, Alaric, the leader of the Visigoths, seized and plundered Rome. The darkness that fell in his wake shadowed all of Italian life in the early Middle Ages, and bread making lost its virtuosity.

Spices fell into disuse until the Venetians went to sea and brought back pepper, cinnamon, cloves, nutmeg, mace, and ginger from the exotic East. Some flavorings were used by the poor to pep up monotonous dishes, and by the twelfth century spices gave strength and taste to a whole range of foods, including the still popular *panforte*, a fruitcake-like confection bursting with dried fruits and nuts flavored with coriander, cloves, cinnamon, ginger, mace, and even white pepper. Spices were much in demand as symbols of conspicuous consumption because they were so expensive and hard to get ("as dear as pepper" was a common saying); some of them were considered aphrodisiacs; and, of course, they also served to preserve fish and meat and masked the smells of rotting food. To this day the Ligurians' preference for fresh greens and herbs can be traced to the reaction of Genoese sailors subjected to the powerful odors of spices collected in ships' holds. The spice merchants, however, profited mightily: Spices were so important to Venice that an entire stock market based on their value was set up on the Rialto. Speculation gave pepper and cinnamon a value way beyond what they were worth, and all kinds of secret deals based on fluctuating prices were made until the bubble of this craze for kitchen spices inevitably burst, or at least leaked and then declined dramatically once Vasco da Gama broke the Venetian monopoly. Cinnamon and ginger ceased to be such great rarities.

All the historic spices continued to be used in Italian baking. Nowadays they aren't tossed into the dough and mixtures with quite so free a hand, but they do lend their flavors to any number of breads and desserts.

ANISE SEEDS/*SEMI DI ANICE.* Anise seeds, according to mythology, have a magical effect on the digestive system, which probably explains why they turn up at the end of the meal in so many desserts. They taste of licorice and are part of an entire tradition of spicing, and range from Udine far north to Sardinia, Sicily, and Calabria in the south. They are what give a special flavor to the *brigidini* of Tuscany and the *biscotti anici* of Sicily and Sardinia.

CINNAMON/*CANNELLA.* Cinnamon, in stick form and powder, is used in a number of Italian sweets and breads, but it has nothing like the popularity it enjoys in American baking. It is, in fact, usually one of several spices blended together.

CLOVES/*CHIODI DI GAROFANO.* Part of the arsenal of spices from medieval and Renaissance spicing that remains today, cloves are used frequently in desserts. They are almost always used whole in Italy, hardly ever, ground.

MACE/*MACIS.* The filament covering the nutmeg is ground and used only in a few Italian desserts.

NUTMEG/*NOCE MOSCATA.* Ever since the Venetians brought spices back from the East, nutmeg has had a prominent place in the cooking of Italy. It is used in both sweet and savory dishes, often bringing out the flavors of spinach and cheeses. Better flavor is achieved by grating a whole new nutmeg each time you need one. Ground nutmeg is hard to find in Italy because good cooks know most of the flavor and aroma is lost as it sits in the tin or bottle.

PEPPER/*PEPE.* Black peppercorns are called for in all these recipes. They should always be ground freshly at the time of cooking. The only exception is *panforte*, in which white pepper is traditional; you don't even know it's there, but it wouldn't be *panforte* without it.

TOMATOES
Pomdori

CANNED TOMATOES/*POMODORI IN SCATOLA.* Even Italians, who live in the land of the sun-ripened tomato, must use canned tomatoes for their sauces in the dead of winter. You should look, as they do, for canned plum tomatoes from San Marzano. Failing this, canned tomatoes from America, although less ripe and less sweet, are a good substitute.

SUN-DRIED TOMATOES/*POMODORI SECCHI.* These are tomatoes allowed to ripen on the vine, and then dried out of direct sunlight. You may find them covered with extra virgin olive oil and spiced with Ligurian herbs. A less expensive alternative is loose dried tomatoes, which you should steep in boiling water for a minute to soften, then either use straight away or cover with oil.

TOMATO PASTE/*CONCENTRATO DI POMODORO.* Tomato paste is a concentrate of tomatoes, and you don't need much to get the desired taste. Don't try using twice as much to get twice as much taste of tomato; it will only tend to drown out other flavors.

Additional Ingredients Essential for Pastries and Cookies

ALMONDS
Mandorle

ALMOND PASTE/*PASTA DI MANDORLE.* Without almond paste there would be no *amaretti, brutti ma buoni, torta deliziosa,* or any number of Italian desserts to satisfy the famous Italian sweet tooth. You may either make your own (page 125), which will have lots of flavor but never be as smooth as the commercial product, or you can buy almond paste, a very fine, flavorful mixture of blanched almonds, sugar, and glucose, to which almond extract may be added. Odense and Solo are good brands.

BITTER ALMONDS/*ERMELLINE.* Bitter almonds are used in the making of *amaretti* because they concentrate the powerful flavor of almonds. They grow freely in the Mediterranean basin, but since they are toxic in their natural state, they are outlawed in the United States. You may substitute kernels from peach or apricot pits, but it is recommended that you blanch them and then toast them in a low 250°F to 275°F oven for about 10 minutes, until they are a pale golden color.

MARZIPAN/*PASTA DI MARZAPANNE.* This is essentially almond paste, which has been rolled even finer and sweetened more. Its name is said to come from *marci panis*, Latin for "St. Mark's bread," and that's what *marzapane* is actually called in Venice, where St. Mark is the city's patron saint. Marzipan is said to have been invented in the early fifteenth century during a grain shortage, when a clever baker made "flour" by grinding almonds to a powder, adding sugar, and kneading to make a kind of bread.

WILD CHERRIES
Amarena
These ripe wild cherries preserved in syrup (preferably) or brandy are moist and fleshy. The Fabbri brand is imported from Italy.

AMMONIUM CARBONATE
A leavening agent like baking soda, known as hartshorn, this makes very crisp cookies. Use only a little, since it has a pronounced ammonium smell, and be sure to crush the crystals well. It works best for thin cookies, helping a drop cookie spread smooth and fine on a cookie sheet.

BUTTER
Burro
Italian butter is sweet, so that all the pastry recipes are written to use unsalted butter. If you use butter with salt, be sure to cut down on the salt called for in the list of ingredients.

CANDIED CITRON
Cedro Candito
Citron, a citrus fruit that grows in the Mediterranean, is as big as a quince and has a bumpy thick rind. It is often used in sweet breads and desserts, and many specialty shops carry it.

CANDIED ORANGE AND LEMON RIND

Arancia Candita e Limone Candito

Among the revelations that come with eating in Italy is the chance to taste all kinds of candied fruits and the candied rinds of Sicilian oranges, lemons, and citrons that are used in numerous sweet breads and desserts. The rinds are fat and full of flavor, and the fruits have a concentrated sweetness and clean fresh taste that is irresistible. And the colors: The deep red-orange of Sicilian oranges is as seductive to the eye as it is to the tongue.

CHOCOLATE

Cioccolata

Chocolate doesn't appear as frequently in Italy as it does in other European countries, but that isn't to say that it isn't delicious when it does turn up. The secret is to use a good-quality chocolate, such as Perugina, Tobler, or Lindt. Most of the chocolate called for in this book is bittersweet and should have a rich, deep flavor and silky texture.

COCOA

Cacao

Italian bakeries use cocoa fairly frequently to give the flavor of chocolate to cookies and pastries. Use Dutch-process cocoa, which is the pure unsweetened powder of cocoa beans that have been roasted, their oils extracted, and then ground very fine. The style is darker and mellower tasting than regular cocoas. If you want to add cocoa to a recipe to give a chocolate taste, subtract 7 ounces (200 grams) of flour for every 3½ ounces (100 grams) of cocoa that you add.

EGGS

Uova

All the eggs used in these recipes are the large size and they should be at room temperature when they are used. If you've forgotten to take them out of the refrigerator or decided to make a recipe at the last minute, soak the eggs in a bowl of warm water for about 10 minutes to warm them up.

ESSENCES AND AROMAS

Essenze e Aromi

The Italians flavor all sorts of sweets and sweet breads with highly potent, concentrated essences. They include essence of panettone and aroma of *colomba*, special mixtures of the combinations of spices that give these sweet breads their taste signatures. There are also aromas of lemon, sweet orange, orange flower, bitter orange, as well as bitter lemon, as well as essence of bitter almond, which is wonderfully bracing to smell.

POTATO STARCH
Fecola

A starchlike flour made from grinding potatoes, potato starch is extremely fine and makes a lovely silky pasta *frolla* for elegant tarts and tortes. Sometimes it can be found in supermarkets; otherwise, health-food stores often carry potato starch as well as ethnic markets.

RICE
Riso

More than fifty kinds of rice are produced in Italy, but only one is really important for pastries. *Originario*, the most common and least expensive type, is a round-grain rice that cooks in 12 to 16 minutes and absorbs about three times its weight in liquid. Use it for *torta di riso*. If you don't have *originario*, use long-grain rice.

TURBINADO SUGAR
Zucchero

The Italians use baking sugar on top of any number of their sweet breads and cakes to give them a wonderful crunch and lightly sweetened taste. The ordinary sugars we buy at the supermarket melt under high temperatures, but turbinado sugar, the raw unrefined sugar crystals washed with steam, keeps its texture even when put in roaring hot ovens.

VANILLA SUGAR
Vaniglia

The strong sweet smell in Italian *pasticceria* comes from vanilla sugar, which flavors cakes and cookies and has its own very special qualities. Italian housewives use little packets of vanilla sugar; bakers have a very fine powder, like superfine granulated sugar made with vanilla flavor. There are now some fine crystallized vanilla sugars, very delicately flavored, available in America, but since we are so used to using vanilla extract, the trick is to find a really good one that gives the lovely delicate flavor of vanilla.

The Basic Three Tools

SCALE

Use a scale that is calibrated in both metric grams and American ounces and pounds, so that ingredients can be accurately weighed for measurement.

DOUGH SCRAPER

This is simply a rectangular piece of stainless steel with a rolled steel or wooden handle and a sharp edge. It is one of the great inventions of modern life, since it can be used for everything from lifting and kneading the dough to cutting it and cleaning the surface on which you have been working.

POROUS BAKING STONE OR QUARRY TILES

These effectively replicate the brick floor of a baker's oven. Made of natural clay stoneware fired at extremely high temperatures, they distribute high heat evenly and absorb the moisture of the dough, thereby producing heavier crisper crusts, especially pizza.

EQUIPMENT FOR PIZZA

BAKING PANS   Black steel bakeware is the best choice for pizza making because it absorbs and retains heat and distributes it evenly, resulting in pizza crusts that are deliciously crisp. Brush the pan lightly with vegetable oil to season it before each baking session, and don't be disconcerted by the mottling and discoloration that are inevitable with these pans. They come in 10-inch, 12-inch, and 15-inch rounds, and in 12-inch and in 16-inch square and deep-dish pans, as well as 12- × 16-inch rectangular pans for focaccia. (If you have a baking stone in the oven, keep it in your oven, then you can omit the pan and bake the pizza on the stone.)

MEZZALUNA If you want to be authentically Italian, you might want to do all your chopping and mincing with a *mezzaluna*, a half-moon shaped knife with two handles that works by rocking the blade back and forth over the parsley, garlic, herbs, or raisins in question.

CUTTING WHEEL A heavy duty, finely honed cutting wheel cuts through a pizza with ease. The Dexter is sturdy and has a replaceable blade, which makes it worth its price.

OILCAN Pizza bakers brush dough with oil before and after baking. Bakers coat forms tightly with oil, and you can be sure that the fine spout of an oilcan allows just the right few drops to take care of the problem of brushing the pizza's crusts after baking.

SPECIAL EQUIPMENT FOR PASTRY BAKING

NUT GRINDER Nothing works as well as a real nut grinder—not a food processor, which tends to separate the oils, not a well-aimed knife, not a blender. The grinder can make delicate flour out of nuts for pastry and for nut pastes, and you can chop chocolate in lovely fine even flakes with it.

GRATER For all the lemon and orange zest that appears in pastries and breads, use the flat fine-tooth grater with one-size hole instead of the four-sided boxy version. It is much easier to handle and is just right for laying directly over the bowl, grating the lemon or orange right into the dough without having to transfer it and risk losing some of the essential oils and zest. Farberware makes an easy-to-use grater.

TART PANS Tart pans with removable bottoms significantly reduce the risk of breaking a crust. They come in heavy tinned steel and in black steel, which absorbs heat quickly and retains it; they can be found in a variety of sizes, including 8-inch and 9-inch diameters, individual 4-inch tartlets, 2-inch-deep 9-inch tart pans, and 11- × 7-inch rectangles. Springform pans function similarly, although they are almost always deeper than tart pans and never have fluted edges.

COOKIE CUTTERS These are oval and round, fluted and smooth, range from 1 inch to 3 inches, and should have fine, sharp edges so they cut cleanly through the dough. In a pinch, you can use the plastic top of a spice jar.

PASTRY BRUSHES There really isn't a substitute for a brush that will dust flour onto or off the surface of the dough; a brush that lets you glaze the tops of tarts, cookies, and even breads; a brush that washes the interior edges of cookies or calzoni so that they stick together during the baking.

PASTRY BAG WITH TIPS Treat yourself to a plastic-coated cloth pastry bag with a sizable capacity, which is easy to fill and easy to clean. You will need several basic tips, along with a plastic coupler and nut for the special long-nosed nozzle used to inject zabaglione cream into Focaccia Veneziana. (Otherwise, just slice the cake into three horizontal layers, lace each with zabaglione cream, and put it back together.)

FLOUR SIFTER You should never sift flour for bread and always sift it for pastries. If you don't have a sifter, simply use a widemouthed fine-mesh sieve, which works perfectly for the task. It will do the same for sifting powdered sugar over the tops of tarts, cakes, and cookies.

PLASTIC DOUGH SCRAPER This moves along with the contours of the bowl and gets out the very last drop of filling or dough.

Techniques for Baking Bread

DISSOLVING THE YEAST

Those little packets of active dry yeast or small cubes of fresh compressed yeast that you buy at the store give life to bread, but they must be reactivated to do their work. Almost every recipe begins by telling you to dissolve the yeast in a small amount of warm water. Compressed cake yeast is best stirred into water that is 90°F to 100°F, while active dry yeast returns to life at a slightly higher 105°F to 115°F. Don't worry too much about getting the temperature precisely right; just make sure that it is warm to the touch—neither hot nor cool. If you are using dry yeast, sprinkle it over the water in a bowl and stir in the granules with a small whisk. Cake yeast should be crumbled directly into the water and stirred to dissolve it. Add ½ teaspoon of sugar. Let the mixture stand for about 10 minutes, when it will look creamy, then whisk it briefly to mix it all up.

TEMPERATURE OF OTHER INGREDIENTS

Warm water is used to dissolve the yeast, but other ingredients should be at room temperature. Italian bakers consider 75°F the ideal temperature for the water and insist that successful bread is best made with the average of all ingredients—water, flour, and room temperature—at that same 75°F. This means that if you are baking in the cold of winter, you may need to heat up the water and warm the flour in the oven, while in summer you should use cool, or even cold, water to keep the same balance.

MIXING THE DOUGH

Mixing the dough itself is straightforward. Dissolve the yeast in the water as directed, add whatever other wet ingredients are called for—olive oil, milk, lard—and mix them in well with a wooden spoon, if you are working by hand, or with the paddle of the mixer. When you mix in the flour, please reserve a bit of it until the end; the dough may come together and you might not need it all. If you are mixing the dough by hand, you may want to use a big widemouthed bowl so that you can knead in it as well as spare yourself the crusty counter that has to be cleaned.

KNEADING

BY MIXER. Once your ingredients have come together to form a consistent dough, change from the paddle to the dough hook for the actual kneading. Begin by kneading at a low speed, but be sure to follow the recipe instructions; some call for subsequent kneading at a higher speed. When the dough is all kneaded and feels the way the instructions describe, scoop it out of the mixer bowl and knead it briefly by hand on a lightly floured surface. I use a heavy-duty KitchenAid mixer. Hand mixers will not do the job; bread dough will simply burn out the motor.

RISING

Like wine or cheese, bread is a natural product that needs to mature at its own pace in an undisturbed spot where it can rise slowly. When the yeast comes back to life and begins to breathe, it emits carbon dioxide bubbles that become trapped in the elastic gluten network built up in the kneading, and they leaven and lighten the dough, pushing it up so that it rises to double or triple its original size. These breads have at least two rises, and a few have three. The rises allow the flavor of the wheat to mature so that the full taste of the grain permeates the finished loaves. They also encourage the chewy country loaves with big holes in the interior to develop their character. Be sure to choose a bowl large enough to permit this astonishing transformation. Lightly oil its interior so the dough won't stick to it. Cover tightly with plastic wrap secured with a rubber band, so that the heat and moisture generated by the process are contained in the bowl; you'll be able to watch it all happening as the steamy moisture is trapped on the plastic wrap. Italian bakers let their dough rise at room temperature, 70°F to 75°F, which is quite a bit cooler than the usual American practice and you should do the same. It will take a bit longer, in some cases, but the final flavor of the bread is well worth it.

TIMING

If you find that things are simply not moving along with the speed you want, you can set the bowl with your dough in a larger bowl containing warm water, and cover it well. If you find the rise is going too fast—maybe you have to go out and don't want to take the chance of over rising—you can always put it in a cool place or, even better, in the refrigerator, and let it rise very slowly there. Cold doesn't ever kill yeast; it just slows its action. When you are ready, take the dough out, let it warm to room temperature, which will take between 2 and 3 hours, and proceed with the recipe. You can do this for the first rise, the second rise, after the bread has been shaped, or even the third rise, if the dough gets that many.

SHAPING

In 1 to 2 hours, in most cases, the dough will have doubled in volume. It will look soft and spongy. You should punch it down in the bowl—you'll see it deflate instantly—then turn it out on a lightly floured surface, divide it into the requisite number of pieces by cutting them with a dough scraper, and punch them down a bit more to release the carbon dioxide built up in blisters inside. Now the yeast can begin to work again, after the loaves have been shaped, and the bread can rise a second time before being baked. Because almost all of these loaves are freestanding—unlike most American breads, which are baked in pans or molds—it is very important to give them enough structure in the shaping so they can keep their form. Start by taking the piece of dough and flattening it, and then, using your thumbs as a guide in the center, roll it up toward you into a flat cylinder. Roll it up once again until you have a thick sausage shape. The real secret in shaping the dough into a firm ball is to roll the dough tightly across the surface of the table with cupped hands, then pull it back firmly against the work surface, always using your cupped hands to help form and maintain its firm round shape. Repeat several times until you have the desired taut ball. What you have really done is to pull the gluten net tight and given the dough the shape it will ultimately take. Professional bakers have learned to be ambidextrous and can shape two small round loaves or rolls at the same time, one in each hand, so quickly that you can hardly comprehend what you are watching.

Every loaf of bread has a smooth side and a rough wrinkled side, where the dough being pulled downward in the shaping process is collected. Once you have your shaped dough, you will place it with the smooth or rough side up. Often the attractive veining of the flour on top of the rustic country loaves comes from a bread having risen smooth side down in a light bed of flour, then, when the dough is inverted onto the baking stone or baking sheet, the smooth surface is up, with a pattern of flour on top and the rough seam side on the bottom.

SECOND RISING

The dough now gets a second rise, during which most will again double in volume, but in considerable less time than the first rise taking about 45 minutes to 1 hour. A very few get a third rise, but there are exceptions.

Read the recipe carefully for each particular bread.

If it is to have its second rise on a baker's peel, or a piece of cardboard or wood, be sure to have sprinkled the surface with semolina, cornmeal, or flour.

If the dough is to bake on a baking sheet, be sure it is oiled before placing the dough on it to rise.

If it is to bake on a preheated heavy baking sheet, be sure to sprinkle it with semolina or cornmeal just before baking.

Parchment paper is a real friend, especially with moist, delicate dough.

Shape the loaf and set it on parchment paper that has been floured and set on a peel or the back of a baking sheet, and cover it with a towel. When the time comes for baking, you can slide the parchment paper right onto the baking stone and slip the paper out 15 to 20 minutes later, when the dough has set.

Some of the breads are set in oiled or buttered molds or baking tins. The dough should only fill half the mold or tin, the bread will look small and somewhat un-promising, but in no time it will have risen to the top. Be sure to cover the top of the shaped dough to keep it from developing a skin, which would be at the end of its expansion.

SLASHING

Some breads have a pattern slashed on their tops before they are set in the oven. The secret of slashing is to hold a razor at a diagonal slant to the dough and to slash quickly with a firm motion that slices deep. You can always go back and slash again if you are not happy with your first effort, but the single definite gesture is much more successful.

BAKING

The last transformation takes place in the oven, where the dough gets its final rise. Italian bakers slide the risen loaves directly onto a hot brick floor while jets of steam are shot into the oven for the first few minutes of baking. All that vapor lets the yeast work a little longer, giving the loaves an extra burst of volume while delaying the setting of the crust.

To make outstanding bread you don't need to have a brick-lined oven that heats to 750°F as long as you take advantage of several secrets from the Italian baker. It makes no real difference whether your oven is gas or electric; what matters is the brick interior. Baking stones or quarry tiles distribute the heat evenly, absorb moisture from the bottom of the loaves, and produce crunchy crusts. If you have neither, you still have good options. The easiest is to let the dough rise and bake directly on a heavy baking sheet. Alternatively, you can set a heavy baking sheet or even a ⅜-inch-thick griddle in the oven, heat it for 30 minutes, then transfer the dough to it. Unless it is Teflon-coated, sprinkle it with cornmeal or semolina just before sliding the dough on top.

If you have baked the breads in a form or special pan, you might want to unmold them for the last 10 to 15 minutes to let them bake directly on a stone and take some color.

GETTING THE DOUGH INTO THE OVEN

Italian bakers often use a long-handled wood peel to set the dough in the oven. With the dough on it, they stick it in the oven and, with a single expert motion, jerk it back, leaving the dough on the oven floor. You can slide your risen dough onto a baking stone in the oven with a peel, a piece of cardboard, or a wooden board, depending on what they have risen on, or you may choose to deposit a dough that has risen on the back of one baking sheet onto a second baking sheet that has been heated. Or you may simply bake on the baking sheet that the bread rose on. If your dough has risen on parchment paper, you'll find it especially easy to get it onto the baking stone; it is easy to transfer paper and all.

ADDING MOISTURE

There are several ways to get steam into the oven. You can place a broiler pan with 1 cup of boiling water on the floor of a gas oven or the bottom shelf of an electric oven 10 minutes before you put in the loaves. Set the bread inside, close the door, and the steam will continue to mist the interior for about 10 minutes. By the time the crust has set, the water will have evaporated, and the rest of the baking will be done in a hot dry oven. If you prefer, toss several handfuls of ice cubes onto the broiler pan as you place the loaves in the oven; they will melt and emit steam for about 10 minutes. The easiest solution is to fill a plant atomizer with cold water and spray the loaves during the first 10 minutes of baking. Whatever you do, don't toss ice cubes on the oven floor, it will warp, and be certain not to spray the oven light while you're doing this humidifying because it might explode.

WHEN THE LOAVES ARE DONE

The traditional method of determining when loaves are done is to knock on the bottoms of the loaves and listen for the resonant hollow that indicates that they have cooked through. If you are uncertain, you can stick an instant-read thermometer into the center of the loaf; by constant checking I have discovered that breads are done between 200°F and 210°F, although the crust reaches temperatures of about 325°F.

COOLING

Cool the bread on a wire rack so that steam doesn't soften the bottom.

STORING

Breads made with only flour, water, yeast, and salt are best eaten the day they are baked. Age—just a few hours sometimes—does, in fact, cause them to go stale. If you make more than you can consume quickly or give away to friends, you can freeze the bread with very good results. The best-keeping breads are those made with starters and those made with a little milk, olive oil, or butter. They seem to stay fresh longer than their plainer, earthier relatives and can be stored in a paper (not plastic) bag in a cool, dark spot.

Many of these breads—the *ciabatta, pugliese, Genzano*, and *coccodrillo*, for instance—make spectacular toast, as well as wonderful croutons to be sautéed in butter and oil and set in the bottom of a bowl of Italian soup. Italian folklore is full of warnings about the horrible fate in store for anyone who wastes a single crumb of bread, so it is hardly surprising that there are numerous dishes based on leftover bread.

ITALIAN PRODUCTS FROM ITALY

If specialty shops and gourmet stores in your area haven't got the dried mushrooms, the fresh creamy cheeses, or the olives you need, here is an excellent source of supplies:

Dean and Deluca
121 Prince Street
New York, NY 10012

Dean and Deluca have an unerring eye for the finest quality. The fabulous range of Italian products that they have brought to America includes dried porcini mushrooms; olives and olive oils; wonderful anchovies packed in olive oil; sun-dried tomatoes; olive paste; and outstanding pesto from Crespi in San Remo; Originario rice; herbs and spices; Pagani tomato paste.

Pani Regionali e Rustici
(Regional and Rustic Breads)

D o they really exist; those mahogany-colored wheels of country bread with creamy interiors, crackly crusted chewy loaves that still taste intensely of the grains of the fields? The question can only be answered both yes and no. For many people, those fragrant loaves belong to a fleeting moment in the golden past when life was slower and simpler, when bread was made by hand and eaten with a glass of wine and a few slices of good local cheese. Today that bread can still be endangered; during the 1950s and 1960s, mass production and industrialization and centralized baking threatened to do away with these more complicated breads. Fortunately, artisan bakers all over the country have revived them, so that their tastes remain part of another generations' patrimony.

These are the traditional regional breads of Italy, made with only flour, water, yeast, and salt. Most get their taste from a starter that has been allowed to mature and grow slightly sour, so that the loaves will have the deep mellow taste of the grain itself. You will need to start these breads a half day or day before you plan to bake by making a starter. The dough from these rustic breads will be a new experience for American cooks who are accustomed to firm bread dough. The biggest challenge is that it is wet and sticky. Be ready with a small mound of flour nearby to sprinkle on the sticky dough, and be sure to keep the work surface floured and your dough scraper handy. Scrape the surface clean so that the little ragged pieces of dough that stick do not tear away at your dough. Parchment paper on baking sheets or peels makes turning the dough over or sliding them onto the baking stone so much easier than shaking them off a peel.

Pane di Como

(COMO BREAD)

MAKES 2 ROUND LOAVES

This is a spectacularly delicious white bread with a crunchy dome and a feathery floury top that tastes of the sweetness of wheat. It is excellent for breakfast. The loaf is engraved with the delicate pattern of the basket in which it is given its final rise, and the interior is honeycombed with irregular holes.

Como is a beautiful town situated on the shores of Lake Como. The breads of Como are more than slightly confusing. Both the ciabatta *and the* pane francese *are also breads from Como, but this Como bread is what is made and eaten there today.*

STARTER. THIS STARTER IS SPECIFICALLY USED
TO MAKE COMO BREAD.

1 teaspoon active dry yeast or ⅓ cake	⅓ cup warm water
(6 grams) fresh yeast	⅔ cup milk, at room temperature
1 scant teaspoon malt syrup	1 cup unbleached all-purpose flour

Stir the yeast and malt into the water; let it stand until foamy, about 10 minutes. Stir in the milk and beat in the flour about 100 strokes with a rubber spatula or wooden spoon until smooth. Cover with plastic wrap and let stand until bubbly, at least 4 hours or preferably overnight.

DOUGH

2 cups water, at room temperature	1 tablespoon salt
6 cups unbleached all-purpose flour	Cornmeal

By Mixer—Mix the starter and the water with the paddle for 5 minutes until the starter is well broken up. Add the flour and mix for 2 to 3 minutes at low speed. The dough will be smooth but won't pull away from the side of the bowl. Change to the dough hook and knead at medium, scraping down the sides of the bowl as necessary, until the dough is elastic but still slightly sticky, 3 to 4 minutes. Finish kneading by hand on a floured work surface.

First Rise—Place in a well-oiled bowl, cover tightly with plastic wrap, and let rise until doubled, about 1 hour. The dough is ready when it is very bubbly and blistered.

Shaping and Second Rise—Cut the dough in half on a floured surface and shape into 2 round loaves. Place in an oiled and floured 8-inch-round banneton or in baskets lined with kitchen towels generously covered with flour. Cover with towels and let rise until fully doubled and up to the tops of the bannetons, about 1 hour.

Baking—Thirty minutes before baking, heat the oven with a baking stone in it to 400°F. Sprinkle the stone with cornmeal. Very carefully invert the loaves onto the stone and bake until the loaf sounds hollow when the bottom is tapped, about 1 hour. Cool on wire racks.

Pane di Como Antico o Pane Francese

(COMO BREAD OF THE PAST, KNOWN TODAY AS "FRENCH BREAD")

MAKES 2 LONG LOAVES

It is said that the legendary taste of Como bread owes a lot to the air and water of the famous lake. But, even without those particular ingredients, this bread is a remarkable and delicious loaf with a big-holed chewy interior and a crunchy crust. Today it is known all over Italy as pane francese, *or French bread. When it was still called Como bread, it was the only food that brought a rapprochement of sorts between the contentious regions of Lombardy and Piedmont. Each was fiercely proud of its culinary specialties, creating quarrels over every dish and gastronomic tradition, but they did relax their differences long enough to speed this bread from the Paduan plain where it was baked to the far reaches of both areas.*

Serve this bread with stews and meats with rich sauces, with green salads, fresh cheeses, sliced salami, and smoked meats.

1 cup *Biga* (pages 25–6), made with half the yeast	3 to 3¼ cups unbleached all-purpose flour
1½ cups water, at room temperature	2 teaspoons salt
1 cup whole wheat flour	Cornmeal

By Mixer—Mix the starter and all but 1 or 2 tablespoons of the water with the paddle in a large mixer bowl. Mix in the flours and then the salt dissolved in the remaining water. Change to the dough hook and knead at a medium speed until soft, moist, and sticky but obviously elastic, about 4 minutes. Finish kneading by hand on a floured surface, sprinkling with additional flour, until smooth but still soft.

First Rise—Place the dough in a lightly oiled bowl, cover with plastic wrap, and let rise until doubled, 1 to 2 hours. The dough is ready when it has numerous bubbles and blisters under the skin.

Shaping and Second Rise—Divide the dough in half on a floured surface and knead it briefly. Shape into 2 round loaves. Let them relax under a cloth for 20 minutes. Line baking sheets or peels with parchment paper and flour the paper generously. Roll each ball into a fat cylinder and place seam side down on the paper. Dimple the loaves all over with your fingertips or knuckles, as for *focaccia*, to keep the dough from springing up. The dough should feel delicate but extremely springy. Cover the loaves and let rise until doubled, with many visible air bubbles, 1 to 1½ hours.

Baking—Thirty minutes before baking, heat the oven with a baking stone in it to 425°F. Sprinkle the baking stone with cornmeal. Carry the peel or baking sheet to the oven and very gently invert the dough onto the stone. Gently remove the parchment paper. Immediately reduce the heat to 400°F and bake until golden, 35 to 40 minutes. Cool on wire racks.

Ciabatta

(SLIPPER-SHAPED BREAD FROM LAKE COMO)

MAKES 4 LOAVES, EACH ABOUT THE WIDTH
OF A HAND AND THE LENGTH OF THE ARM
FROM WRIST TO ELBOW

Ciabatta means slipper in Italian; one glance at the short stubby bread will make it clear how it was named. Ciabatta is a remarkable combination of rustic country texture and elegant and tantalizing taste. It is much lighter than its homely shape would indicate, and the porous chewy interior is enclosed in a slightly crunchy crust that is veiled with flour.

1 teaspoon active dry yeast or ⅓ small cake fresh yeast	1 tablespoon olive oil
	2 cups *Biga* (pages 25–6)
5 tablespoons warm milk	3 cups unbleached all-purpose flour
1 cup plus 3 tablespoons water, at room temperature	1 tablespoon salt
	Cornmeal

Stir the yeast into the milk in a mixer bowl; let stand until creamy, about 10 minutes. Add the water, oil, and starter and mix with the paddle until blended. Mix the flour and salt, add to the bowl, and mix for 2 to 3 minutes. Change to the dough hook and knead for 2 minutes at low speed, then 2 minutes at medium speed. Knead briefly on a well-floured surface, adding as little flour as possible, until the dough is velvety, supple, very springy, and moist.

First Rise—Place the dough in an oiled bowl. Cover with plastic wrap, and let rise until doubled, about 1½ hours. The dough should be full of bubbles, very supple, elastic, and sticky.

Shaping and Second Rise—Cut the dough into 4 equal pieces on a well-floured surface. Roll up each piece into a cylinder, then stretch each into a rectangle, about 10 by 4 inches, pulling with your fingers to get it long and wide enough. Generously flour 4 pieces of parchment paper on peels or baking sheets. Place each loaf seam side up on a paper. Dimple the loaves vigorously with your fingertips or knuckles so that they won't rise too much. The dough will look heavily pockmarked, but it is very resilient so don't be concerned. Cover loosely with dampened towels and let rise until almost doubled, 1 to 2 hours. The loaves will look flat and definitely unpromising, but don't give up for they will rise more in the oven.

Baking—Thirty minutes before baking, heat the oven with baking stones in it to 425°F. Just before baking, sprinkle the stones with cornmeal. Carefully invert each loaf onto a stone. If the dough sticks a bit, just work it free from the paper gently. Bake for 20 to 25 minutes, spraying 3 times with water in the first 10 minutes. Cool on wire racks.

Pane al'Olio

(OLIVE OIL BREAD)

MAKES 2 RINGS OF 6 OR 7 ROLLS EACH OR
12 TO 14 INDIVIDUAL ROLLS

A *little good olive oil makes a tasty white bread, especially when the top is sprinkled with granules of sea salt. Serve with sliced salami, sausages, smoked meats, roast veal, ham, or an-tipasti.*

2½ teaspoons (1 package) active dry yeast or 1 small cake fresh yeast	2 to 3 teaspoons lard, at room temperature
1 cup plus 3 tablespoons water	3 cups unbleached all-purpose flour
3 tablespoons plus 1 teaspoon olive oil	2 teaspoons salt
	Sea salt

Stir the yeast into a cup of warm water; let stand until creamy, about 10 minutes. Stir in the oil and lard with the paddle; then mix in the flour and salt. Change to the dough hook and knead for about 5 minutes, half at low speed and half at medium speed. Scrape down the sides of the bowl as necessary. The dough should be elastic and velvety.

First Rise—Place the dough in a lightly oiled bowl, cover with plastic wrap, and let rise until doubled, about 2 hours. The dough should be moist and velvety.

Shaping and Second Rise—Divide the dough into 12 to 14 equal pieces, each about the size of a lime, and shape into small balls. Arrange the balls about 1½ inches apart in 2 free-form circles on oiled or parchment-lined baking sheets, or place in oiled ring molds that have been sprinkled with sea salt. Cover with plastic wrap and then a towel and let rise until doubled, 1 to 1½ hours.

Baking—Heat the oven to 400°F. If you have made the free-form rings, brush the tops of the rolls with olive oil and then sprinkle lightly with sea salt. Bake 35 minutes for the wreath, 20 minutes for the individual rolls. Cool on wire racks.

Pane Toscano o Pane Sciocco
(SALTLESS TUSCAN BREAD)

MAKES 1 LARGE WHEEL OR 2 OVAL LOAVES

Tuscans eat thick slabs of local prosciutto that is much stronger and saltier than that of other regions, and their finocchiona sausages are more highly flavored than other Italian varieties. The saltless Tuscan bread is the perfect foil for both. The sauces for Tuscan meats and stews are extremely spicy and flavorful, and the saltless bread sets a perfect balance when steeped in the gravies. The bread dries out very quickly, but it is very tasty soaked in a dressing or liquid for a salad or soup, such as panzanella *or* ribollita.

STARTER

1 teaspoon active dry yeast or 1 small cake fresh yeast	About 1⅓ cups unbleached all-purpose flour
⅔ cup warm water	

Stir the yeast into the water in a small bowl; let stand until creamy, about 10 minutes. Add the flour and stir about 100 strokes of a wooden spoon, or stir with the paddle of an electric mixer for about 1 minute. Cover with plastic wrap and let rise until tripled, 6 hours to overnight.

DOUGH

1 teaspoon active dry yeast or 1 small cake fresh yeast	3 cups unbleached all-purpose flour
⅓ cup warm water	Pinch of salt, optional
1 cup water, at room temperature	Cornmeal

Stir the yeast into the warm water in a small bowl; let stand until creamy, 10 minutes. Add the dissolved yeast and 1 cup water to the starter in a large mixer bowl and mix with the paddle. Beat in the flour and continue beating until thoroughly mixed, 1 to 2 minutes. Add the salt, if desired, and beat 1 more minute. Change to the dough hook and knead until the dough is elastic, resilient, and somewhat velvety, about 4 minutes. Finish kneading by hand on a floured surface.

First Rise—Place the dough in an oiled bowl, cover tightly with plastic wrap, and let rise until doubled, 2 to 3 hours.

Shaping and Second Rise—Cut the dough into 4 equal pieces on a floured surface and shape each piece into a round loaf. Cut 4 pieces of parchment paper and place on baking sheets; flour the paper. Place the loaves rough side up on the paper. Cover loosely with towels and rest for 30 minutes. Dimple the loaves with your fingertips or knuckles; then oil the tops lightly and cover with plastic wrap. Let rise until very blistered with sizable air bubbles visible, about 2 hours. Remove the plastic wrap for the last 10 to 15 minutes of rising time to allow the loaves to develop a slight skin.

Baking—Thirty minutes before baking, heat the oven with a baking stone to 400°F. Just before baking, sprinkle the stone with cornmeal. Very gently invert each loaf onto a stone and remove the parchment paper. Bake until golden brown, 35 to 40 minutes, spraying the loaves with water 3 times in the first 10 minutes. Cool on wire racks.

Pane Tipo Altamura ✣

(DURHAM FLOUR BREAD FROM ALTAMURA)

The golden bread of Altamura, a handsome town in the region of Puglia on the heel of the Italian boot, is famous all over Italy. Made of the high-gluten durum wheat that grows across the Tavoliere plain, the bread is typically rustic with a hard crust but chewy interior that exudes the intense, pungent smell of the tasty wheat.

1¼ teaspoons active dry yeast or	1 tablespoon salt
1 small cake fresh yeast	Unbleached all-purpose flour, for
2 cups warm water	kneading
1½ cups *biga* (pages 25–6)	Cornmeal
About 2 cups durum flour	

Stir the yeast into the warm water in a large mixer bowl; let stand until creamy, about 10 minutes. Add the starter and mix with the paddle until the starter (i.e. *biga*) is broken up and the liquid is chalky white. Add the durum flour and salt and mix until the dough pulls away from the side of the bowl, about 2 minutes. Don't add extra water, although you will be tempted, for this flour absorbs moisture slowly. If after mixing for 2 minutes it still seems dry, mix in 1 teaspoon water at a time. Change to the dough hook and knead 2 minutes on low speed, then 3 to 4 minutes on medium speed. The dough should be smooth to the touch but very blistered on top. It will feel like Silly Putty and be slightly tacky even when fully kneaded. Knead lightly by hand on a surface floured with all-purpose flour.

First Rise—Place the dough in an oiled bowl, cover with plastic wrap, and let rise until doubled, 1 to 2 hours.

Shaping and Second Rise—Turn out onto a lightly floured work surface and cut the dough in half. Shape each piece first into a round, then to an oval that is higher and plumper in the center and slightly tapered at the ends. Make a deep slash down the middle of each loaf with a razor. Let rise, cut side down and cover with a towel, on a well-floured board or peel until doubled, 45 minutes to an hour.

Baking—Thirty minutes before baking, heat the oven with a baking stone to 400°F. Turn the dough over and cut the slash again if it has closed during the rise. Sprinkle the stone with cornmeal and gently slide the loaf cut side up onto the stone. Bake for 35 minutes. Cool on a wire rack.

Pane Pugliese ✦

(BREAD OF PUGLIA)

MAKES 2 LARGE FLAT LOAVES OR
3 SMALL ROUND LOAVES

These big, crusty wheels of country bread originated from much darker loaves, a legacy of Turkish conquerors that baked their chewy porous bread in wood-burning stoves. In Italy, today, they still bow to tradition by making these loaves with less refined flours. Because this is the bread of the poor, it is served with the typical food of the region: greens, fish, cheese, and fruit. More prosperous Italians eat it with stews and meats and with strong sauces and gravies, steaks, and even carpaccio.

1¼ teaspoons active dry yeast or	7½ cups unbleached all-purpose
½ small cake fresh yeast	flour
¼ cup warm water	1 tablespoon plus one teaspoon
3 cups water, at room temperature	salt
⅕ cup *biga* (pages 25–6)	Cornmeal

Stir the yeast into the warm water in a large mixer bowl; let stand until creamy, about 10 minutes. Add the 3 cups water and starter and mix with the paddle until well blended. Add the flour and salt and mix until the dough comes together and pulls away from the side of the bowl, 1 to 2 minutes. You may need to add another 1 to 2 tablespoons flour. Change to the dough hook and knead it at medium speed for 3 to 5 minutes. The dough will be very soft and elastic but will never pull away entirely from the bottom of the bowl.

First Rise—Place the dough in a lightly oiled large bowl or plastic tub, cover tightly with plastic wrap, and let rise until tripled, about 3 hours.

Shaping and Second Rise—Flour your work surface generously, flour a dough scraper, and have a mound of flour nearby for your hands. Pour the dough out of the bowl, flour the top, and cut into 2 or 3 equal pieces, depending on how many loaves you are planning. Flatten each piece of dough and roll it up lengthwise, using your thumbs as a guide for how tight the rolls should be. Turn the dough 90°, pat it flat, then roll up again still using your thumbs as a guide. Shape each piece into a ball by rolling the dough between your cupped hands and using the surface of the worktable to generate tension and pull the dough taut across the skin of the dough.

Place the loaves on floured parchment paper set on baking sheets or peels, cover with a heavy towel or cloth, and let rise until doubled, about 1 hour.

Baking—Thirty minutes before baking, heat the oven with a baking stone to 450°F. Five to ten minutes before baking, flour the tops of the loaves and dimple them all over with your fingertips. Let stand 5 to 10 minutes. Sprinkle the stones with cornmeal. Italian bakers turn the dough over into the oven very carefully with a swooping motion that scoops up some flour on the peel. You may prefer to slide the loaves onto the baking stones without turning them over, or, if they are on the baking sheets, the loaves can be baked directly on the pans. Bake until golden brown and crusty, 50 to 60 minutes for the larger loaves, 30 to 35 minutes for the smaller ones. Check by knocking each loaf and listening for the hollow ring. Cool on wire racks.

Pane Siciliano

(SICILIAN BREAD)

MAKES 2 LOAVES

This bread has a golden crust with crunchy sesame seeds that give a faint peanutlike taste to the bread. The Sicilians make it with semolina flour milled especially for the bread, but because our semolina is coarser than theirs, I use durum flour. Don't use the coarse semolina, for it simply won't make the bread. The bread is especially good with sausages, salami, oysters, and mussels.

2½ teaspoons active dry yeast or
   1 small cake fresh yeast
   (18 grams)
¼ cup warm water
1 tablespoon olive oil
1 teaspoon malt syrup
1 cup water, at room temperature

About 2½ cups durum flour of very
   fine semolina for pasta
1 cup plus 1 tablespoon unbleached
   all-purpose flour
2 to 3 teaspoons salt
⅓ cup sesame seeds
Cornmeal

Stir the yeast into ¼ cup warm water in a large mixer bowl; let stand until creamy, about 10 minutes. Add cup of room temperature water. Stir in the oil and malt with the paddle; then add the flours and salt and mix until smooth. Change to the dough hook and knead on medium speed until the dough is firm, compact, and elastic with lots of body, 4 to 5 minutes. Finish by kneading by hand on a lightly floured surface.

First Rise—Place the dough in a lightly oiled bowl, cover tightly with plastic wrap, and let rise until doubled, about 1 hour. The dough should be springy and blistered but still soft and velvety.

Shaping and Second Rise—Punch the dough down, knead it briefly, and let it rest for 5 minutes. Flatten it with your forearm into a square. Roll it into a large fairly narrow rope, 20 to 22 inches long. The dough should be so elastic that it can almost be swung and stretched like a jump rope.

Place the loaves on floured parchment paper, peels sprinkled with cornmeal, or oiled baking sheets. Brush the entire surface of each loaf lightly with water and sprinkle with sesame seeds; pat the seeds very gently into the dough. Cover with plastic wrap, then a kitchen towel, and let rise until doubled, 1 to 1½ hours.

Baking—Heat the oven to 425°F. If you are using baking stones, turn the oven on 30 minutes before baking and sprinkle the stones with cornmeal just before sliding the loaves onto them. Bake for 10 minutes, spraying 3 times with water. Reduce the heat to 400°F and bake 25 to 30 minutes longer. Cool on wire racks.

Pane alle Olive

(OLIVE BREAD)

MAKES 2 LOAVES

Along the coast of the Italian Riviera near Genoa, the hillsides are covered with endless ranks of silvery green olive trees interrupted only by tile-roofed pink villas, sharp outlines of palm trees, and flashes of brilliant geraniums. The strong sun and warm earth of the region produce the exceptional olives that find their way into the bread. In the past, sailors took the bread to sea because the rich olive oil kept it fresh and the tiny pungent black and sweeter green olives gave it its flavor.

There are two ways to make this bread: Mix Sicilian-style pitted green olives, which are easy to find, into the dough so their moisture becomes part of the dough, or knead in half tiny black Ligurian olives with green olives by hand. Serve with carpaccio, green salads, antipasti, and lamb. This bread makes wonderful sandwiches.

3½ teaspoons active dry yeast or 1⅓ small cake fresh yeast

¼ cup warm water

¼ cup olive oil

12 ounces Sicilian-style green olives, pitted, or 6 ounces tiny black Ligurian olives, such as Ardoino

or Crespi Olivelle, 6 ounces green olives, pitted; reserve several whole olives for garnish

3¾ cups unbleached all-purpose flour, ⅓ cup reserved for kneading

1½ teaspoons salt

Cornmeal

Stir the yeast into the water in a large mixer bowl; let stand until creamy, about 10 minutes. Add the oil, pitted olives, flour, and salt. Mix with the paddle for 2 minutes on low speed, then change to the dough hook and mix 4 to 5 minutes until the olives are well broken down. The olives will exude their liquid, which will give the dough enough moisture. If necessary, add up to 1 tablespoon additional water. Finish kneading briefly by hand on a lightly floured surface, adding the reserved flour as needed, until the dough is firm. The dough will feel soft but never smooth.

First Rise—Place the dough in an oiled bowl, cover with plastic wrap, and let rise until doubled, 1 to 2 hours.

Shaping and Second Rise—Cut the dough in half for 2 oval loaves or 16 to 18 equal pieces for the rings. To make the loaves, fatten each half of the dough and fold into thirds, like a business letter. Roll the dough toward yourself, using your thumbs to guide the dough and create tension in the rolling process. Roll with both hands to a cigar shape that is plumper in the middle and tapered at the ends. Place the loaves on oiled baking sheets or peels sprinkled with cornmeal. To make the rings, roll each piece of the dough into a ball and arrange 1 inch apart in 2 rings on oiled baking sheets or in 2 oiled ring molds. Press the reserved olives hard into the tops. Cover with a towel and let rise in a warm spot for about 1 hour. The dough should relax and the skin should not be tight when it goes into the oven.

Baking—Heat the oven to 450°F. If you are using a baking stone, turn the oven on 30 minutes before baking and sprinkle the stone with cornmeal just before sliding the loaves onto it. Place the loaves into the oven and reduce the heat to 400°F. Bake for 35 to 40 minutes. Cool on wire racks.

Piccia Calabrese
(CALABRIAN BREAD)

MAKES 1 LARGE OR 2 SMALLER LOAVES

This is the bread from Calabria, the southern region in which my mother and father were born. The bread has a beautiful golden crust and an interior fragrant with all the tastes of the south, but it isn't nearly as overwhelming as the list of ingredients would lead you to believe. It tastes particularly good with fresh mozzarella, ricotta, Monterey Jack, or another smooth fresh cheese.

1 package dry active yeast or 1 small cake fresh yeast	6 little cocktail onions, chopped
¼ cup warm water	2 tablespoons chopped tiny artichokes
1¼ cups *biga* (pages 25–6)	3 gherkin pickles, chopped
2 tablespoons lard or olive oil	2 strips roasted sweet red pepper, fresh or canned, chopped
2 tablespoons sliced mushrooms	1 tablespoon dried oregano
1 tablespoon olive oil	About 2¼ cups unbleached all-purpose flour
3 tablespoons chopped canned tomato with juices	1 teaspoon salt
½ large or 1 small anchovy, boned and chopped, or 1 teaspoon anchovy paste	¾ teaspoon freshly cracked pepper
1 tablespoon capers, rinsed and chopped	Cornmeal

Stir the yeast into the water in a large mixer bowl; let stand until creamy, about 10 minutes. Add the starter and mix with the paddle until well blended. Add the lard or olive oil and mix. Sauté the mushrooms briefly in 1 tablespoon of olive oil and let cool. Add the mushrooms, tomato, anchovy, capers, onions, artichokes, pickles, red pepper, cooled cooked mushrooms, oregano, and mix thoroughly. Add the flour, salt, and pepper and mix slowly until the dough comes together. Change to the dough hook and knead at medium speed until velvety, moist, and elastic, about 3 minutes. If you want, finish kneading by hand on a floured surface, sprinkling with ½ to ⅔ cup additional flour as needed.

First Rise—Place the dough in an oiled bowl, cover with plastic wrap, and let rise until doubled, 1 to 1½ hours.

Shaping and Second Rise—Shape the dough on a floured surface into 1 large or 2 smaller round loaves by rolling the dough first into a fairly taut log, then shaping it into a round loaf. The dough will be slightly sticky; sprinkle the dough and the work surface with flour while shaping it. Place each loaf on a peel sprinkled with cornmeal, cover with a slightly dampened towel, and let rise until doubled, about 50 minutes.

Baking—Thirty minutes before baking, heat the oven with baking stones to 425°F. Just before baking, cut an even slash around the shoulder of the loaf or 3 slashes across the top with a razor. Sprinkle the stones with cornmeal and slide the loaves onto the stones. Bake, spraying 3 times with water in the first 10 minutes, for 45 minutes. Cool on wire racks.

Casatiello

This spicy bread, flecked with chunks of salami and freshly ground pepper, was originally made for Easter in the countryside of Naples, but it is now eaten year-round except during the steamy months of summer. The traditional casatiello *was peppery rustic bread, shaped like a large doughnut and with eggs still in the shell held in place on top with two crossed bands of dough. This version can certainly be made with eggs set on the top, but as the eggs harden during the baking, they will sink into the bread.*

SPONGE

4¼ teaspoons active dry yeast or 1⅔ small cakes fresh yeast	4 eggs yolks
1 tablespoon plus 1 teaspoon sugar	About 2¼ cups unbleached all-purpose flour
1¼ cups warm water	1¼ teaspoons salt

Stir the yeast and ½ teaspoon sugar into the water in a mixing bowl; let stand until foamy, about 10 minutes. Add the egg yolks and the remaining sugar and stir until smooth. Stir in half the flour and beat until smooth. Add the remaining flour and the salt and stir until a soft dough is formed. Knead gently on a lightly floured surface for 3 to 4 minutes, or with the dough hook of an electric mixer at low speed for 1 to 2 minutes. Cover tightly with plastic wrap and let rise 45 minutes to 1 hour.

DOUGH

4 large eggs	2 ounces Parmesan cheese, grated
½ cup plus 1½ tablespoons sugar	1 ounce Gruyère cheese, grated
1⅓ teaspoons salt	2 ounces Provolone, cut into small cubes
About 4¼ cups unbleached all-purpose flour	3½ ounces Milano salami, thinly sliced and finely chopped
2 sticks plus 2 tablespoons unsalted butter, at room temperature	1 teaspoon coarsely ground black pepper
2 ounces Pecorino Romano cheese, grated	1 egg white, beaten

Beat the eggs, sugar, and salt together with the paddle in a large mixer bowl. Add the sponge and mix until blended. Add the flour and mix to a shaggy mass. Add the butter and continue beating with the paddle until a rough dough is formed. Sprinkle the grated Pecorino, Parmesan, and Gruyère over the dough and mix until roughly blended. Change to the dough hook and knead at medium speed until elastic, supple, and fairly smooth, 3 to 4 minutes.

First Rise—Place the dough in a lightly oiled bowl, cover with plastic wrap, and let rise until almost tripled, 1 to 1½ hours.

Shaping and Second Rise—Turn out onto a lightly floured surface and pat and roll the dough out to a large rectangle, ½ inch thick. Sprinkle half the Provolone, salami, and pepper over the surface. Fold into thirds, like a business letter; then roll the dough out again 1 inch thick. Sprinkle the dough with the remaining Provolone, salami, and pepper and fold into thirds. Gently knead for 2 to 3 minutes to distribute the cheese and salami evenly. Cut the dough in half and, with the cut side up, knead each half gently into a small round ball by rolling the dough between cupped hands on the work surface and pulling the skin of the dough taut. Place each ball in a buttered 2-quart soufflé dish. The dough should fill about half the mold. Cover with a towel and let rise to the tops of the molds, 1 to 1½ hours.

Baking—Heat the oven to 400°F. Brush the tops of each loaf with the beaten egg white. Bake for 45 minutes; remove from the molds and cool on wire racks.

Ciabatta ai Funghi

(MUSHROOM BREAD)

MAKES 2 LARGE OVAL LOAVES

The two secrets of getting the most flavor into this bread are using the soaking water from the porcini and allowing the flavor to develop over long rises. You may find the bread growing powerfully in its second rise; if so, just dimple it gently to deflate it slightly, and allow the rise to go the full 3 hours.

4 to 6 dried porcini mushrooms	1¼ teaspoons active dry yeast or 1
1¾ cups warm water	small cake fresh yeast
8 ounces fresh mushrooms,	3¾ cups unbleached all-purpose
sliced	flour
1 teaspoon minced garlic	1 tablespoon salt
1 to 2 tablespoons olive oil	Cornmeal

Soak the *porcini* in the warm water for at least 1 hour; drain but save the liquid. Strain the liquid through cheesecloth 2 or 3 times and measure 1 cup. Roughly chop the porcini and pat dry. Sauté the fresh mushrooms and garlic in as little of the oil as possible and set aside to cool. Warm the porcini liquid to 105°F to 115°F.

Stir the yeast into the warm porcini liquid in a mixer bowl; let stand until creamy, about 10 minutes. Mix the flour and salt and add to the yeast mixture. Mix with the paddle until the flour is absorbed. Change to the dough hook and knead for 2 minutes at low speed and 2 minutes at medium speed. You will have to stop several times to scrape down the dough in the bowl. Finish kneading briefly by hand on a floured surface, adding the porcini and a little extra flour to bring the dough together.

First Rise—Place the dough in a lightly oiled bowl, cover tightly with plastic wrap, and let rise for 3 hours.

Shaping and Second Rise—Pour the dough onto a floured surface, punch it down, and knead briefly. Divide the dough in half and shape each half into a big flat oval. Scatter the sautéed mushrooms over both ovals and roll the dough up, tucking in the ends. Pat each loaf flat, roll it up again, and shape into an oval. The loaves will be compact and quite small initially, but they will rise. Dimple each loaf with your fingertips or knuckles, being careful not to expose the mushrooms. Place on a baking sheet or peel sprinkled with cornmeal, cover with a dampened towel, and let rise for 3 hours.

Baking—Thirty minutes before baking, heat the oven with the stone to 400°F. Just before baking, sprinkle the stone with cornmeal. Slide the loaves onto the stone and bake for 50 minutes to 1 hour, spraying 3 times with water in the first 10 minutes. The loaves can also be baked on an oiled baking sheet. Cool on wire racks.

Pane Integrale con Noci e Passi

(WHOLE WHEAT BREAD WITH NUTS AND RAISINS)

2½ teaspoons yeast or 1 package dry yeast

1⅓ cups water

¼ cup honey

¼ cup vegetable oil

3½ cups whole wheat flour

1¼ teaspoons salt

¼ cup nonfat dried milk

1 cup each nuts and raisins

Proof the yeast in a KitchenAid bowl in water and honey and then add oil. Add the flour, salt, dried milk, and the nuts and raisins with the mix with the paddle and mix for 5 minutes.

First Rise—Place in an oiled bowl and cover with plastic wrap. Let rise for 1 hour.

Shaping and Second Rise—Divide the dough in half. Place each half in a large loaf pan. Cover with plastic wrap and let rise for 1 hour.

Baking—Bake for 1 hour at 350°F.

Pane al Formaggio

(CHEESE BREAD)

MAKES 2 ROUND OR 2 LONG, THIN LOAVES

Take two of Italy's best cheeses—aged Parmesan and the saltier, more pungent pecorino—fold them into a dough enriched with eggs and a little olive oil, and you have a superb cheese bread to eat with smoked meats, soups, green salads, and even fresh fruit.

2½ teaspoons active dry yeast or 1 small cake fresh yeast	2 teaspoons salt
1 cup warm water	¾ cup grated Parmesan cheese
2 eggs, at room temperature	½ cup grated pecorino cheese
2 tablespoons olive oil	Cornmeal
3¾ cups unbleached all-purpose flour	1 egg white, beaten

Stir the yeast into the water in a mixer bowl; let stand until creamy, about 10 minutes. Mix in the eggs and oil with the paddle, and then the flour, salt, and cheeses. Change to the dough hook and knead until firm, velvety, and elastic, 3 to 4 minutes. The texture may be slightly gritty from the cheeses.

First Rise—Place the dough in a lightly oiled bowl, cover with plastic wrap, and let rise until doubled, about 2 hours.

Shaping and Second Rise—Punch the dough down on a lightly floured surface and knead it briefly. Cut the dough in half and shape each piece into a round loaf or log that is fatter in the middle and tapered at the ends. Place on a baking sheet or peel sprinkled with cornmeal, cover with a towel, and let rise until doubled, about 1 hour.

Baking—Thirty minutes before baking, heat the oven with a baking stone to 425°F. Just before baking, brush the loaves with the beaten egg white. Slash the long loaves with 3 parallel cuts, using a razor. Sprinkle the stone with cornmeal and slide the loaves onto it. Bake 40 minutes, spraying 3 times with water in the first 10 minutes. Cool on wire racks.

Pan Completo o Pan Graham

(GRAHAM BREAD)

MAKES TWO 9- × 5-INCH LOAVES

Graham flour is named for the nineteenth-century reformer Sylvester Graham who was such a fanatic crusader for the benefits of whole grain that his name has become synonymous with whole wheat in some places. Graham bread is enjoying a vogue in big cities in Italy, not only for the obvious reasons of health but also because it is a rich, nutty loaf with a lighter texture than might reasonably be expected. It is wonderful toasted. Variations of whole wheat bread made at Gianfornaio in Milan include pan graham baked with yogurt, flax seeds, soy flakes, which combine with the grain in a way so that the bread has the protein value of a sizable beef steak. If you can't find the graham flour, substitute fine stone-ground whole wheat flour. Eat the bread with salami and smoked meats, mushrooms, or sliced salmon.

STARTER

¾ teaspoon active dry yeast
or 1 small cake fresh
yeast

¾ cup warm water

¾ cups water, at cool room
temperature

3¾ cups graham or stone-ground
wheat flour

Stir the yeast into the 1 cup of warm water in a mixing bowl; let stand until creamy, about 10 minutes. Stir in ¾ cup of water and then the flour. Cover with plastic wrap and let rise overnight. The dough will be initially stiff, but it will have relaxed by morning.

DOUGH

½ teaspoon active dry yeast or
⅛ small cake fresh yeast

1 tablespoon warm water

About 2 cups graham or
stone-ground whole wheat flour

1 teaspoon salt

About ⅓ cup unbleached
all-purpose flour, for
kneading

Stir the yeast into the water in a small bowl; let stand until creamy, about 10 minutes. Stir the dissolved yeast into the starter with the paddle. Mix the graham flour and salt and add to the starter. Mix until the dough comes together. Change the dough hook and knead for 3 to 5 minutes at medium speed. Finish kneading briefly by hand on a floured work surface, sprinkling with all-purpose flour, until the dough is no longer sticky.

First Rise—Place the dough in a lightly oiled bowl, cover tightly with plastic wrap, and let rise until doubled, 1¾ hours.

Shaping and Second Rise—Punch the dough on a floured surface and cut it in half. Knead briefly and shape each half into an oval loaf to fit in a 9 × 5 inch loaf pan. Place the loaves, seam sides down, in the oiled pans and cover with a towel. Let rise for 40 minutes.

Baking—Heat oven to 375°F. Make several parallel slashes on top of each loaf. Bake 40 minutes. Cool completely on wire racks.

Fruit and Nut Breads

Pane di Noci
(WALNUT BREAD)

MAKES 1 RING OR ROUND LOAF

The lovely dark color of this bread comes entirely from walnuts that saturate the bread with their irresistible delicate and nutty flavor. Be sure to toast your walnuts lightly to ring out the flavor before you chop and knead them into the dough. Baking the bread in a little ring mold with a few whole walnuts on the bottom makes an appealing loaf when it is unmolded. The Italians like eating this bread with soft, fresh cheese.

2 cups walnut pieces, plus 4 to 6
    perfect halves for the ring
    loaf
1 package active dry yeast or 1 small
    cake fresh yeast
¼ cup honey

1⅓ cups warm water
2 tablespoons olive oil
3¾ cups unbleached all-purpose
    flour
1½ teaspoons salt
Cornmeal

Toast the walnuts on a baking sheet in a 400°F oven for 10 minutes. Chop the walnuts to coarse crumbs with a sharp knife or in a food processor fitted with a steel blade. Reserve the perfect halves for the ring loaf, if using.

Stir the yeast and honey into the water in a mixer bowl; let stand until foamy, about 10 minutes. Stir in the oil with the paddle. Add the flour, salt, and walnuts and mix until the dough comes together. Change to the dough hook and knead until soft, moist, and fairly dense, 4 to 5 minutes. Knead briefly by hand on a lightly floured surface.

First Rise—Place the dough in an oiled bowl, cover tightly with plastic wrap, and let rise until doubled, about 1 hour.

Shaping and Second Rise—Turn the dough out onto a lightly floured surface. Without punching it down or kneading it, shape it into a log and join the ends to make a ring. You may place the ring in an oiled ring mold with 4 to 6 walnut halves set in the bottom, so that when the bread is baked and turned out of the mold the nuts are on the top. The dough can also be baked in a free-form ring or round loaf. Place the free-form loaf on a floured peel or oiled baking sheet. Cover the dough with plastic wrap and let rise until doubled, about 1 hour.

Baking—Heat the oven to 400°F. If you are using a baking stone, turn the oven on 30 minutes before baking and sprinkle the stone with cornmeal just before sliding the loaf onto it. Bake for 10 minutes. Reduce the heat to 350°F and bake 40 minutes longer. If you are baking the bread in a ring mold, bake the loaf out of the pan on a baking sheet or stone for the last 10 minutes to brown the bottom and sides. Cool completely on wire rack.

Pan Tramvai o Pane All'uva 🌿

(RAISIN BREAD)

This raisin bread makes delicious focaccia *and it keeps extremely well, although most people love the bread so much they never find that out.*

About 3 cups golden or dark raisins	2 teaspoons unsalted butter, at room temperature
3¾ teaspoons active dry yeast or ½ small cake fresh yeast	3¾ cups unbleached all-purpose flour, plus 2 to 3 tablespoons for the raisins
1 teaspoon malted grain syrup or liquid malt extract	1½ teaspoons salt
1 tablespoon sugar	Cornmeal

Soak the raisins in water to cover (cool water for golden raisins, warm water for dark raisins) at room temperature for 1½ hours. Drain the raisins; mix raisins in ¼ cup flour to prevent them from falling to the bottom, warm 1⅓ cups of the raisin water for the yeast.

Stir the yeast, malt, and sugar into the raisin water in a mixer bowl; let stand until foamy, about 10 minutes. Stir in the butter with the paddle. Add 3 cups flour and the salt and mix until the dough comes together. Change to the dough hook and knead until firm, elastic, and silky, 2 to 3 minutes.

First Rise—Place the dough in a lightly oiled bowl, cover tightly with plastic wrap, and let rise until doubled, 1½ to 2 hours.

Filling—Turn the dough out onto a lightly floured surface. Without punching the dough down or kneading it, pat it gently with your palms or roll it with a rolling pin into a circle about 14 inches in diameter. The dough will be slightly sticky and tacky. Pat the raisins dry and toss with 2 to 3 tablespoons flour. Save ¼ cup of the raisins. Work the raisins over the dough, turn in the sides, and roll it up. Flatten the dough with your palms and sprinkle with half the remaining raisins. Roll up, then let the dough rest under a towel until relaxed and easy to work again, about 15 minutes. Pat the dough as flat as you can and sprinkle with the remaining ¼ cup of raisins.

First Rise—Place the dough in a lightly oiled bowl, cover tightly with plastic wrap, and let rise until doubled, 2 hours.

Shaping and Second Rise—Punch the dough down on a floured surface and cut it in half. Knead briefly and shape each half into an oval loaf to fit in a 9- × 5-inch loaf pan. Place the loaves seam side down into the oiled pans and cover with a towel, let rise, 40 minutes.

Baking—Heat the oven to 375°F. Make several parallel slashes on top of each loaf. Bake for 40 minutes, the last 10 minutes on a baking sheet to brown the sides and bottoms. Cool completely on wire rack.

Sweet and Holiday Breads

Easter Bread
("CUDDURACCI")

I remember the Easters of my young childhood when my mother and father would bake very special Easter breads. I learned in my adulthood that these very traditional Easter breads are baked in every province of Calabria and are called in the Calabrian dialect, cuzzupa. However, in the province of Reggio di Calabria, the hometown of my parents, these breads are called cudduracci. The fundamental element of this sweet bread is the embedding of whole eggs in their shells into the loaves, because the eggs are symbols of rebirth or resurrection.

4 teaspoons active dry yeast	¾ cup olive oil or vegetable oil
1½ cups milk, at room temperature (lukewarm)	6 large eggs (and place aside 6 large eggs in their shells)
5 cups all-purpose unbleached flour	1 lemon, grated for zest only (avoid bitter white pith)
2 cups granulated sugar or Splenda	

In a bowl, dissolve the yeast in the lukewarm milk, add 1 cup flour, and mix well. Cover with plastic wrap and let rest for 1 hour in an unheated oven. (I use my KitchenAid bowl.) Then add the sugar, oil, eggs, and the remaining 4 cups flour. Mix well with the paddle. Change to the dough hook and knead on medium speed for 10 minutes. Add the lemon zest while the dough is being kneaded.

Place the dough onto a lightly floured surface and knead by hand for 5 minutes. Place the dough in a stainless steel bowl that has been lightly greased with olive oil or vegetable oil spray. Cover tightly with plastic wrap and allow to rise in an unheated oven for 2 hours.

Punch down the dough and on a lightly floured surface divide the dough into halves. Shape each half into a wreath. Carefully embed 3 eggs into each wreath of dough and cover partially with dough.

Place the wreaths onto a rimmed cookie sheet covered with parchment paper. Cover each loaf with a damp kitchen towel. Return to an unheated oven for a third rise for 1 hour. Brush the surfaces with a beaten egg yolk.

Preheat the oven to 400°F. Bake for 40 minutes. Remove from the oven and let the loaves cool on a cookie sheet for 10 minutes. Place the loaves on a wire rack and allow to cool at room temperature for 1 hour.

, cut into slices with a serrated knife. The slices with the whole egg are he eldest and the youngest in the family to ensure good health and long

accompaniment with this sweet bread is either a glass of sweet vermouth resso coffee for the adults. For the children, serve hot chocolate or cold special sweet bread is served as the main desserts after Easter dinner.

Panettone

MAKES 1 PANETTONE

Panettone is a delicate and porous rich egg bread studded with raisins and bits of candied citron and orange that is traditionally eaten by the Milanese on Christmas. These days it can be found all over Italy and in the United States as well and not only during the holidays. Many panettones from Italy are made with a special natural yeast, and they seem to last forever.

No bread has more stories of its origins. The most reasonable explanation of the name is that the Milanese passion for terms of affection led them to call regular bread panett, so that when larger or richer bread was made, it was inevitable that it be called panettone. Some point to the Middle Ages when bakers were divided into two groups: those who baked for the poor with millet and other inexpensive grains and those who baked for the rich with wheat flour. Only at Christmas could bakers for the poor make enriched bread with butter, eggs, sugar, raisins, and candied fruit, which became known as pan di tono, or rich and fancy bread.

The most famous story of the origins of panettone involves a wealthy young Milanese noble in the fifteenth century who fell in love with the daughter of a poor baker named Tony. He wanted to marry the girl, so he put at her father's disposal the means to buy the best flour, eggs, and butter, as well as candied orange and citron and fat sultana raisins. The bread he created, known as pan di Tonio, was a great success. It made Tony's reputation as well as his fortune, and, as a dividend, Tony's backer got the baker's daughter.

SPONGE

1 package active dry yeast or 1 small cake fresh yeast	⅓ cup warm water
	½ cup unbleached all-purpose flour

Stir the yeast into the water in a small bowl; let stand until creamy, about 10 minutes. Stir in the flour. Cover tightly with plastic wrap and let rise until doubled, 20 to 30 minutes.

1 package active dry yeast or 1 small
    cake fresh yeast

3 tablespoons warm water

2 eggs, at room temperature

1¼ cups unbleached all-purpose flour

¼ cup sugar

½ stick unsalted butter, at room
    temperature

Stir the yeast into the water in a mixer bowl; let stand until creamy, about 10 minutes. Add the sponge, eggs, flour, and sugar and mix with the paddle. Add the butter and mix until the dough is smooth and consistent, about 3 minutes. Cover with plastic wrap and let rise until doubled, 1 to 1½ hours.

SECOND DOUGH

2 eggs

3 egg yolks

¾ cup sugar

2 tablespoons honey

1½ teaspoons vanilla extract

1 teaspoon salt

2 sticks unsalted butter, at room
    temperature

About 3 cups unbleached all-purpose
    flour, plus ⅓ cup for kneading

Add the eggs, egg yolks, sugar, honey, vanilla, and salt to the first dough and mix again until smooth. Mix in the butter and flour until smooth. The dough will be soft, about 2 minutes. Finish by kneading on a lightly floured work surface, using a little additional flour as necessary.

First Rise—Place the dough in a lightly oiled bowl, cover with plastic wrap, and let rise until tripled, 2½ to 4 hours. The dough can also rise overnight at a cool room temperature (65° to 68°F).

FILLING

1½ cups golden raisins

½ chopped candied citron

½ chopped candied orange
    peel

Grated zest of 1 orange

Grated zest of 1 lemon

2 to 3 tablespoons unbleached
    all-purpose flour

At least 30 minutes before the end of the first rise, soak the raisins in cool water to cover. Drain and pat dry. Combine the raisins, candied citron, candied orange peel, orange and lemon zests and dust with the flour. Pat dough into an oval and sprinkle with one-quarter of the fruit mixture. Roll up into a log. Gently flatten the dough again to create as much surface as possible, sprinkle with the remaining fruit mixture, and roll up again.

Shaping and Second Rise—Shape dough into a ball and slip into a well-buttered springform 10-inch pan. For this panettone, which is as light and airy as traditional bakery panettone, the pan is very important; you must use a 10-inch springform pan. Flatten dough to cover bottom completely. Cut an X in the top of the loaf with a razor. Cover with a towel and let rise until doubled, about 2 hours. If your kitchen is cold, warm the oven at the lowest possible setting for 3 minutes, place a large pan of hot water on the lowest rack, and let the dough rise in the warm, slightly moist atmosphere. With a gas oven, the heat of the pilot light may be enough, i.e. 90°F.

Baking—Heat the oven to 400°F. Just before baking, cut the X in the loaf again. Some bakers insert a nut of butter into the cut. Bake for 10 minutes. Reduce the heat to 350°F and bake until a tester inserted in the center comes out clean, 30 minutes. Cool on a rack for 30 minutes, then carefully remove from the pan and place the loaf on a wire rack to cool completely.

Columba Pasquale

(EASTER BREAD)

MAKES 1 SHAPED LOAF

Everyone agrees that the columba pasquale *is a sweet bread made at Easter from a dough almost identical to panettone; it is shaped like a dove and veiled with crystallized sugar and studded with toasted unpeeled almonds. There are, however, two very different stories about its origins. One traces the* columba *of Milan to the victory of Legnano in 1176 when the cities of the Lombard League finally defeated Frederick Barbarossa, who was intent on capturing Italy for the Holy Roman Empire. It is said that two doves, symbolizing the Holy Spirit, appeared during the battle on the halter of the chariot carrying the battle standards and that the* columba *memorializes that event and victory. Others say that while the panettone comes from Milano, the* columba *clearly derives from nearby Pavia during the time when Alboin conquered the city. As tribute, they say, he exacted an enormous number of precious jewels as well as twelve girls to do with as he pleased. All except one girl wept and sobbed at her fate, but the one who used her head took some eggs, yeast, sugar, flour, candied fruits, and spices and made a sweet cake in the shape of a dove. When the king called her to his bed, the story goes, she brought him her* columba, *which he ate with pleasure and then allowed her to go free. Yet another story says that she baked him a sweet cake shaped like a dove, the symbol of peace, and Alboin made Pavia his capital and spared it from destruction.*

SPONGE

3½ teaspoons active dry yeast or 1⅓ small cakes fresh yeast	½ cup warm water
1 tablespoon sugar	3 egg yolks
	½ cup unbleached all-purpose flour

Stir the yeast and sugar into the water in a large mixing or mixer bowl; let stand until foamy, about 10 minutes. Vigorously stir in the egg yolks and flour and continue stirring until smooth. Cover tightly with plastic wrap and let rise until doubled, about 30 minutes.

1 teaspoon dry yeast or ⅓ small cake fresh yeast	3 tablespoons unsalted butter, at room temperature
5 tablespoons warm water	1½ cups unbleached all-purpose flour

Stir the yeast into the water in a small bowl, let stand until creamy, about 10 minutes. Stir the dissolved yeast into the sponge. Stir in the butter and flour. Cover tightly with plastic wrap and let rise until doubled, 1 to 2 hours.

SECOND DOUGH

½ cup plus 3 tablespoons sugar	1 stick unsalted butter, at room temperature
1 tablespoons honey	Scant 2 cups unbleached all-purpose flour
3 egg yolks	
1½ teaspoons vanilla extract	1 teaspoon salt
Grated zest of 2 oranges	1 cup chopped candied orange peel

Add the sugar, honey, egg yolks, vanilla, orange zest, and butter to the first dough in the mixer bowl. Mix with the paddle until smooth. Add the flour and salt and beat until a soft dough is formed. Change to the dough hook and knead briefly. Knead gently by hand on a floured surface until elastic.

First Rise—Place the dough in an oiled bowl, cover tightly with plastic wrap, and let rise until tripled, about 3 hours. The dough will have lots of air bubbles beneath the surface when it is fully risen.

Shaping and Second Rise—Cut the dough in half on a lightly floured surface. Pat each piece flat and sprinkle the candied orange peel over the surface. Roll up each piece into a log. Pat the dough flat again and roll up one piece into a 10-inch log with a slightly tapered end, the other into a fatter 7-inch log with slightly tapered ends. Place the shorter log across the other, shaping them into a stylized dove, on a lightly oiled or buttered baking sheet. Make a slight indentation in the bottom log where the top leg crosses it. Cover with a towel and let rise until doubled, 2 to 3 hours. If your kitchen is very cold or dry, let it rise in a slightly warm oven (85° to 90°F) over a pan of steaming water.

5 tablespoons blanched almonds	1 to 2 egg whites
2 to 2½ tablespoons bitter almonds or apricot kernels	¼ cup whole unpeeled almonds
½ cup plus 2 tablespoons granulated sugar	1 to 2 tablespoons turbinado sugar
	Confectioners' sugar

Process the blanched almonds, bitter almonds or apricot kernels, and sugar in a food processor fitted with a steel blade. Alternatively, grind the almonds and apricot kernels in a nut grinder until fine; place in a small bowl and add the sugar. Stir in enough of the egg whites to make the mixture easily spreadable but not runny. Delicately brush the topping over the fully risen dough. Dot with the whole almonds and then sprinkle with the turbinado sugar. Sift the confectioners' sugar lightly over the top.

Baking—Heat the oven to 400°F. Bake for 10 minutes. Reduce the heat to 350°F and bake 40 minutes longer. Cool completely on a rack.

Other Shapes—The dough can also be shaped into a round loaf and baked in a buttered 2-quart mold or soufflé dish. Bake 15 minutes longer at 350°F.

Pizza e Focacce
(Pizza and Focaccia)

What are pizzas and *focacce* but primitive rustic food made of the tastiest ingredients harvested from the fields, the vines of the hillsides, and the seas? These crisp or chewy country breads are the food of peasants and wily city dwellers with little money but lots of imagination. Flavored with oils from local olives, cheeses from herds that graze neighboring pastures, tomatoes planted in the nearby countryside, and herbs that grow in wild tangles or are cultivated in gardens and window boxes that punctuate the facades of houses all over the country, pizza and focaccia represent a triumph of *fantasia* and strategy over a scarcity of ingredients, the instinct for survival transformed into an infinite variety of tastes. Clever Italians simply take a little dough, sprinkle it with products of the countryside, and turn it into a delicious and edible plate; flat or slightly raised with rims, they are easier to eat out of hand than with knife and fork. In one of those delicious bits of irony, these most basic of rustic breads have become popular and chic, symbols of the relaxed easy pleasure of eating with friends.

Perhaps it has always been so. The thin, chewy bread that Italians call *focacce* are as old as Neolithic man and indicate that even before recorded time, Italians were grinding grain between stones, mixing it with water, and boiling it into a mush much like polenta. This mush was probably left out one night and an adventurous Neolithic baker must have decided to cook it under the embers or roast it, pancake style, over the stones.

Although we are still in the realm of educated guessing, we know that the Egyptians discovered the miracle of fermentation, but we don't know how. It is probable that the flour and water mixed together for a batch of breads was left out and trapped the wild yeast of the air, which transformed yesterday's ingredients to a puffy mass. Cooks and scholars surmise that someone—an insolvent slave or perhaps an angry one—tossed a bit of the risen mass into the fresh dough and in a single inspired offhand gesture, discovered the process of leavening dough. This is a long preamble to the fact that pizza and focaccia are simply branches of the family of bread once made without leavening and are now parts of the baker's art that are treated a bit differently than the wheels and loaves of the Italian repertoire. They are flat round breads seasoned with oil and cooked in the oven or oven embers and are called pizza in the south and focaccia in the north.

Pizza seems to date to an era when the Greeks settled the region in the south of Italy that has become known as Magna Grecia because it was so purely Greek. The Greeks taught the Romans the secret of their trade, for they were very inventive bakers who made breads with many flavorings and baked them in a variety of forms. At about the time that the Etruscans, who settled initially in the north of Italy, were baking flat *focacce* and *schiacciata*-like breads, the Italians of the south, including the early Neapolitans of that time, were probably eating an ancestor of pizza called *laganum* by the poet Horace. Virgil, who lived in Augustan Rome and went to Naples to visit, wrote a poem celebrating *moretum*, a flat disk of dough that was baked on a griddle and covered with an herb sauce of garlic, parsley, rugula, coriander, and a dry cheese, all ground together in a mortar and bound together with olive oil and a few drops of strong vinegar. The topping certainly sounds very much like pesto without the basil. Had the rustic *moretum* been leavened, it would be a direct relative of pizza, even though it was cooked first and sprinkled with the herb mixture just before eating.

The *piadina* of Romagna is yet another ancestral flat bread, which still appears at every country festival and rustic celebration in the area contained between the low hills east of the Apennines and quiet flat coast of the Adriatic Sea. The thin tortilla-like circle of dough, originally baked not in an oven but on a thick piece of terracotta called a *testo*, is yet one more flat peasant bread that can claim ancestry. Today you can still find *piadine*, folded over fat slices of country salami or wrapped around boiled or sautéed greens, in restaurants as well as at local *sagras* all over the countryside. All these unleavened rustic breads are predecessors of the *focacce* and *pizzas* we eat today and reach far back into the history of Italy.

The focaccia of today derives its name from focus, the Latin word for hearth, for focaccia, which began life long before ovens were common, was made by patting the dough into a flat round and cooking it directly on a hot stone or under a mound of hot ashes on the hearth itself. *Schiacciata*, the term still used in Tuscany, simply means flattened or crushed. One look at these low crisp, crunchy rounds is convincing evidence that the word was well chosen. The word *pizza* may simply mean pie; it can be sweet or savory, flat or risen, although it is most frequently encountered in the plate-shaped circle of dough with a raised edge that has conquered America. The word has several derivations, although the Italian Encyclopedia of Science, Literature, and Art virtually shrugs its shoulders in dismay and says only "uncertain etymology." Pizza comes from the Roman *placenta*, a flat focaccia, like a dish made, as Cato described it, of wheat flour, cheese, and honey and baked over a low fire, but it also comes from *pices*, a Greek adjective that describes the dark black coating left on the bottom of the dough by the burning ashes of the early ovens. Pizza, according to many sources, is simply the Neapolitan dialect for the Greek word *picea*, which denotes both the pie and the black color of the ash that cooked it.

Now that it is clear, perhaps it would be better not to acknowledge the fact that stuffed dough such as *calzone, pizza rustica*, and fried stuffed turnovers also have the name pizza. There is method to the madness, but it helps to know the history to understand, for instance, how the half-moon-shaped turnovers that are today's *calzoni* got their name. *Calzoni*, meaning pant legs, were originally long narrow tubes of dough enclosing sausages or salamis; they looked very much like the baggy pants Neapolitan men wore in the eighteenth and nineteenth centuries. *Panzarotti*, fat envelopes of pizza dough stuffed with various fillings, are named for the Neapolitan dialect word for stomach, because when they are fried in extremely hot oil, they suddenly swell up like big full bellies.

The word *pizza* is not found in the Italian dictionary because it is made with flour and because it is a specialty of the Neapolitans and of the very city of Naples itself. If you want to know what a pizza is, take a piece of dough, roll it out, then pull or spread it a bit with a rolling pin or push it out with the palm of your hand, put whatever comes into your head to put on it, season it with oil or lard, bake it in the oven, eat it, and you will know what a pizza is. Though more or less the same, the focaccia and *schiacciata* are "embryos of the art." So said Sir Emanuele Rocco in the anthology *Use e Costumi di Napoli*, compiled in 1950 by a Frenchman named De Bourchard, whose chauvinistic convictions reflect his attachment to the pizzas of Naples baked at the little stalls and shops of his day.

A few years previous, Alexander Dumas, author of *The Three Musketeers*, wrote in his *Grand Dictionnaire du la Cuisine*, "Pizza is a sort of bun like the ones made at Saint-Denis. It is round in shape and made with the same bread dough. It seems simple enough, but on closer inspection, it is really very complicated." He continues, enumerating its ingredients. "Pizza is made with oil, bacon, lard, cheese, tomato or small fish. It is the yardstick by which the whole food market is measured; prices rise and fall according to the prices of these ingredients." Imagine what a vast public pizza must have had to make such an impact on the prices of its flavorings. Did hamburgers ever influence the price paid for beef on the hoof in the stockyards of Chicago or fried chicken change the economy of the South? Dumas's appreciation for pizza was great, but, as any number of eminent authorities have pointed out, he was off-base in one of his observations. Dumas thought that *pizza oggi a otto* was made eight days before it was eaten; actually, it was and still is eaten hot out of the oven but paid for eight days later, easy financial terms provided then as now by neighborhood *pizzaioli* to local residents who as likely as not are a bit strapped for money. Not only is the arrangement light on the wallet but it also guarantees that your last pizza is free if you die before eight days have elapsed. In another bit of financial strategy, canny Neapolitans frequently use anchovies on pizzas because the little fish can easily be caught from the sea virtually free. Anchovies not only give the taste of salt for very little money but they also spare the pizza maker the expensive tax the government used to levy on salt, the most basic of all seasonings.

The first pizzas as we know them today were probably flavored very simply with oil, garlic, mozzarella, and anchovies or tiny local fish called *cincinielli*. The wit of Neapolitan bakers soon spawned a much greater variety of combinations. The single most famous story of toppings and pizza concerns Queen Margherita, who traveled with King Umberto I to Naples in 1889 when he was on a visit to the lands of his kingdom. The queen, who had heard about pizza, was anxious to sample the dish, but, because she could hardly go off to an open-air pizza stand or pizzeria, the primier pizza maker of the time called upon her. Don Raffaele Esposito, owner of the pizzeria Pietro il Pizzaiuolo, and his wife went to the Capodimonte Palace with several varieties of pizza for the queen to taste. She was most enthusiastic about the pizza made with mozzarella, tomatoes, and fresh basil, which was red, white, and green, the colors of the Italian flag. In the flush of success, don Raffaele christened it pizza Margherita in her honor. It didn't take long for word to spread through the kingdom and make pizza Margherita an instant success. Whether the tale is apocryphal or not, pizza Margherita helped put pizza on the national culinary map of Italy.

Today, pizza is so various and widespread that *pizza alla napoletana, pizza alla romana, pizza pasquale*, and *pizza rustica* only hint at its protean forms. From the *sfinciuni* of Sicily—pizza dough covered with tomato sauce, cheese, onions, oil, and bread crumbs and baked in the oven—to the Sardenaria of San Remo, named for its topping of local sardines or *sardine pase*, pizza expressed the extraordinarily diverse tastes of regional traditions. The focaccia of Recco, which has put the little town outside Genoa on the gastronomic map, is made with a strudel-like dough, while the pizza named for the admiral Andrea Doria is made with durum flour and black olives.

Some of the most basic pizzas and variations from the south to north are included in these recipes, but you should use your own imagination and be guided by the desires of your own taste buds to make your own toppings. Formal recipes are much less important than the flavorful ingredients at hand. Neapolitans start with the sun and the mist from the gulf and add strong local tastes without intricate mystery or shadings—let that be your guide. You can add anchovies to one pizza or mozzarella to another; you can use fontina instead of mozzarella or add prosciutto, mushrooms, clams, pesto, or mussels. Pizza is really only a platter of bread topped with the foodstuffs of the countryside and mixed with real passion and imagination.

Pizza

Pizza alla Napoletana

(PIZZA OF NAPLES)

MAKES ONE 15- TO 16-INCH PIZZA,
2 MEDIUM, OR 5 TO 6 INDIVIDUAL PIZZAS

Like the discoverer of fire or the maker of the wheel, the creator of pizza remains unknown. We do know that by the eighteenth century, pizza was the food of Naples, an extravagantly delicious dish combining the simplest and cheapest ingredients with fabulous imagination. The crisp, slightly smoky tang of the pizza, made as it should be, depends on the hands and secrets of the pizzaioli locali, heirs of a tradition passed orally from one baker to the next, as well as heirs of the oils of their olives and the lard of their pigs, the waters of their hills, the tomatoes of their vines, the leaves of basil ripened by their sun, the mozzarella of their buffalo, and the wood-burning fires of their brick-lined ovens.

The pizzas are as big as a plate, with rings of dough raised at the outer edges (all the better to grasp them with). Ask a Neapolitan and he'll tell you that pizza is a grace note of life, a subtle piece of magic transmuted by the alchemy of fire into a delicacy for the nose, mouth, and eyes.

Numerous pizzerias dot the streets, the narrow curving vicoli and mazes of tiny dark lanes that wind through the labyrinthine heart of the city, but once pizza vendors wandered through Naples carrying dozens of pizzas, each one folded in half in the shape called a "libretto," because it looked like a pocketbook, and calling out phrases describing their wares in ringing tones, rhyming couplets, double entendres, and simple descriptive phrases. Though few of the troubadours with the slang and song and come-ons are left, the circle of dough, holding within it a world of southern tastes, still dazzles the taste buds and remains the remarkably rustic treat that conquered the world.

A couple of tips: To shape the dough, you may use either a rolling pin (the easiest) or your fists by draping the dough over them and then moving them apart to within an inch of the rim, slowly and gently turning them and stretching the dough to ³⁄₈ inch thick. The experts get it even thinner. The edge, called cornicine (like a big picture frame), is a favorite of babies and gastronomes, and it should be a bit thicker to keep the sauce and ingredients in their place. Always brush the rim of the pizza with a bit of olive oil when it is still hot from the oven so that the entire dish glistens.

1¼ teaspoons active dry yeast or	3 cups unbleached all-purpose
⅔ small cake fresh yeast	flour
Pinch of sugar	1½ teaspoons salt (if using anchovies
1⅓ cups warm water	in the topping, reduce the salt to a
¼ cup olive oil, plus additional for	pinch)
brushing the crust	Cornmeal

Stir the yeast and sugar into the water in a mixer bowl; let stand until foamy, about 5 minutes. Stir in the oil with the paddle. Mix the flour and salt and add to the yeast mixture. Mix until the dough comes together. Change to the dough hook and knead at medium speed until soft and satiny but firm, about 3 minutes. Finish kneading briefly by hand on a lightly floured surface.

First Rise—Place the dough in a lightly oiled bowl, cover tightly with plastic wrap, and let rise until not quite fully doubled, 45 minutes to 1 hour.

Shaping and Second Rise—You may shape the dough with a rolling pin or your hands. Knead the dough briefly on a lightly floured surface to expel the air bubbles, 1 to 2 minutes. Divide the dough if you are making more than 1 pizza. Roll each piece into a ball and then flatten into a thick disk. With a rolling pin, roll out the dough to ⅜ inch thick, leaving a 1-inch rim. Place the dough in an oiled pizza pan or on a peel that has been sprinkled with cornmeal or flour. To shape by hand, push the dough out from the center on a lightly floured surface, working around the circle and pushing to within an inch of the edge. When the dough is a bit more than 1 inch thick, place it over your fists and start moving them gently away from each other, stretching the dough between them. Move your fists back to the center, turn the dough a bit (you might even make it jump a bit in the air to accomplish this), and then move your fists apart again, being careful not to tear the fine dough in the middle. When it is almost the size you want, place it in an oiled pizza pan or on a peel that has been sprinkled with cornmeal or flour. Finish shaping the dough with your fingers.

Cover the dough with a towel and let rise for no longer than 30 minutes. The dough should be puffy and softly risen.

Topping—Select one of the topping recipes that follow, or, if you have gotten into the spirit of Italian baking, use whatever combinations of mushrooms, cheese, greens, onions, anchovies, and herbs that strike your imagination.

Baking—Heat the oven to 400°F. Use a baking stone if you have one (turn the oven on 30 minutes before baking) and sprinkle the stone with cornmeal just before sliding the pizza onto it. You can bake the pizza in a pan or on the back of a baking sheet, but you won't get a true crisp crust of a Neapolitan pizza without the stone. Bake large pizzas for 25 to 30 minutes and smaller ones for 15 to 25 minutes. The pizza is done when the crust is golden brown and crisp with little burst blisters visible and the cheese, if you used it, is melted and bubbling. Immediately brush the crust with oil.

PIZZA AGLIO E OLIO TOPPING

MAKES ENOUGH TO TOP PIZZA ALLA NAPOLETANA DOUGH

This is the simplest and most traditional topping of all.

¼ cup fruity olive oil

3 to 6 cloves fresh garlic, very thinly sliced

1 tablespoon chopped fresh oregano or 1 teaspoon dried oregano

1½ teaspoons salt

Freshly ground black pepper

Drizzle a little of the oil over the dough and sprinkle with the garlic, oregano, salt, and pepper to taste. Bake at 450°F for 25 to 30 minutes.

PIZZA ALLA NAPOLETANA TOPPING

MAKES ENOUGH TO TOP PIZZA ALLA NAPOLETANA DOUGH

2 to 3 tablespoons olive oil

1½ pounds fresh medium tomatoes, peeled, seeded, and roughly chopped, or 1 can (14 ounces) plum tomatoes, drained and roughly chopped

2 large cloves garlic, very thinly sliced

1½ teaspoons dried oregano or 7 to 8 fresh basil leaves

1 teaspoon salt

1 teaspoon freshly ground black pepper, optional

Drizzle a little of the oil over the dough and spread the tomatoes over the top. Sprinkle with the garlic, oregano or basil, salt, and pepper, if desired, then drizzle with more oil.

Bake at 450°F for 25 to 30 minutes.

PIZZA MARGHERITA TOPPING

MAKES ENOUGH TO TOP PIZZA ALLA
NAPOLETANA DOUGH

2 to 4 tablespoons olive oil
1 to 1½ pounds fresh medium
   tomatoes, peeled, seeded, and cut
   into strips, or 1 can (14 ounces)
   plum tomatoes, drained and cut
   into strips

8 ounces sliced fresh mozzarella or
   Italian fontina
¼ cup freshly grated Parmesan or
   pecorino, optional but tasty
7 to 10 fresh basil leaves
1 teaspoon salt

Lightly moisten the dough with a bit of oil. Spread the dough with the tomatoes, grated cheese, and basil and sprinkle with salt. Drizzle the remaining olive oil over the top. If you are making 1 large pizza, top it with all the ingredients but the mozzarella. Bake for 10 to 15 minutes, top with cheese, and bake until done. Because mozzarella is high in butterfat, it tends to burn before the crust is done, but this baker's secret solves the problem. Save a few basil leaves to dapple the cheese with.

Bake at 450°F for 15 to 30 minutes, depending on the size of the pizza.

PIZZA ALLA MARINARA TOPPING

MAKES ENOUGH TO TOP PIZZA ALLA
NAPOLETANA DOUGH

1 cup olive oil
1 to 1½ pounds fresh medium
   tomatoes, peeled, seeded, and cut
   into strips, or 1 can (14 ounces)

plum tomatoes, drained and cut
   into strips
2 cloves garlic, very thinly sliced
4 to 6 anchovy fillets or to taste

Brush a little of the oil onto the dough. Spread the tomatoes and garlic over the top, then sprinkle with small pieces of anchovy or use the whole fillets or cut them in half to make a sunburst pattern on top. Drizzle with the remaining oil.

SICILIAN PIZZA DOUGH

2½ teaspoons (1 package) dry yeast

1½ teaspoons sugar

1½ cups plus 1 tablespoon lukewarm
    water

1 tablespoon olive oil

1½ teaspoons salt

4¼ cups unbleached all-purpose
    flour

First Rise—Stir the yeast and sugar into the water in a mixing bowl. Let stand until creamy, 10 minutes. Mix in the oil with the paddle. Add the salt and flour and mix for 2 minutes. Change to the dough hook and knead at medium speed for 4 minutes.

Rising—Place the dough in a lightly oiled bowl. Cover tightly with plastic wrap and let rise for 1 hour. Punch it down, cover again, and let rise for 20 minutes.

Sfinciuni alla Palermitana
(SFINCIUNI FROM PALERMO)

MAKES ONE 15-INCH-ROUND PIZZA OR ONE
12- × 17-INCH PIZZA

Sfinciuni *is the quintessential pizza of Palermo. Some versions, like this one that uses Sicilian pizza dough, are rustic and countrified, while others, such as the one made famous by the nuns of the monastery of San Vito, which encloses a meat filling between two very fine layers of dough, are much more elegant. People pick up a slice or two at bakeries or fast-food shops to eat as they walk around the city, and sometimes there are even vendors in side squares selling* sfinciuni *right off their carts. They are usually baked in big rectangular pans and cut into whatever size matches the buyer's appetite.*

TOMATO SAUCE

2 medium yellow onions, chopped

4 cups water

2 tablespoons tomato paste

2 tablespoons olive oil

1 anchovy, chopped, or 1 teaspoon
  anchovy paste

Simmer the onions in the water in a covered heavy saucepan for at least 30 minutes but preferably 1 hour. Stir in the tomato paste, oil, and anchovy and simmer covered for at least 1 hour more; the longer you cook the sauce, the lighter and sweeter its taste will be. Cool to room temperature.

SFINCIUNI

Pizza alla Siciliana dough (page
  105), made through the first
  rising

1 to 2 tablespoons olive oil, plus
  additional for brushing the crust

3 to 4 tablespoons grated fresh

Caciocavallo or mild Provolone
  cheese

3 ounces artichoke hearts (packed in
  oil), drained and chopped

¼ cup plain fresh bread crumbs,
  lightly toasted

Shaping—Knead the dough briefly on a lightly floured surface and shape it into a thick disk. Roll it out to fit a 15-inch-round pizza pan, leaving a thick edge. Lightly oil the pan and place the dough in the pan. Cover with a towel and let rise for 30 minutes.

Sprinkle the cheese and artichoke hearts over the dough, then spoon on the tomato sauce and sprinkle with bread crumbs. Drizzle the oil over the surface.

Baking—Heat the oven to 400°F. Using a baking stone, if you have one, turn the oven on 30 minutes before baking and place it directly on the preheated stone. Bake until the dough is golden, 20 to 25 minutes. Immediately brush the crust with oil. Serve hot.

Pani Nuovi (New Breads)

I n Italy, where *fantasia* is the rule and bakers are artists, there has been a real revolution in bread baking in the last twenty-one years. Bakers have given their imaginations free rein and simply started kneading all the best products of the country's markets right into their dough, adding a new wave taste to the world's oldest food. Mounds of sweet peppers, fat bunches of basil, wheels of aged Parmesan cheese, nuts, and exotic grains have all found new homes in unusual loaves.

Vegetable and Herb Breads

Pane al Pesto
(PESTO BREAD)

MAKES 2 ROUND LOAVES

Let's sing the praises of the unknown baker who first stirred fresh pesto into bread dough. This recipe for pesto is stronger and more concentrated than most because it must retain its fragrance and taste even through the process of being baked into bread. And it does!

PESTO

1 cup fresh basil leaves (basil leaves must be packed down into cup)	2 tablespoons pine nuts or chopped walnuts
¾ cup grated Parmesan cheese	1½ teaspoons minced garlic
½ cup olive oil	⅛ teaspoon salt
	⅛ teaspoon black pepper

Puree all the ingredients in a food processor fitted with the steel blade or a blender. Measure 1 cup of pesto for this recipe.

DOUGH

1 package active dry yeast or 1 small cake fresh yeast	3¾ cups unbleached all-purpose flour with one teaspoon of salt
1 cup plus 2 tablespoons warm water	2 teaspoons cornmeal
Scant 2 tablespoons olive oil	2 tablespoons plain bread crumbs

Stir the yeast into the water in a mixer bowl; let stand until creamy, about 10 minutes. Stir in the oil and the cup of pesto thoroughly with the paddle. Mix the flour, salt, cornmeal, and add to the yeast mixture. Mix until well moistened. Change to the dough hook and knead until the dough is velvety and medium soft, 3 to 4 minutes. Finish kneading briefly by hand on a lightly floured surface. Shape into a round loaf. Sprinkle with bread crumbs. Drizzle the oil over the surface. Place loaf into an oiled pan.

Baking—Heat the oven to 400°F. Use a baking stone if you have one (turn the oven on 30 minutes before baking) and place the pan directly on the preheated stone. Bake until the dough is golden, 20 to 25 minutes. Immediately brush the crust with oil. Serve hot.

Focaccia

(FOCACCIA ALLA GENOVESE—FOCACCIA FROM GENOA)

MAKES ENOUGH DOUGH FOR THREE
9- TO 10-INCH-ROUND FOCACCE OR
TWO 10- × 15-INCH THINNER FOCACCE
(RECTANGULAR FOCACCE)

*F*ocaccia *has become a national dish. This disk or large rectangle of leavened dough is found from the tiny towns of the Italian Riviera to Naples on the Mediterranean and Ostuni on the Adriatic, but its true home is Genoa, which is to focaccia what Naples is to pizza. It is called* focaccia *in Genoa and much of Liguria, but it changes names elsewhere. It is known as* sardenaira *in Provence and as* sardenara *or* sardinaira *in most western parts of Liguria, which feel a magnetic attraction to the French tradition just over the border,* schiacciata *in Florence and pockets of Puglia, and* pinze *in the south. The* fougasse *of France and hearth cakes of England share the same ancestry, for as the Romans extended their empire, they brought with them not only their carefully reasoned city plans, their temples, and amphitheaters but their* focacce *and flat disks of bread as well.*

Focacce are simplicity itself, herbs of the countryside and the golden oils of Liguria flavor the interior, while a little local garlic or tiny savory olives stud its surface. In Puglia a variety called puddica *is enriched with the ingredients of a pastoral people—tomatoes, garlic, oregano, capers, and oil and variations on that theme. Anchovies from the sea and cheeses from herds tended by local shepherds flavor other southern specialties. The bakers of Italy, never willing to rest on their laurels, are always using their fertile imaginations to create other possibilities, and you, too, should combine appealing ingredients—pancetta, grated cheeses, shreds of basil, or sweet onions sweated in oil—according to your own desires. Focacce are usually savory, seasoned with oil or other fats, but there are sweet ones as well, such as the focaccia from Bologna made from simple brioche-like dough that becomes the envelope for ice cream sandwiches, Italian style. Try making* Pan Tramvai *(raisin bread), pages 86–7, as a focaccia with a hail of crystallized or turbinado sugar on top. This innovative departure makes sensational breakfast bread.*

Focacce can be soft or crisp, thick or thin, light and almost plain or topped with any number of condiments, but they are always rustic and a convivial treat eaten as a snack. When I bake them at home, the entire house is lightly perfumed by their cooking, bringing the flavors of the countryside dancing in the air, tickling the nose, and encouraging the taste buds to prepare for a treat.

Bakers sometimes tuck flavoring right into the dough and sometimes then only dapple the top. The dough is always stretched in a well-oiled pan, then dimpled with the fingertips, leaving little indentations to collect the oil and salt on top. Sprinkle water, oil, and salt over the surface just before baking so that the focaccia emerges golden, moist, and perfectly cooked from the oven. When this rustic dish is ready for eating, you'll undoubtedly be inspired to take it on country outings and picnics, to slip it to the children for lunch and snacks, and to keep it for eating with salads, cheeses, roast chickens, and meat, along with a glass of good earthy wine.

2½ teaspoons (1 package) active dry yeast or 1 small cake (18 grams) fresh yeast	2 tablespoons olive oil
¼ cup warm water	About 7 cups unbleached all-purpose flour or ½ all-purpose flour and ½ bread flour
2¼ cups plus 1 to 2 tablespoons water, at room temperature	1 tablespoon (15 grams) fine sea salt or table salt

Stir the yeast into the ¼ cup warm water in a mixer bowl; let stand until creamy, about 10 minutes. Stir in 2¼ cups plus 1 tablespoon water and the oil with the paddle. Add the flour and salt and mix until the dough comes together, 1 to 2 minutes, adding 1 tablespoon water if needed. Change to the dough hook and knead at low speed for 1 to 2 minutes, then at medium speed for another 3 minutes, stopping to push the dough down from the collar. The dough should be velvety and elastic.

First Rise—Place the dough in a lightly oiled bowl, cover tightly with plastic wrap, and let rise until doubled, about 1½ hours.

Shaping and Second Rise—For round focacce, cut the dough into 3 equal pieces on a lightly floured surface. Shape each piece into a thick disk; roll out each disk to a 9- or 10-inch circle and place in the bottom of an oiled 9- or 10-inch pie plate. For rectangular focacce, cut the dough in half and shape to fit 2 oiled 10½- × 15½-inch pans. Cover the dough with towels and let rise for 30 minutes.

Dimpling and Third Rise—Dimple the dough vigorously with your fingertips, leaving indentations that are as deep as ½ inch. The bakers of Genoa do this to trap the little pools of oil and salt that flavor the surface. Cover the tops with moist towels and let rise until doubled, about 2 hours.

Topping—Select one of the topping recipes that follow. One baker of Genoa told me that the great secret of keeping these doughs so moist and yet cooking them thoroughly is to cover the tops with equal amounts of olive oil and water mixed with salt; the water evaporates solely during the cooking, allowing the interiors to cook fully without drying out. Alas, home ovens don't get hot enough to make use of this wonderful piece of advice, but you can paint the tops with oil and sprinkle with salt, and, when you place the focacce in the oven, spray them with water, 3 times for the first 10 minutes of baking.

Baking—Heat the oven to 400°F. Use baking stones if you have them (turn the oven on 30 minutes before baking) and place the pans directly on the preheated stones. Bake for 20 to 25 minutes, spraying with water 3 times in the first 10 minutes; immediately invert the focacce onto racks to cool so that the bottom crusts don't get soggy. Bakers in Genoa set them on bamboo racks to cool because they leave no taste. Eat focacce warm or at room temperature the same day you bake them, no matter what, don't refrigerate; they simply won't taste right.

Focaccia alla Salvia

(FOCACCIA WITH SAGE)

MAKES THREE 9- TO 10-INCH-ROUND
FOCACCE OR TWO 10$^{1}/_{2}$- × 15$^{1}/_{2}$-INCH
RECTANGULAR FOCACCE

24 to 30 fresh sage leaves or
  1½ tablespoons dried sage
  leaves, crumbled (not
  powdered, which is much
  too pungent)

Focaccia alla Genovese dough
  (page 111)
2 tablespoons olive oil
1½ tablespoons salt
Whole fresh sage leaves

Work the crumbled chopped sage leaves into the dough in the first kneading. Follow the directions for *Focaccia alla Genovese* through the third rise. Just before baking, brush the dimpled dough with oil and sprinkle with the salt. Decorate the tops with the whole sage leaves. Bake as directed for Focaccia alla Genovese.

Variation—To make *Focaccia al Rosmarino*, substitute 1½ tablespoons chopped fresh rosemary or 2 teaspoons dried chopped rosemary for the chopped sage. Decorate each focaccia with several sprigs of fresh rosemary, if desired.

Focaccia alle Olive

(FOCACCIA WITH OLIVES)

MAKES THREE 9- TO 10-INCH-ROUND
FOCACCE OR TWO 10$^1/_2$- × 15$^1/_2$-INCH
RECTANGULAR FOCACCE

8 ounces black Ligurian olives or a
combination of black and green
olives, preferably Ponentine,
Ardoino, or Niçoise

Focaccia alla Genovese dough
(page 111), made through the
third rise
2 tablespoons olive oil

Pit the olives and push the olives into the dimpled doughs just before baking.
Brush the doughs with olive oil. Bake as directed for *Focaccia alla Genovese*.

Focaccia al Gorgonzola

(GORGONZOLA FOCACCIA)

MAKES TWO 9- TO 10-INCH-ROUND FOCACCE
OR ONE 12- × 17-INCH FOCACCIA

This focaccia *is very appealing to look at as well as to eat. It is about 1½ to 2 inches high and the Gorgonzola covering settles slightly unevenly on the surface, creating irregular valleys with deep golden cheese patches and high raised sections lightly brushed with the topping.*

DOUGH

3½ teaspoons active dry yeast or	¼ cup olive oil
1⅓ small cakes (24 grams) fresh yeast	3¾ cups unbleached all-purpose flour
1½ cups warm water	2½ teaspoons salt

Stir the yeast into the water in a mixer bowl, let stand until creamy, about 10 minutes. Stir in the oil with the paddle, then the flour and salt. Change to the dough hook and knead until smooth and elastic, about 3 minutes.

First Rise—Place the dough in an oiled bowl, cover tightly with plastic wrap, and let rise until doubled, 1 to 1½ hours.

Shaping—Cut the dough in half and place each piece in a lightly oiled 9- or 10-inch pie plate. Flatten and stretch the dough to cover as much of the bottom as possible; then dimple the tops quite vigorously with your fingertips to stretch it some more. Cover with a towel and let it relax for 10 minutes. Dimple and stretch the dough more, so that it really covers the bottom, let rest under a towel for another 20 to 25 minutes.

TOPPING

¼ cup whipping or heavy cream	⅛ teaspoon freshly grated nutmeg
8 ounces Gorgonzola cheese	Olive oil, for brushing the tops
½ teaspoon dried thyme	

Mix the cream, cheese, and thyme in a food processor fitted with the steel blade. With the paddle of an electric mixer, mash the cheese in a mixing bowl and beat in the cream and thyme. Spread the cheese mixture equally over the doughs with a rubber spatula or wooden spoon.

Second Rise—Brush the tops lightly with oil, cover with a towel, and let rise until well puffed, 50 minutes to 1 hour.

Baking—Heat the oven to 425°F. Bake for 10 minutes. Reduce the heat to 375°F and bake until the topping is golden brown and just starting to bubble, about 10 minutes. Unmold immediately onto a rack. This focaccia is best hot but can also be served warm or at room temperature. Do not refrigerate.

Variations—To make *Focaccia al Sale*, omit the Gorgonzola topping. Sprinkle the top of the dough with coarse salt and brush with olive oil. Brush again with oil after baking.

To make *Focaccia alle Cipolle*, substitute 2 finely sliced and sautéed yellow onions for the topping. Sprinkle with salt and brush with olive oil. Brush again with oil after baking.

To make *Focaccia ai Peperoni*, sauté 2 to 3 finely sliced red and yellow bell peppers in 3 tablespoons olive oil and 1½ tablespoons butter over medium-low heat until soft, about 15 minutes. Substitute the sautéed pepper mixture for the Gorgonzola topping. Brush the focacce with oil after baking.

To make *Focaccia alla Ricotta*, mix 8 ounces ricotta, ½ cup diced prosciutto, ⅓ cup grated *pecorino* or Parmesan cheese, 5 tablespoons milk, and ⅛ teaspoon freshly grated nutmeg as directed for the Gorgonzola topping.

Schiacciate Integrali
(WHOLE WHEAT FLAT BREADS)

MAKES 5 TO 6 PIZZETTE; TWO 10-INCH
SCHIACCIATE; OR ABOUT 60 FOCACCETTE

These Florentine schiacciate are simply tasty flat breads made of whole wheat flour; top them with sweet red onions flavored with thyme or wash the tops with garlic-scented olive oil. If you bake them without toppings, these make wonderful buns for sandwiches; just cut them in half, stuff with slices of prosciutto and cheese, and warm them briefly. Whether you make them as big as pizzas or as small as hors d'oeuvres, you can be sure you're making the Tuscan equivalent of focacce in the stylish whole wheat variation.

2½ teaspoons active dry yeast or
   1 small cake fresh yeast

1½ cups warm water

1 tablespoon plus 1 teaspoon lard or
   olive oil

About 2¾ cups unbleached all-
   purpose flour

1 cup less 2 tablespoons whole wheat
   flour

1½ teaspoons salt

Olive oil, for brushing the tops

Stir the yeast into the warm water in a mixer bowl; let stand until creamy, about 10 minutes. Stir in the lard with the paddle. Mix in the flours thoroughly; add the salt and mix until incorporated. Change to the dough hook and knead until velvety and elastic, 2 to 3 minutes. If you want, finish kneading briefly by hand on a floured surface.

First Rise—Place the dough in a lightly oiled bowl, cover tightly with plastic wrap, and let rise until puffy but not doubled, 1 to 1¼ hours.

Shaping—Knead the dough briefly on a lightly floured surface. Cut the dough in half for two 10-inch schiacciate or into 5 or 6 pieces for pizzette. Shape each piece into a ball on a lightly floured surface or stretch the dough over your fists to a 10-inch circle for schiacciate or a 5-inch circle for pizzette, leaving a thick edge. Place on floured baker's peels or lightly oiled pizza pans, pie plates, or baking sheets. You may need to stretch the dough, let it relax for a few minutes under a towel, then stretch it again. Brush the tops with oil.

To make focaccette—Roll the dough out thin on a floured surface and cut out circles with a 1¼- to 1½-inch cookie cutter. Place on lightly oiled baking sheets. Do not oil the tops. Cover with towels and let rise without any topping.

Topping for schiacciate or pizzette—Sauté 2 thinly sliced large red onions in 2 tablespoons olive oil and 1 tablespoon unsalted butter over very low heat for 15 to 20 minutes; spread the onions over the dough and sprinkle with a fat pinch of dried thyme. Or sauté 2 whole large cloves garlic in 2 to 2½ tablespoons olive oil over medium heat for 4 to 5 minutes; discard cooked garlic, brush the dough with the oil and sprinkle with 2 tablespoons chopped fresh sage or rosemary or 1 tablespoon sea salt.

Second Rise—Cover the dough with towels and let rise until puffy but not doubled, about 45 minutes. Dimple and stretch the dough again with your fingers. Before baking and after the second rise, dimple the focaccette with your index fingers; then oil the tops and sprinkle with a bit of fine sea salt.

Baking—Heat the oven to 400°F. Use baking stones if you have them (turn the oven on 30 minutes before baking) and place the baking pans directly on the preheated stones. Bake the schiacciate for 22 to 25 minutes, the pizzette for 15 to 18 minutes, and the focaccette for 12 to 15 minutes. Serve hot or cool on racks to room temperature.

Calzone di Messina

(CALZONE MESSINA SICILY STYLE)

2 pounds prepared pizza dough

2 pounds skinless Italian sausage

3 large onions, diced

1 cup pitted oil-sured black olives

½ cup dry red wine

1 tablespoon tomato paste or
 sauce

1 egg yolk, beaten

Oil a baking tin and line with 1 pound rolled-out pizza dough. Fry the sausage in a large nonstick skillet until crisp and remove. Fry the onions on moderate heat until soft. Add the wine, adjust the heat to high, and evaporate the wine; stir with a wooden spoon. Add the tomato paste, cook 10 minutes on moderate heat, and add the olives. Stir well and allow to cool. Pour the filling (sausage, onions, tomato mixture) over the bottom crust. Cover with 1 pound rolled-out pizza dough and press the edges together. Make slits in the top crust (steam vents). Brush with the beaten egg yolk. Bake in a 450° oven for 25 minutes. Remove and let stand for 15 minutes. Slice into squares and serve.

Crostata di Formaggio e Pancetta

(CHEESE AND ITALIAN BACON PIE)

2 frozen 9-inch piecrusts	4 large eggs, at room temperature
6 thin slices pancetta or bacon	1 cup low-fat or skim milk
1 medium onion, diced	1 teaspoon salt
8-ounce package Sargento natural six-cheese Italian shredded cheese	¼ teaspoon ground nutmeg
	⅛ teaspoon hot crushed pepper

Preheat the oven to 425°F. Bake the empty crusts at 425°F for 5 minutes. Adjust the oven temperature to 450°F. Remove the partially baked crusts.

Meanwhile, fry the pancetta or bacon until crisp. Drain all the grease except for 1 tablespoon. Sauté the onion in grease until soft.

Sprinkle 4 ounces of cheese in each pie shell. Sprinkle half of the bacon and onion on top of the cheese. Beat the eggs with milk, salt, nutmeg, and hot crushed pepper and pour evenly between the two crusts.

Bake at 450°F for 15 minutes, lower the oven to 350°F, and bake for another 15 minutes. Shut off the oven and let the pies set for the last 15 minutes. Remove, cool to room temperature, slice, and serve. This is a super appetizer.

Introduction To Pastries

Stroll down any street in an Italian town and you'll see unmistakable evidence of the famous Italian sweet tooth. Bakeries and *pasticcerie* on almost every block boast windows and shelves full of rustic tarts and richer creamier *dolci*, examples of the satisfying simple desserts and the more ornate category of sweets that includes confections dreamed up to celebrate saints' day holidays, festivals, and feast days. Who could be surprised? Even the Romans had a bakers' guild and loved their layer cakes, flat cheesecakes, little tarts filled with custard or cheese, and baked pastries sweetened with honey or grape must. (Must is grape juice heated to a thick syrup.)

The craze for sweets has been an Italian tradition for a very long time. The entire tradition of cooking with sugar began particularly early in Italy as a result of the Crusades and the voyages of Venetian traders. Sugar came to Sicily with the Arabs, who brought their elaborate pastries, as well as sugarcane and almond paste and transformed Palermo into a city of sumptuous pastries made of lemons and sweet oranges, almonds, dates, and figs. Venice was the great center of the medieval spice trade, and its cooks were apt pupils who quickly learned the secrets of Arab pastry baking. When sugar first arrived, it was called *il sale dolce*, sweet salt, and the Italians used it as a flavoring in all food, not just desserts. The sweet foods were not set aside until the end of a meal, as they are now, but interspersed with other courses. Both sugar and spices were first sold in pharmacies, because they were considered medicinal wonders with benefits for health, although they were also destined for luxurious preparations on the tables of the rich. By 1300, Florence allowed only one hundred special bakers to work with sugar and spices and make marzipan, the base of almost all medieval and modern baking. Marzipan was called *fruta di martorana*, from the convent in Palermo famous for its extraordinary "fool the eye" fruits, vegetables, and animals.

Pastry baking became an art separate from bread baking in the late fifteenth century—the pastry cooks' guild was formed in 1492—but *torte* then were both sweet and savory—there was *pasta frolla* wrapped around meats and poultry, mushrooms, and dried fruits seasoned with spices. Four and twenty blackbirds really were baked in a pie; the recipe was published in the first European cookbook, *De Honesta Voluptate e Valetudine* in 1474 (in Italy, of course). The monks of early medieval Siena may have been enjoying their *panforte*, in which spices and pepper joined forces with sweet fruits and nuts, but it wasn't until the Renaissance that most true sweets came into their own. Bartolomeo Scappi, the chef of Pope Pius IV, wrote an enormous treatise that contained the first in-depth look at pastry making. It even had a recipe for dough layered with lard and rolled and folded like the puff pastry we make today. Pastry cooks appeared in the kitchens of great houses and courts and created radical innovations in the art of desserts.

Soon the secrets of the pastry baker spread to the West. As a young bride, Maria de Medici took her cooks to France where they taught the French cooks so well that a century later, when La Varenne wrote his first careful cookbook with its meticulous measurements and instructions, the French had become the acknowledged masters of the art. Now we tend to forget the importance of Italy's contributions. What after all is a *genoise* but the pastry of Genoa given a Gallic name? It is much easier to see the culinary stamp of other countries. *Pan di spagna*, Spanish bread, is sponge cake brought by the Spaniards when they conquered Sicily in the fifteenth century, and plum cake came from England with the Duke of Wellington who didn't want to leave his cake behind. These sweets mingling with the indigenous specialties and tastes of individual regions came to life as the Genoese made sweet *focaccia* with raisins, the Venetians invented the *zaletti* they still eat today, and the Sicilians made the *cannoli* and *cassate* that bear the culinary stamp of the earlier Normans and Arabs.

The monasteries and nunneries of Sicily played such a crucial role in the making of sweets that they had a virtual monopoly on the most important recipes of the region. Until the unification of Italy in 1860, cookies, cakes, and numerous pastries were made only in these religious retreats. And it was only as the nuns began to move out of the convents that the tradition began to change.

The Italian passion for sweets has had centuries to develop, so it is no surprise that every celebration comes with dessert. Easter couldn't arrive in Naples without *pastiera* or in Palermo without *cassata*. *Panforte* is the quintessential sweet of Christmas in Siena. For birthdays, marriages, confirmations, and baptisms, the art of the pastry baker is always at the table.

Crostate (Tarts)

Of the two traditions of baking sweets in Italy, one is based on the simple and homey desserts that families make year after year for friends and guests. These simple desserts are much cozier than the Italian extravaganzas that look more designed than baked, architectural marvels tucked full of pastry creams and sumptuous frothy interiors. The more domestic sweets have perfumed the mountain houses in the Val d'Aosta, the simple farmhouses near Bologna, villas in the Tuscan countryside, and apartments in Rome. Emanating from a simple way of life, they almost invariably start with *pasta frolla,* the basic sweet dough of Italy, which dates back to the late Renaissance.

Crostate are tarts. They are made only with *pasta frolla,* and each dessert takes its name from the fruit or jam that fills the crust. These *crostate* are, in fact, sold at the *forni,* bakeries where both bread and pastries are made, and the baking tends to be simple and straightforward. Nuts, fruits, and jams are the bases of most of the tarts, although bakers can transform the simplest ingredients into extravagant fare. The *torta del nonno* is essentially chocolate pudding tucked in a soft, buttery crust. Even the *torta Dumont* is a simple dessert from the mountains of France that found its way over the border and into the Italian tradition. Of course, you will not be surprised that a few lemons may be transformed into a cool lemon soufflé set in a baked "cup," or that hazelnut filling may be glazed with chocolate. Italian bakers are given to invention and can create tantalizing tastes from the simplest ingredients.

Pasta Frolla Semplice 🌿

(TENDER PIE OR TART DOUGH)

1 stick unsalted butter, softened, or ¾ cup vegetable oil

4 tablespoons granulated sugar or Splenda

Beat until pale yellow.

Add:

1 large egg

¼ cup milk, whole or skim

Beat until smooth.

Add:

one 16-gram Paneangeli vanilla-flavored baking powder (for a substitute,
dissolve 1 teaspoon baking powder and 1 teaspoon vanilla extract in the milk

Add:

2 cups all-purpose flour or whole wheat

Blend until the dough comes together.

For the Tart: Press the dough with your fingers into a greased 11- × 8-inch tart
pan with a removable bottom. Preheat the oven to 350°F. With the tines of a fork,
prick the bottom of the dough thoroughly. Bake for about 1 hour until golden
brown. Let rest for 1 hour. Fill with any precooked filling you desire.

For the Pie: Press into deep-dish 9-inch Pyrex pie dishes. Cook as directed by
your pie recipe.

For the Cookies: Roll out a double recipe of dough on a floured surface. Cut into
any shape desired. Place on parchment paper–cookie sheets and bake according to
the directions for your cookie recipe. For plain cookies, bake at 350°F for 15 to 20
minutes. To top with a lattice, cut the dough into 1-inch strips.

Pasta di Mandorle
(ALMOND PASTE)

MAKES ABOUT 2 POUNDS OR 3 $^{1}/_{4}$ CUPS

1 pound 2 ounces blanched almonds,
very lightly toasted

¾ cup confectioners' sugar, plus
additional for kneading

2 cups granulated sugar

½ cup water

¼ cup light corn syrup

½ teaspoon almond extract

Grind the almonds to a coarse powder in a nut grinder, blender, or food processor fitted with the steel blade. (If you use the processor, process with 1 tablespoon of the confectioners' sugar.) Then add the rest of the confectioners' sugar and grind to a fine powder. Remove to a mixer bowl.

Heat the sugar, water, and corn syrup in a small heavy saucepan over low heat and stir. When the sugar dissolves, turn up the heat to bring the syrup to a boil and cook until it registers 234°F to 236°F on a candy thermometer (a drop of the syrup should form a soft ball when dropped into a glass of cold water). Pour the sugar syrup over the almond mixture and mix by hand or with the paddle at the lowest speed until blended. Cool to room temperature. Mix in the almond extract. Knead well on a surface sprinkled with confectioners' sugar until soft and elastic, 2 to 3 minutes. Shape into a thick disk and wrap securely in plastic wrap. It will keep for months in the refrigerator.

Apricot Glaze

⅓ cup best-quality apricot jam or
   preserves

½ teaspoon water or fresh lemon
   juice

Heat the preserves and water in a small heavy saucepan over moderate heat until the mixture comes to a boil. Strain it through a sieve. Use the glaze while it is still warm. Any leftover glaze will keep indefinitely in a covered jar; heat it again before using. This recipe is easily doubled.

Crostata Di Marmellata

(JAM TART)

MAKES ONE 11- × 8-INCH TART;
12 SERVINGS

The famous Italian sweet tooth is indulged by the baker's art, but desserts made and served at home are usually extremely simple—a bowl of fresh fruit, a platter of cookies, or this simple jam tart, an unpretentious sweet pastry shell filled with homemade preserves. The quality of the jam is very important, because the fruit is not complicated with other flavorings. In Rome this crostata is made with visciole, a sour dark cherry that resembles amarena; in Emilia Romagna, Liguria, and Tuscany you will most likely find the tart filled with fruit or berry preserves.

3 cups best-quality raspberry or
   apricot jam
11- × 8-inch partially baked tart
   shell, with dough reserved for

lattice Pasta Frolla Semplice
   (page 124)
½ cup Apricot Glaze (page 126)

Spread the jam ½ inch thick over the tart shell. Make the lattice as directed on page 124.

Baking—Heat the oven to 400°F. Bake until the lattice is golden brown, 15 to 20 minutes. Immediately brush the top with the glaze. Cool to room temperature on a rack.

Variations—To make *Torta di Marmellata* or *Tartine alla Marmellata*, partially bake a 9- or 10-inch tart shell or 1½-inch tartlet shells made with Pasta Frolla Semplice, page 124, flavored with rum instead of vanilla. You will need about 2 cups jam for the 9- or 10-inch tart and 1½ to 2 cups jam for 10 to 12 tartlets. Make the lattice as directed on page 124. Bake as directed above; the tart will be done in 20 to 25 minutes and tartlets in 15 to 20 minutes. Glaze and cool as directed.

Crostata di Frutta

(BAKED FRUIT TART)

MAKES ONE 11-× 8-INCH TART; 12 SERVINGS

Use any of the fruits of summer to make this tart: golden pink peaches, brilliant strawberries or raspberries, blackberries, or cherries.

1¼ to 1½ cups apricot jam

11-× 8-inch partially baked tart shell, with dough reserved for lattice

Pasta Frolla Semplice (page 124)

3½ to 4 cups fresh fruit, such as sliced peaches; halved

strawberries; whole raspberries, blackberries, or blueberries; or sliced pitted cherries

1 egg, beaten

½ cup Apricot Glaze (page 000)

Spread the jam ¼ inch thick in the bottom of the tart shell. Arrange the fruit in an attractive pattern over the jam. Make the lattice as directed on page 124. Brush the lattice with the beaten egg.

Baking—Heat the oven to 425°F. Bake until the lattice is medium brown, 20 to 25 minutes. Immediately brush the top with the glaze. Cool to room temperature on a rack.

Variations—For a 9-inch tart, use about ¾ cup jam and 3 cups fruit. For 10 to 12 tartlets, use 1 to 1¼ cups jam and 8 ounces to 1 pound fruit.

Torta di Frutta Fresca ✦

(FRESH FRUIT TART)

MAKES ONE 9- OR 10-INCH TART, 6 TO 8
SERVINGS

A *fresh fruit tart is a fresh fruit tart in any language you care to name, but this one comes from Italy, the land of Botticelli and Bellini, so make it as glorious to look at as it is to eat. Set curved slices of golden peaches and scarlet plums within an enclosure of pastry dough, weave pointillist fantasies of dark blueberries and red raspberries, or fan slices of strawberries in radiating circles and shine them all with apricot glaze.*

¾ to 1 cup Pastry Cream (page 132)	strawberries, peaches, or plums;
9- or 10-inch fully baked tart shell (see	or whole raspberries, blueberries,
Pasta Frolla Semplice, page 124)	or blackberries
2 to 3 cups fresh fruit, such as sliced	¼ cup Apricot Glaze (page 126)

Spread the pastry cream ¼ inch thick in the bottom of the tart shell. Arrange the fruit in concentric circles over the cream. Brush the fruit with the glaze.

Variations For an 11-× 8-inch tart, use about 1 to 1⅓ cups pastry cream and 3 to 4 cups fresh fruit. For 10 to 12 tartlets, use about 2 cups pastry cream and 1⅓ to 2 cups fresh fruit. If you are using strawberries for the tartlets, arrange the slices in concentric circles to make a pyramid shape.

Torta di Nocciole con cioccolata 🌿

(HAZELNUT CAKE WITH CHOCOLATE GLAZE)

This cake is rich, densely nutty, and flavored with just a touch of orange. It is wonderful unadorned or sprinkled with a fine shower of confectioners' sugar, although it would be hard to imagine anyone objecting to the smooth dark chocolate glaze, which gives it an entirely different elegant life.

1 cup hazelnuts, plus additional for
  garnish
½ cup plus 2 tablespoons sugar
⅓ cup chopped candied orange peel
1 stick plus 2 tablespoons unsalted
  butter, at room temperature

1 large egg, at room temperature
2 large egg yolks, at room
  temperature
9-inch partially baked tart shell
  (Pasta Frolla Semplice, page 124)

Heat the oven to 350°F. Toast all the hazelnuts on a baking sheet until the skins blister, 10 to 15 minutes. Rub the skins off the nuts in a kitchen towel, or place the nuts in a food processor fitted with the plastic blade and process with 1 or 2 pulses until the skins come off. Set aside 10 to 12 perfect nuts for garnishing the cake.

Process the nuts and 2 tablespoons sugar in the food processor fitted with the steel blade to a coarse powder. Add the remaining sugar and the orange peel and process until finely ground. Remove to a mixer bowl, add 1 stick plus 2 tablespoons butter and cream with the paddle until very light and fluffy, about 5 minutes. Change to the whisk if your mixer has one. Add the egg and egg yolks, one at a time, beating thoroughly after each addition. Beat at medium to high speed for 3 to 4 minutes. Pour the cake batter into the tart shell and smooth the top.

Baking—Heat the oven to 350°F. Bake until a skewer inserted in the center comes out clean, 35 to 40 minutes. Cool completely on a wire rack.

GLAZE

5 ounces dark bittersweet chocolate
6½ tablespoons unsalted butter, at
  room temperature

1½ teaspoons corn syrup or clear
  glucose

Melt the chocolate in the top of a double boiler over simmering water. When the chocolate is completely melted, stir in the butter, 1 tablespoon at a time, waiting until each tablespoon of butter melts before adding the next, and then add the corn syrup. The glaze should be stiff and shiny. Pour the hot glaze over the cake to set the glaze quickly. Garnish with the perfect whole hazelnuts.

Variations—This cake can also be baked with a top crust of pastry. Roll out 10 ounces of pastry dough ¼ inch thick. Place over the batter before baking and trim the edges. Press onto the tart shell. Cut out small shapes from the leftover dough with a ravioli cutter or small knife and arrange on the pastry. Make a hole in the center to allow steam to escape. Brush the top with 1 egg yolk mixed with 1 tablespoon water and decorate the edge with skinned whole hazelnuts. Bake as directed.

Pastiera di Grano

(EASTER COOKED WHEAT PIE DI CLELIA
FROM CLELIA LA BOZZETTA'S COLLECTION)

CRUST

2 cups all-purpose flour or whole
  wheat
¾ cup granulated sugar or Splenda
1 stick unsalted butter or ¾ cup
  vegetable oil
One 16-gram pack of Paneangeli

vanilla-flavored baking powder or
substitute for Paneangeli vanilla-
flavored baking powder, dissolve
1 teaspoon baking powder and
1 teaspoon vanilla extract in ¼ cup
milk

Mix all the ingredients well. Knead for 5 minutes on a lightly floured surface. Shape into a round disk ¼ inch thick, wrap in plastic wrap, and refrigerate for ½ hour. Roll out the dough to fit into a 12½- × 1½-inch pie tin.

PASTRY CREAM

½ cup sugar or Splenda
¼ cup cornstarch
1 teaspoon vanilla extract

2 egg yolks
1 quart milk, whole or skim

Beat the sugar, cornstarch, vanilla, and egg yolks with a wire whisk in a large saucepan. Place on medium heat, add the milk, and whisk until the mixture comes to a boil and thickens. Remove from the heat and refrigerate. Meanwhile, make the filling:

FILLING

1 pound ricotta, whole or part skim
½ cup sugar or Splenda
1 can cooked wheat berries (found in
  Italian specialty shops)
Dilute the wheat berries with:
  1 tablespoon milk

1 teaspoon orange flour water or
  orange juice
2 egg yolks
1 teaspoon vanilla extract
½ cup candied citron, finely diced
¼ cup brandy (any kind)

Beat all the ingredients well. Fold in the pastry cream. Pour into a prepared pie tin. Bake for 1 hour at 350°F. Allow to cool. This can be frozen and thawed to room temperature before serving.

Torte (Cakes)

Crostata di Ricotta

(ITALIAN CHEESECAKE OR RICOTTA TART)

MAKES ONE 9^{1}/$_{2}$-INCH CHEESECAKE;
8 TO 10 SERVINGS

Although it seems unlikely that such an elegant cake could come from humble beginnings, this cheesecake, from the mountains of the Garfagnana region of Tuscany, is based on the highly prized ricotta of that rustic area. Its popularity survives in various forms in Italy today.

½ cup golden raisins

3 to 4 tablespoons Marsala

1 pound ricotta, preferably whole milk

1 cup sugar

1 tablespoon unbleached all-purpose flour

4 eggs separated, at room temperature

¼ cup heavy or whipping cream

¼ cup sour cream

1 teaspoon vanilla extract

¼ teaspoon salt

Deep 9½-inch unbaked pastry shell (Pasta Frolla Semplice, page 124), made with 2 tablespoons Marsala and 1 teaspoon grated lemon zest instead of the vanilla

Soak the raisins in the Marsala for at least 15 minutes. Drain but reserve the Marsala. Press the ricotta through a wire-mesh sieve into a mixing bowl, or process with several pulses in a food processor fitted with the steel blade until smooth and transfer to a mixing bowl. Add the sugar and flour and beat with a wooden spoon until creamy. Add the egg yolks, heavy and sour creams, reserved Marsala, and the vanilla; stir until thoroughly blended. Stir in the raisins. Beat the egg whites and salt until the peaks are stiff and fold into the ricotta mixture. Pour the filling into the tart shell and smooth the top.

Baking—Heat the oven to 350°F. Bake until the filling is set and the pastry golden brown, 50 to 60 minutes. Turn off the oven and let the cake cool with the oven door open for 30 minutes. This cake is so much better served warm that I urge you to bake it for 2 to 3 hours before serving or at least the same day you plan to eat it. If you must refrigerate it, warm it at 350°F for 20 to 30 minutes before serving.

Torta di Riso

(RICE TART)

MAKES 1 DEEP 8-INCH TART; 8 SERVINGS

Rice tarts are a very ancient tradition in Italian desserts, but no one knows whether they actually date back to Marco Polo's voyage to the East when Venetian traders, merchants, and sailors began bringing rice back from the Orient in ever-increasing amounts. By the sixteenth century there was an explosion of rice planting in the countryside around Venice, and housewives gave free reign to their imaginations and dreamed up elaborate rice dishes to satisfy their culinary fantasies. Perhaps that explains the origin of a venerable Venetian dessert exotically named torta alla Turchesa, *a Turkish tart, which combines with rice cooked in milk, butter, sugar, raisins, almonds, a few dates, and pine nuts and then bound with eggs and egg yolks. It sounds remarkably similar to this* torta di riso, *which is but one of many variations on the menu available in Italy today. Almonds are often de rigueur in this particular dessert and can certainly be added to this tart as well.*

3 cups milk

1¼ cups water

½ cup plus 2 tablespoons sugar

2 strips lemon zest

Pinch of salt

1 cup plus 1½ tablespoons
Originario or long-grain rice

1 heaping cup raisins

¼ cup Marsala or rum, plus 1 to 2
tablespoons for brushing the top

2 large eggs, separated, at room
temperature

1 teaspoon vanilla extract

5 tablespoons unsalted butter, at
room temperature

Deep 8-inch tart shell (Pasta Frolla
Semplice, page 124), baked 20 to
25 minutes

Heat the milk, water, sugar, lemon zest, and salt to a boil in a medium heavy saucepan. Stir in the rice and reduce the heat to very low. Simmer covered, stirring occasionally, until all the liquid is absorbed, 35 to 40 minutes. Spread the rice on a dinner plate to cool and discard the lemon zest.

While the rice is cooking, soak the raisins in ¼ cup Marsala for at least 30 minutes. When the rice has cooled to room temperature, whisk the egg yolks and vanilla in a mixing bowl until blended. Stir in the rice. Add the butter and raisins with the Marsala and mix thoroughly. Beat the egg whites until the peaks are stiff but not dry and fold into the rice mixture. Pour the filling into the tart shell.

Baking—Heat the oven to 400°F. Bake just until lightly creamy inside (a skewer inserted in the center should not come out completely clean), about 30 minutes. If the top is too pale, you can brown it briefly under the broiler. Cool on a wire rack, and brush the surface with 1 to 2 tablespoons Marsala, making a few holes with a toothpick to allow the liquor to penetrate the interior. Serve at room temperature.

Variations To make *Budini di Riso*, bake the rice pudding in 6 fully baked tartlet shells at 400°F for 20 minutes.

Torta Rustica di Noci e Caffè
(A RUSTIC COUNTRY CAKE OF ESPRESSO AND WALNUTS)

MAKES ONE 8-INCH CAKE OR
SMALL CAKE RING; 6 TO 8 SERVINGS

This simple, moist cake of walnuts and espresso was once commonly made at home on the Tuscan coast north of Viareggio; it has since become almost a memory and today only the old people still eat and remember it.

About 1⅔ cups walnut pieces

7 tablespoons unsalted butter, at room temperature

½ cup plus 2 tablespoons sugar

2 large eggs

1¾ cups less 1 tablespoon all-purpose flour

½ teaspoon baking powder

½ teaspoon salt

½ cup warm strong brewed espresso or 3 tablespoons instant espresso powder, dissolved in ½ cup warm water

1 teaspoon vanilla extract

Finely grind about 10 of the walnut pieces and set aside for the top; chop (but not finely) the remaining walnuts.

Cream the butter and sugar with a wooden paddle or electric mixer until light and fluffy. Add the eggs, one at a time, beating thoroughly after each addition. Sift the flour, baking powder, and salt together. Beat in the flour mixture alternately with the coffee and vanilla in 3 additions, beginning and ending with the flour. Stir the chopped walnuts into the cake batter.

Butter and lightly flour an 8-inch cake pan or 6-cup ring mold. Pour the cake batter into the prepared pan and sprinkle with the ground walnuts.

Baking—Heat the oven to 350°F. Bake the cake until a skewer inserted in the center comes out clean, 40 to 60 minutes for the 8-inch cake or 40 to 50 minutes for the ring mold. Cool completely on a wire rack.

Torta Speziata

(SPICE CAKE)

MAKES ONE 8-INCH CAKE

Spice cake, Italian style, is very moist and tender and is delicious with rum-flavored whipped cream.

⅔ cup raisins

7 tablespoons unsalted butter, at
room temperature

½ cup granulated sugar

1 large egg

1¾ cups less 1 tablespoon all-purpose
flour

½ cup plus 1 tablespoon best-quality
Dutch-process cocoa

2 teaspoons baking powder

1 heaping teaspoon ground
cinnamon

1 teaspoon ground nutmeg

¼ teaspoon ground cloves

¾ teaspoon salt

¾ cup plus 1 teaspoon warm strong
brewed espresso or 3 tablespoons
instant espresso powder dissolved
in ¾ cup of water plus 1 scant
tablespoon plus 1 teaspoon hot
water

Confectioners' sugar

Soak the raisins in warm water to cover for 15 to 30 minutes; drain. Cream the butter and sugar with a wooden paddle or electric mixer until light and fluffy. Add the egg and beat thoroughly. Sift 1¾ cups flour, the cocoa, baking powder, cinnamon, nutmeg, cloves, and salt together. Beat in the flour mixture alternately with the espresso in 3 additions, beginning and ending with the flour. Toss the raisins with 1 tablespoon flour and fold into the batter.

Butter and flour an 8-inch cake pan; pour the batter into the pan and smooth the top.

Baking—Heat the oven to 350°F. Bake until the cake shrinks slightly from the side of the pan; it should still be slightly moist inside, 40 minutes to cool. Cool on a wire rack. Invert the cake onto a serving plate and sieve confectioners' sugar over the top.

Crostata di Pasta di Mandorle
(ALMOND PASTE TART)

1 package 7-ounce Odiense almond
   paste, grated
½ cup sugar or Splenda
1 stick unsalted butter, softened, or
   ¾ cup vegetable oil

3 large eggs
½ cup cake flour (Pillsbury's Soft as
   Silk) or whole wheat flour
Zest of 1 lemon or orange

Beat the almond paste, sugar, and butter with an electric mixer on low speed. Add the eggs, one at a time, until well incorporated. Add the flour. Beat on high speed for 3 minutes. Mix in the citrus zest. Pour into a well-greased 8-inch tart pan.

Baking—Bake for 35 minutes at 350°F. Cool at room temperature and serve. This freezes well—do *not* reheat—thaw and serve at room temperature.

Crostata di Fichi Freschi
(FRESH FIG PIE)

Make the crust from Pasta Frolla recipe, page 124, and bake according to the directions.

1½ cups half-and-half or milk

1½ teaspoons honey

1 teaspoon vanilla extract

7 tablespoons sugar or
  Splenda

3 tablespoons plus 1 teaspoon
  cornstarch

1 whole egg and 1 egg yolk

3 pints fresh figs, washed and
  chopped roughly

In a heavy saucepan cook the half-and-half or milk, honey, and vanilla. Bring to a boil; lower the heat and simmer for 5 minutes. Remove from the heat, let cool for 10 minutes, and whisk in the sugar, cornstarch, 1 egg and egg yolk. Return to medium heat, whisk constantly, bring back to a boil, and simmer for 3 minutes, constantly whisking. Remove and cool in the refrigerator for ½ hour. Mix in the chopped figs. Refrigerate for 1 hour. Fill the baked crust. Cut and serve at room temperature.

Torta di 500 grami

(POUND CAKE)

> 2 sticks softened butter or 1 cup vegetable oil
> 1½ cups sugar or Splenda

Cream together with an electric mixer until pale yellow.

> 4 eggs

Mix in one at a time until each is absorbed.

> ½ cup milk, whole or skim
> 2 teaspoons pure vanilla extract

Mix in until smooth.

> 2 cups flour and 2 teaspoons baking powder (whole wheat is okay)

Sift over batter. Beat until smooth. At this point you may add:

> 1 cup chopped nuts (walnuts are preferable)
> 1 cup raisins, soaked in hot water for 15 minutes and drained

Mix for about 10 minutes on high speed.

Preheat the oven to 350°F.

Pour the batter into a well-greased tube pan. Bake at 350°F for 1 hour. Remove from the oven and let rest for 10 minutes. Turn out of the pan.

This also freezes well. Follow the same procedure for freezing cheesecake, on the following page.

Torta di Ricotta
(RICOTTA CHEESECAKE)

2 pounds ricotta, drained in a
  colander for ½ hour
1 pound powdered sugar or 2 cups
  Splenda, for baking
6 large eggs
2 teaspoons vanilla extract

3 tablespoons all-purpose flour or
  whole wheat
¼ pound or 4 ounces candied fruit,
  optional
Three 9-inch frozen deep-dish pie
  pastry

Beat the drained ricotta along with the sugar or Splenda until smooth. Add the eggs, one at a time, until absorbed. Add the vanilla and flour and blend well with the electric whisk attachment. Fold in the candied fruit, if using.

Preheat the oven to 380°F.

Pour into three 9-inch frozen pie pastry shells.

Place each pie on parchment paper–covered cookie sheets.

Bake at 380°F for 1 hour. Remove, let cool on the cookie sheet for 20 minutes, then place the pies on a wire rack to cool completely. Refrigerate or freeze with heavy-duty aluminum foil. When ready to use, thaw the frozen pie in the refrigerator overnight and allow to come to room temperature before serving. A knife dipped in hot water is very helpful here.

Torta di Ricotta di Guglielmo Napoli

(ITALIAN RICOTTA CHEESECAKE)

3 pounds whole milk ricotta

1½ cups granulated sugar or Splenda, for baking

6 large eggs

1 heaping tablespoon all-purpose flour or whole wheat

½ teaspoon cinnamon

½ cup chocolate chips, or ½ cup bittersweet or butterscotch morsels

½ cup candied fruit

3 teaspoons vanilla extract

½ teaspoon almond extract

In the bowl of a heavy-duty standing mixer with a whisk, beat the ricotta and sugar or Splenda until smooth. Add the eggs, one at a time until absorbed. Add the flour, cinnamon, chocolate chips, or bittersweet morsels, candied fruit, and vanilla and almond extracts. Beat until smooth.

Preheat the oven to 350°F.

Grease a 10-inch springform pan heavily with vegetable oil spray.

Sprinkle plain bread crumbs into the pan to coat the bottom and sides. Shake out any excess bread crumbs.

Pour the ricotta mixture into the pan. Bake for 1 hour. Open the oven door and let the cake rest for 25 minutes. Remove and allow to cool at room temperature for 2 hours. Run a butter knife all around the perimeter of the pan to loosen. Unsnap the sides; remove the side. Refrigerate. This may be frozen by wrapping tightly with heavy-duty aluminum foil. Defrost in the refrigerator overnight. Let thaw at room temperature for 1 hour and serve.

Torta di Formaggio Dolce e Zucca
(PUMPKIN CHEESECAKE)

CRUST

1½ cups sugarless cookie crumbs

¼ cup Splenda sweetener

Zest from 1 small lemon

1 teaspoon ground nutmeg

FILLING

Three 8-ounce packages low-fat
cream cheese

1 cup Splenda sweetener

3 large eggs

½ cup low-fat sour cream or plain
yogurt

1½ cups canned pure pumpkin
puree

½ teaspoon cinnamon

½ teaspoon ground ginger

½ teaspoon salt

¼ teaspoon ground nutmeg

Heat the oven to 350°F. Spray the bottom of a 10-inch springform pan with vegetable spray (not the sides). Wrap with heavy-duty aluminum foil outside the pan. In a medium bowl, stir together all the ingredients for the crust. Press evenly over the bottom and ½ inch up the sides. Bake for 10 minutes.

In a KitchenAid bowl, beat room temperature cream cheese until smooth. Scrape down the sides of the bowl. Beat in the Splenda. Add the eggs one at a time. Beat in all the other ingredients until smooth and scrape down the sides of the bowl.

Place the aluminum-covered springform pan in a large roasting pan. Fill the roasting pan with very hot water to ½ inch up the sides of the springform pan. Bake for 70 minutes. Remove from the oven. Remove from the roasting pan. Cool completely on a wire rack. Refrigerate overnight. Remove the sides of the springform pan. Cut and serve.

Torta di dolce Formaggio di Carmela

(CARMEL'S CHEESECAKE [NO BOTTOM CRUST])

My niece Carmel O. Ferrante gave me this marvelous cheesecake recipe. I like it for it does not require a bottom crust and is very richly delicious.

Three 8-ounce packages regular cream cheese	6 jumbo eggs
Two 8-ounce packages low-fat Neufchâtel cream cheese	1½ cups sugar or Splenda
	1½ teaspoons vanilla extract (pure *not* imitation)

In a heavy-duty stand-up mixer, place all of the ingredients and beat with the wire whisk attachment for 10 minutes on medium speed.

Preheat the oven to 350°F.

Spray a 10-inch springform pan with a light coating of vegetable oil spray.

Pour the mixture into the pan. Bake for 1 hour. Remove and cool for 20 minutes. Unlock the pan and wrap in heavy-duty aluminum foil to freeze. It will keep for a long time in the freezer. When ready to use, remove from the freezer and allow to thaw overnight in the refrigerator. Of course, you may simply refrigerate the cake and serve it for dessert at dinner.

Torta di Noccioline Amercane Pecan

(PECAN PIE)

My niece Jo-Anne, who lives in Encino, California, gave me this recipe.

1 cup Karo light corn syrup or
    sugarless maple syrup
1 cup granulated sugar or Splenda,
    for baking
3 large eggs, slightly beaten

2 tablespoons melted butter
1 teaspoon vanilla extract
1½ cups shelled pecans
One 9-inch frozen deep-dish
    piecrust

Preheat the oven to 350°F.

Beat the first 5 ingredients until well blended. Stir in the pecans. Pour into the piecrust. Bake for 55 minutes on a cookie sheet covered with parchment paper. Remove and let rest on the cookie sheet for ½ hour. Take the pie and place on a wire rack at room temperature for 1 hour. Serve warm. This may be frozen—follow the directions on page 143.

Torta al Rhum

(ITALIAN RUM CAKE)

5 large eggs, separated	1¼ cups all-purpose unbleached flour
¾ cup sugar or Splenda	2 teaspoons baking powder
½ cup rum	⅛ teaspoon salt

In a stand-up mixer, beat with the wire whisk, egg yolks, sugar, and rum. Beat the egg whites until stiff with ¼ cup sugar.

Sift the flour and baking powder over the wet ingredients and beat until smooth.

Add salt then beat until stiff. Fold in stiff egg whites until the whites are no longer visible.

Pour into a 10-inch springform pan that has been greased with vegetable cooking spray.

Bake in a 350°F oven for 45 minutes. Cool in the pan for 10 minutes. Invert on a wire rack to cool completely.

Torta di Mele di Evelina

(MY SISTER EVELYN'S APPLE CAKE)

1 cup granulated sugar or Splenda	1 teaspoon ground cinnamon
1 stick soft butter or ¾ cup vegetable oil	1 teaspoon salt
	3 teaspoons baking powder
3 large eggs	1½ cups milk, whole or skim
3 cups all-purpose unbleached flour or whole wheat	One 21-ounce can apple pie filling
	1 teaspoon vanilla extract

TOPPING

¼ cup packed light or dark brown sugar	¼ cup chopped nuts
	2 tablespoons melted butter

Preheat the oven to 350°F.

In a stand-up mixer attached with a whisk, beat the sugar with 1 stick of butter until creamy. Add the eggs, one at a time, until very smooth. Sift in the flour, cinnamon, salt, baking powder. Add vanilla extract and milk. Beat until very smooth.

Pour half of the cake batter into a greased rectangular pan. Add the apple pie filling and spread evenly. Top with the second half of the batter. Sprinkle with the topping ingredients. Bake for 45 to 50 minutes. Allow to cool in a pan on a wire rack. When cooled, cut the servings right in the pan and serve.

Torte di Zucca #1 Semplice #2 Originale

(PUMPKIN PIES #1 SIMPLE #2 ORIGINAL)

#1 SIMPLE PUMPKIN PIE

1 can (30 ounces) Libby's pumpkin
   pie mix
⅔ cup (5 ounces) evaporated skim or
   whole milk

2 large eggs, beaten
One 9-inch frozen pie pastry

Mix the pumpkin pie mix, evaporated milk, and the beaten eggs. Pour into a 9-inch frozen pie shell. Bake in 425°F oven for 15 minutes. Reduce the temperature to 350°F and bake for 1 hour. Cool on a wire rack for 2 hours. Serve warm or refrigerate. If refrigerated do not warm in a microwave oven—serve cold.

#2 ORIGINAL OR TRADITIONAL PUMPKIN PIE (2 PIES)

2 frozen 9 inch deep-dish pie shells

Preheat the oven to 450°F.

Beat 6 large eggs, 2 cups granulated sugar or Splenda, and 1 teaspoon salt and beat well. Add 2 cups evaporated skim or whole milk and beat well. Add one 29-ounce can of pureed pumpkin and beat well. Add the following spices: 2 teaspoons cinnamon, ½ teaspoon ground cloves, ½ teaspoon ground nutmeg, and ½ teaspoon ground ginger.

If you wish to add an Italian touch, then sprinkle the pie with slivered almonds (¼ cup for each pie).

Pour into pie shells. Place the pies on parchment-covered cookie sheets.

Bake at 450°F for 10 minutes. Reduce the heat to 350°F and bake for 45 minutes.

Place on a wire rack to cool for 2 hours. Serve warm or refrigerate. Serve at room temperature or, if refrigerated, serve cold—do not microwave.

Biscotti (Cookies)

I talians have given their cookies wonderful names that sound as if they're straight out of fairy tales or nursery rhymes: *brutti ma buoni* (ugly but good), *baci di dama* (lady's kisses), *boche di lupe* (wolves' mouths). Often the same cookie has an entirely different name in a different city or region. *Brutti ma buoni* in Tuscany has unaccountably become *bocconcini del nonno* (little sweets for grandfather) in Rome.

Cookies have been part of the Italian way of eating for a long time. The source of the almond paste cookies that are now favorites from one end of Italy to the other is probably the marzipan of Sicily that came with the Arabs, who also introduced cane sugar, almonds, and spices at about the same time that the crusaders were bringing oranges, lemons, dates, and figs to the island. Normans were refining sugar in Sicily before the twelfth century, and the Arabs brought a tradition of elaborate pastries that transformed Palermo into a city of sumptuous eating. We know that in 1308 at a banquet in honor of Pope Clement V there were at the table two trees full of all kinds of fruit—apples, figs, pears, and peaches—that seemed absolutely real but were actually made of *pasta reale*, or marzipan, made at the nearby monastery of Martorana. It was, in fact, the busy fingers and nimble hands of nuns that kept the tradition of marzipan alive as they made ever more extravagant fantasies: little lambs turned up for Easter, and perfect replicas of prickly pears, salamis, and fine slices of prosciutto proved their finesse with a paste made only of almonds, sugar, and egg whites. The nuns kept their recipes secret as they perfected them, and made all kinds of elegant decorations on little cookies. Their sweets were covered with angels and fruits that resembled bas-reliefs on local churches, and some even had geometric fondant frostings and glazes inspired by local cathedral ceilings.

Today the tradition is dying out, but every region still has its own special almond paste cookies. The *amaretti* of Saronno are famous everywhere, but there are *amaretti* from Piedmont as well, *riciarelli* from Siena, *brutti ma buoni* from Florence, *marasche* from Bologna, and *pignolate* from Sicily. Glass cases in bakeries are full of all kinds of cookies; every little *paese* and town has its own local cookie that is every bit as much a part of the regional tradition as its breads and pastas.

Biscotti Taralle

(FROSTED COOKIES)

6 large eggs

2½ cups granulated sugar

3½ cups all-purpose unbleached
flour or whole wheat

3½ cups cornstarch

2 cups milk

1 pack of Paneangeli vanilla-flavored
baking powder or the substitution
on page 124

1⅔ cups powdered sugar

1 teaspoon vanilla extract

4 tablespoons water

1 tablespoon butter or ¾ tablespoon
olive oil

Preheat the oven to 350°F.

Separate the egg whites from the egg yolks. Beat the yolks with the granulated
sugar until creamy. Sift in the flour and cornstarch and mix well, add the milk, and
blend well. Add the vanilla-flavored baking powder and blend well. Whisk the
egg whites into stiff peaks and fold into the flour mixture. Drop by tablespoonfuls
on cookie sheets covered with parchment paper (spray vegetable oil lightly on the
paper).

Bake in a 350°F oven for 35 minutes.

To make the frosting, dissolve the powdered sugar and vanilla in the water in a
small saucepan and heat to just before boiling. Set aside. Remove the cookie sheet
and frost each cookie with a pastry brush. Return to the oven. Shut off the oven and
shut the door. Let rest for 30 minutes. Remove from the oven and place on a wire
rack to cool completely.

Biscotti di Granoturco di Oreste

(MY BROTHER ORESTE'S CORNMEAL COOKIES)

1 stick butter, softened, or ¾ cup
    vegetable oil

¾ cup sugar or Splenda, cream until
    pale yellow

1 large egg, mix in until absorbed

¼ cup milk, whole or skim

1 teaspoon vanilla extract, mix well

1½ cups all-purpose unbleached
    flour or whole wheat

½ cup cornmeal

1 teaspoon baking powder

¼ teaspoon salt

½ cup raisins, soaked in hot water
    for 15 minutes and drained

Preheat the oven to 350°F.

Blend in all the above ingredients well on medium speed in a standing electric mixer. Drop the batter by teaspoonfuls on a greased cookie sheet 2 inches apart. Bake at 350°F at 15 minutes. Let cool for 10 minutes. Place on a wire rack to cool completely.

Stomatico

(TRADITIONAL REGGIO CALABRIAN COOKIES)

2 cups sugar or Splenda

1 cup caramel, i.e., 1 cup sugar heated on high in a heavy saucepan. When the sugar begins to melt, lower the heat to low and the sugar becomes a light brown syrup.

2 sticks softened butter or 1 cup vegetable oil

1 ounce ammoniated baking soda, dissolved in ½ cup milk

2 pounds all-purpose flour or whole wheat

2 hefty tablespoons powdered cinnamon

1½ cups whole raw almonds

Preheat the oven to 350°F.

To make this recipe you must have a heavy duty KitchenAid mixer. Cream the sugar and caramel with the butter using the paddle. Add the dissolved ammoniated baking soda and mix well. Add the sifted flour and cinnamon. Add almonds. Mix the dough with the paddle until blended. Change to the dough hook and knead for 5 minutes. Turn out onto a lightly floured large wooden cutting board. With a large wood rolling pin, roll into a 1-inch thickness. Cut into any shape desired. Place on greased cookie sheets. Bake at 350°F for 30 minutes. Cool on wire racks. Store uncovered in a very dry area. The longer these dry out the better. Store in brown paper bags.

Biscotti del Mio Papà

(MY FATHER, GIUSEPPE ORSINI'S, COOKIES)

4 large eggs

1 cup sugar or Splenda

½ cup vegetable oil

3 teaspoons vanilla extract, cream
    with electric mixer until smooth

5 cups all-purpose unbleached flour
    or whole wheat

4 tablespoons baking powder

½ teaspoon salt

Preheat the oven to 350°F.

Sift all the ingredients for the batter and mix until you have a stiff dough. You can add up to 1 more cup of flour.

Roll the dough between the palms of your hands into a 1-inch-thick rope. Cut into 4-inch lengths. Place 2 inches apart on greased cookie sheets. Press each cookie lightly with the tines of a fork. Bake at 350°F until light brown for 12 to 15 minutes. Cool on a wire rack. Store in an airtight container. These are great for dipping in hot coffee or sweet vermouth.

Biscotti di Pignoli

(PINE NUT COOKIES)

PASTA DI MANDORLE (ALMOND PASTE)

1 pound raw almonds

¾ cup confectioners' sugar

2 cups granulated sugar or Splenda

½ cup water

¼ cup light corn syrup or sugarless
    maple syrup

½ teaspoon almond extract

In a large food processor fitted with the steel blade, grind the almonds and pow-dered sugar to a fine powder. Transfer to the bowl of a standing electric mixer.

In a small saucepan, heat the granulated sugar, water, and corn syrup on low heat until the sugar is dissolved. Heat to a boil on high heat until the syrup registers 236° on a candy thermometer.

Pour the syrup over the almond paste and mix at low speed until well blended. Let cool to room temperature. Yield: 2 pounds. Reserve what is not immediately used by wrapping in plastic film and refrigerate. Reserved paste must come to room temperature before using in any recipe.

BISCOTTI

1 cup pine nuts

1 pound almond paste, at room
    temperature

2 cups granulated sugar or Splenda

2 tablespoons honey

1 teaspoon pure vanilla extract

3 egg whites

In a standing electric mixer, beat all the ingredients with the paddle until stiff. Line cookie sheets with parchment paper. (For the next step, I use unpowdered la-tex gloves.) Pick out teaspoonfuls of dough and roll into the size of fat cherries, about 2 inches round. Place 3 inches apart. Pat small amounts of pine nuts into each cookie. Bake at 380°F for 15 minutes. Let rest outside the oven for 10 min-utes. Remove with a spatula to a wire rack and allow to cool for 1 hour. Reserve the cookies in a large uncovered container.

Biscotti Quaresimali

(LENTEN COOKIES)

1 pound granulated sugar	1 teaspoon pure vanilla extract
1 pound raw almonds	2 full teaspoons ground cinnamon
1 pound pastry flour or twice sifted whole wheat	1 ounce ammoniated baking soda
	4 large eggs

Mix all the ingredients in a heavy-duty standing electric mixer fitted with a paddle until well blended. (For the next step, I use unpowdered latex gloves.) With wet hands, shape the dough into 6-inch-long sausages. Place very wide apart on parchment-paper cookie sheets. Bake for 1 hour at 300°F. Remove from the oven and with a large serrated knife, cut by pressing down (do not saw) into 1-inch cookies. Allow to cool on a large clean surface. These cookies, once completely cooled, are stored in open paper bags. Do not cover. The more exposed to air, the better.

Buranelli

(COOKIES FROM THE ISLAND OF BURANO—VENICE)

1 stick and 2 tablespoons butter or
  ¾ cup vegetable oil
1 cup and 3 tablespoons sugar or
  Splenda
5 egg yolks

2 teaspoons vanilla extract
1 teaspoon lemon extract
3 cups all-purpose flour or whole
  wheat
1 teaspoon salt

Cream the butter and sugar. Add the egg yolks one at a time. Add the vanilla and lemon extracts.

Sift the flour and salt over the mixture. Mix well with the paddle in the bowl of a standing mixer. Shape the cookies into small S shapes. Place on a cookie sheet covered with parchment paper 1½ inches apart. Bake at 375° for 20 to 25 minutes. Cool on a wire rack.

Ossi di Morti

Bones of the Dead, made in Reggio Calabria on All Souls' Day, November 2. These are re-minders that death is a sweet experience because it is the end of human pain and suffering.

3 egg whites

2 cups powdered sugar

1 tube (7 ounces) Odiense almond
  paste, grated, or 7 ounces of

homemade almond paste
  (p. 125)

2 tablespoons cocoa powder

1 cup *pignoli* (pine nuts)

In a large bowl, beat the egg whites to soft peaks. Add the powdered sugar and whip until just stiff. Add the almond paste, cocoa, and pine nuts and blend well. Drop by teaspoonfuls on a parchment paper–covered cookie sheet 1½ inches apart. Bake at 325°F for 22 minutes. Let cool for 10 minutes. Place on a wire rack to cool completely.

Biscotti con Spezie e Mandorle

(TUSCAN SPICE AND ALMOND BISCOTTI)

Cinnamon, allspice, and almonds are a fine flavor combination.

1 cup toasted almonds	¼ teaspoon allspice
1 cup plus 2 tablespoons all-purpose flour	⅓ cup sugar
	¼ cup butter, softened
¼ teaspoon baking powder	2 tablespoons honey
¼ teaspoon baking soda	1 medium egg
¼ teaspoon salt	½ teaspoon vanilla extract
¼ teaspoon cinnamon	¼ teaspoon almond extract

In a food processor or blender, finely grind half of the almonds. In a bowl, combine the ground almonds, flour, baking powder, baking soda, salt, cinnamon, and allspice. In a large bowl, cream the sugar and butter. Mix in the honey, egg, and vanilla and almond extracts. Gradually blend in the dry mixture and the remaining almonds. Divide the dough in half or thirds. On a well-floured surface, shape into logs. Transfer the logs to a parchment paper–lined or lightly sprayed baking sheet and bake in a preheated 350°F oven for 20 minutes. Cut the logs on the diagonal into ¾-inch slices. Return the slices to the baking sheet, leaving space around each slice, and continue baking for 10 to 15 minutes or until desired crispness. Cool completely on a wire rack.

Biscotti con Cannella e Pasi e Mandorle

(CINNAMON ALMOND RAISIN BISCOTTI)

Ground almonds add richness to these biscotti.

1 cup toasted almonds

½ cup brown sugar, firmly packed

¼ cup butter, softened

2 medium eggs

1 teaspoon vanilla extract

1 teaspoon almond extract

1 cup coarsely chopped toasted
  almonds

1 cup golden raisins

1½ cups all-purpose flour

1½ teaspoons cinnamon

¾ teaspoon baking powder

In a food processor or blender, grind 1 cup of almonds with the brown sugar. In a bowl, cream the butter with the almond mixture. Stir in the eggs, vanilla, and almond extract, 1 cup chopped almonds, and raisins. In a medium bowl, combine the flour, cinnamon, and baking powder and add to the almond mixture. Divide the dough in half or thirds. On a well-floured surface, shape into logs. Transfer the logs to a parchment paper–lined or lightly sprayed baking sheet and bake in a preheated 350°F oven for 20 minutes or until firm and lightly browned. Cool on a rack for at least 5 minutes. Cut the logs on the diagonal into ¾-inch slices. Return the slices to the baking sheet, leaving space around each slice, and continue baking for 10 to 15 minutes or until desired crispness. Cool completely on a wire rack.

Biscotti con Mandorle

(ALMOND BISCOTTI)

These basic biscotti are always delicious.

1 cup all-purpose flour	2 medium eggs
½ cup sugar	½ teaspoon vanilla extract
½ teaspoon baking soda	½ teaspoon almond extract
Pinch of salt	1 cup toasted almonds

In a bowl, combine the flour, sugar, baking soda, and salt. In another bowl, whisk together the eggs and vanilla and almond extracts; stir into the dry ingredients. Add the almonds. Divide the dough in half or into thirds. On a well-floured surface, shape into logs. Transfer the logs to a parchment paper–lined or lightly sprayed baking sheet and bake in a preheated 300°F oven for 30 minutes or until firm and lightly browned. Cool on a rack for at least 5 minutes. Cut the logs on the diagonal into ¾-inch slices. Return the slices to the baking sheet, leaving space around each slice, and continue baking for 15 minutes or until desired crispness. Cool completely on a wire rack.

Biscotti con Noci Macadamia e Rhum

(RUM MACADAMIA NUT BISCOTTI)

Rum and macadamia nuts make these biscotti special.

1 cup sugar	3 cups all-purpose flour
½ cup butter, softened	½ teaspoon baking powder
2 tablespoons dark rum	3 cups coarsely chopped toasted
4 medium eggs	macadamia nuts

In a bowl, cream the sugar and butter. Add the rum and eggs and mix well. In another bowl, combine the flour and baking powder and stir into the rum mixture. Add the nuts. Divide the dough in half or into thirds. On a well-floured surface, shape into logs. Transfer the logs to a parchment paper–lined or lightly sprayed baking sheet and bake in a preheated 350°F oven for 20 minutes or until firm and lightly browned. Cool on a rack for at least 5 minutes. Cut the logs on the diagonal into ¾-inch slices. Return the slices to the baking sheet, leaving space around each slice, and continue baking for 15 to 20 minutes or until desired crispness. Cool completely on a wire rack.

Biscotti con Nocciole e Albicoche

(HAZELNUT APRICOT BISCOTTI)

Ground hazelnuts give these biscotti an extra-rich flavor.

1 cup sugar	1½ teaspoons baking powder
½ cup butter, softened	1½ cups coarsely chopped toasted
2 teaspoons vanilla extract	hazelnuts
4 medium eggs	1½ cups coarsely chopped dried
1 cup finely ground hazelnuts	apricots
3 cups all-purpose flour	

In a large bowl, cream the sugar and butter. Add the vanilla, eggs, and ground hazelnuts. In a medium bowl, combine the flour and baking powder and add to the ground hazelnut mixture. Stir in the chopped hazelnuts and apricots. Divide the dough in half or into thirds. On a well-floured surface, shape into logs. Transfer the logs to a parchment paper–lined or lightly sprayed baking sheet and bake in a preheated 350°F oven for 20 minutes or until firm and lightly browned. Cool on a rack for at least 5 minutes. Cut the logs on the diagonal into ¾-inch slices. Return the slices to the baking sheet, leaving space around each slice, and continue baking for 10 to 15 minutes or until desired crispness. Cool completely on a wire rack.

Biscotti con Acero e Noci Pecan
(MAPLE PECAN BISCOTTI)

Maple adds its distinctive flavor to these crisp biscotti.

½ cup brown sugar, firmly packed	2 cups toasted pecans
¼ cup butter, softened	1½ cups all-purpose flour
2 tablespoons maple extract	¾ teaspoon baking powder
2 medium eggs	

In a bowl, cream the sugar and butter. Add the maple extract, eggs, and pecans. In a medium bowl, combine the flour and baking powder and add to the pecan mixture. Divide the dough in half or into thirds. On a well-floured surface, shape into logs. Transfer the logs to a parchment paper–lined or lightly sprayed baking sheet and bake in a preheated 350°F oven for 15 to 20 minutes or until firm and lightly browned. Cool on a rack for at least 5 minutes. Cut the logs on the diagonal into ¾-inch slices. Return the slices to the baking sheet, leaving space around each slice, and continue baking for 10 to 15 minutes or until desired crispness. Cool completely on a wire rack.

Biscotti con Zucca e Noci Pecan

(PUMPKIN PECAN BISCOTTI)

Add this pumpkin treat to your Thanksgiving repertoire.

½ cup sugar

¼ cup butter, softened

2 medium eggs

½ can (14.5 ounces) pumpkin purée

1½ cups toasted pecans

1½ cups all-purpose flour

1 teaspoon cinnamon

½ teaspoon freshly grated nutmeg

½ teaspoon ground cloves

¾ teaspoon baking powder

In a bowl, cream the sugar and butter. Stir in the eggs, pumpkin, and nuts and mix well. In another bowl, combine the remaining ingredients and add to the nut mixture. Divide the dough in half. On a well-floured surface, shape into logs. Transfer the logs to a parchment paper–lined or lightly sprayed baking sheet and bake in a preheated 350°F oven for 15 to 20 minutes or until firm and lightly browned. Cool on a rack for at least 5 minutes. Cut the logs on the diagonal into ¾-inch slices. Return to the baking sheet, leaving space around each slice, and continue baking for 10 to 15 minutes or until desired crispness. Cool completely on a wire rack.

Biscotti con Tre Tipi di Zenzero e Noci Pecan
(TRIPLE GINGER PECAN BISCOTTI)

These biscotti feature great flavor and the crunch of pecans.

½ cup sugar	2 medium eggs
¼ cup butter, softened	1½ cups coarsely chopped toasted
2 tablespoons ground ginger	pecans
1 tablespoon grated gingerroot	1½ cups all-purpose flour
¾ cup minced crystallized ginger	¾ teaspoon baking powder

In a bowl, cream the sugar and butter. Stir in the gingers, eggs, and pecans. In a small bowl, combine the flour and baking powder and add to the ginger mixture. Divide the dough in half or into thirds. On a well-floured surface, shape into logs. Transfer the logs to a parchment paper–lined or lightly sprayed baking sheet and bake in a preheated 375°F oven for 20 minutes or until firm and lightly browned. Cool on a rack for at least 5 minutes. Cut the logs on the diagonal into ¼-inch slices. Return the slices to the baking sheet, leaving space around each slice, and continue baking for 10 to 15 minutes or until desired crispness. Cool completely on a wire rack.

Biscotti con Sesami e Arancio

(SESAME ORANGE BISCOTTI)

Sesame seeds are a pleasant surprise in these biscotti.

½ cup sugar	½ cup toasted sesame seeds
¼ cup butter, softened	1½ cups all-purpose flour
1 tablespoon grated orange zest	¾ teaspoon baking powder
2 medium eggs	1 teaspoon cinnamon

In a bowl, cream the sugar and butter. Stir in the orange zest and eggs. Add the sesame seeds and flour. Divide the dough in half or into thirds. On a well-floured surface, shape into logs. Transfer the logs to a parchment paper–lined or lightly sprayed baking sheet and bake in a preheated 375°F oven for 20 minutes or until firm and lightly browned. Cool on a rack for at least 5 minutes. Cut the logs on the diagonal into ¾-inch slices. Return the slices to the baking sheet, leaving space around each slice, and continue baking for 10 to 15 minutes or until desired crispness. Cool completely on a wire rack.

Biscotti con Frutti e Noci
(BURSTING-WITH-FRUIT BISCOTTI)

These cakelike biscotti are filled with fruit and nuts.

½ cup golden raisins

⅔ cup dried cranberries

⅔ cup chopped dried apricots

¼ cup sherry wine or sweet
  vermouth

3 medium eggs, separated

1¼ cups sugar

½ cup butter, melted and cooled

2 teaspoons vanilla extract

3 cups all-purpose flour

¾ teaspoon baking powder

½ cup toasted pistachio nuts

½ cup toasted walnuts

In a small bowl, combine the raisins, cranberries, apricots, and sherry; set aside for 30 minutes. In a large bowl, beat the egg yolks with half of the sugar. In another bowl, beat the egg whites; add the remaining sugar and continue beating until a soft meringue forms. Fold the meringue into the egg yolks.

In another bowl, combine several spoonfuls of meringue and the egg yolks with the butter and vanilla; add it back to the meringue and egg yolks. In a medium bowl, combine the flour and baking powder and add to the meringue and egg yolks. Work in the fruits with the sherry and nuts. Divide the dough in half or thirds. On a well-floured surface, shape into logs. Transfer the logs to a parchment paper–lined or lightly sprayed baking sheet and bake in a preheated 350°F oven for 30 minutes or until firm and lightly browned. Cool on a rack for at least 5 minutes. Cut the logs on the diagonal into ¾-inch slices. Return the slices to the baking sheet, leaving space around each slice, and continue baking for 10 to 15 minutes or until desired crispness. Cool completely on a wire rack.

Biscotti con Fichi e Rosmarino e Limone

(FIG LEMON ROSEMARY BISCOTTI)

There's a hint of the Greek countryside in these flavorful biscotti.

1 cup sugar

½ cup butter, softened

1 teaspoon almond extract

1 teaspoon minced fresh rosemary

3 medium eggs

1 cup finely chopped dried figs

½ cup finely chopped candied lemon
   peel

½ cup toasted almonds

2¾ cups all-purpose flour

1½ teaspoons baking powder

In a large bowl, cream the sugar and butter. Stir in the almond extract, rosemary, and eggs. Add the figs, lemon peel, and nuts. In a medium bowl, combine the flour and baking powder and add to the fruit-nut mixture. Cover and refrigerate for 3 hours. Divide the dough in half or into thirds. On a well-floured surface, shape into logs. Transfer the logs to a parchment paper–lined or lightly sprayed baking sheet and bake in a preheated 375°F oven for 20 minutes or until firm and lightly browned. Cool on a wire rack for at least 5 minutes. Cut the logs on the diagonal into ¾-inch slices. Return the slices to the baking sheet, leaving space around each slice, and continue baking for 10 to 15 minutes or until desired crispness. Cool completely on a rack.

Biscotti con Limone e Zenzero

(LEMON GINGER BISCOTTI)

With lots of ginger and nuts, these biscotti are perfect for dessert.

½ cup sugar

¼ cup butter, softened

1 teaspoon vanilla extract

1 teaspoon lemon extract

1 teaspoon grated lemon peel

2 medium eggs

1 cup coarsely chopped crystallized ginger

1 cup toasted walnuts

1½ cups all-purpose flour

¾ teaspoon baking powder

½ teaspoon ground ginger

In a large bowl, cream the sugar and butter. Add the vanilla and lemon extracts, lemon peel, and eggs. Stir in the crystallized ginger and nuts. In a medium bowl, combine the flour, baking powder, and ground ginger and add to the lemon mixture. Divide the dough in half or into thirds. On a well-floured surface, shape into logs. Transfer the logs to a parchment paper–lined or lightly sprayed baking sheet and bake in a preheated 350°F oven for 15 to 20 minutes or until firm and lightly browned. Cool on a rack for at least 5 minutes. Cut the logs on the diagonal into ¾-inch slices. Return the slices to the baking sheet, leaving space around each slice, and continue baking for 10 to 15 minutes or until desired crispness. Cool completely on a wire rack.

Biscotti Tropicali

(TROPICAL BISCOTTI)

The luscious taste of the tropics makes these biscotti special.

½ cup sugar

¼ cup butter, softened

2 medium eggs

1 cup chopped dried pineapple,
   soaked in ¼ cup rum

½ cup unsweetened coconut

½ cup coarsely chopped toasted
   Brazil nuts

2 cups all-purpose flour

¾ teaspoon baking powder

In a large bowl, cream the sugar and butter. Add the eggs and combine well. Add the pineapple and soaking liquid, coconut, and nuts. In a medium bowl, combine the flour and baking powder and add to the pineapple mixture. Divide the dough in half or into thirds. On a well-floured surface, shape into logs. Transfer the logs to a parchment paper–lined or lightly sprayed baking sheet and bake in a preheated 375°F oven for 20 minutes or until firm and lightly browned. Cool on a rack for at least 5 minutes. Cut the logs on the diagonal into ¾-inch slices. Return the slices to the baking sheet, leaving space around each slice, and continue baking for 15 minutes or until desired crispness. Cool completely on a wire rack.

Biscotti di Buona Salute

(NO-GUILT BISCOTTI)

These biscotti contain many good-for-you ingredients.

½ cup bran	2 large eggs
½ cup rolled oats	¼ cup honey
1 cup all-purpose flour	1 teaspoon vanilla extract
½ cup whole wheat flour	⅔ cup finely chopped mixed dried
½ cup brown sugar, firmly packed	fruit
1 teaspoon baking powder	½ cup toasted pecans
1 teaspoon cinnamon	

In a large bowl, combine the bran, oats, flours, brown sugar, baking powder, and cinnamon. In a small bowl, whisk the eggs, honey, and vanilla; add to the dry ingredients. Work in the fruit and nuts. Divide the dough in half or into thirds. On a well-floured surface, shape into logs. Transfer the logs to a parchment paper–lined or lightly sprayed baking sheet and bake in a preheated 325°F oven for 20 to 25 minutes or until firm and lightly browned. Cool on a rack for at least 5 minutes. Reduce the heat to 300°F. Cut the logs on the diagonal into ¾-inch slices. Return the slices to the baking sheet, leaving space around each slice, and continue baking for 15 minutes or until desired crispness. Cool completely on a wire rack.

Biscotti con Noci di Acagio e Arancio

(CASHEW ORANGE CRUNCH BISCOTTI)

A *wonderful orange flavor permeates these nutty biscotti.*

1¼ cups all-purpose flour

½ cup sugar

½ teaspoon baking soda

Pinch of salt

2 medium eggs

2 tablespoons grated orange peel

1 cup toasted cashews

In a bowl, combine the flour, sugar, baking soda, and salt. In a small bowl, whisk the eggs with the orange peel. Stir into the dry ingredients, add the cashews, and mix well. Divide the dough in half or into thirds. On a well-floured surface, shape into logs. Transfer the logs to a parchment paper–lined or lightly sprayed baking sheet and bake in a preheated 300°F oven for 20 minutes or until firm and lightly browned. Cool on a rack for at least 5 minutes. Cut the logs on the diagonal into ¾-inch slices. Return the slices to the baking sheet, leaving space around each slice, and continue baking for 10 to 15 minutes or until desired crispness. Cool completely on a wire rack.

Biscotti con semi di Papaveri e Limone

(LEMON POPPY SEED BISCOTTI)

Poppy seeds and tangy lemon give these biscotti special appeal.

1 cup sugar

½ cup butter, softened

3 medium eggs

2 tablespoons poppy seeds

½ teaspoon lemon extract

1 tablespoon grated lemon peel

3 cups all-purpose flour

1½ teaspoons baking powder

Pinch of salt

In a bowl, cream the sugar and butter. Add the eggs, poppy seeds, and lemon extract and peel. In another bowl, combine the remaining ingredients and add to the lemon mixture. Divide the dough into thirds. On a well-floured surface, shape into logs. Transfer the logs to a parchment paper–lined or lightly sprayed baking sheet and bake in a preheated 375°F oven for 20 minutes or until firm and lightly browned. Cool on a rack for at least 5 minutes. Cut the logs on the diagonal into ¾-inch slices. Return the slices to the baking sheet, leaving space around each slice, and continue baking for 10 minutes or until firm and lightly browned. Cool completely on a wire rack.

Biscotti con Fichi e Noci Pistachi 🌿
(FIG PISTACHIO BISCOTTI)

Figs and pistachios are an exotic and winning combination.

½ cup sugar

¼ cup butter, softened

2 medium eggs

1 teaspoon vanilla extract

1 teaspoon lemon extract

1 cup unsalted toasted pistachio nuts

1 cup chopped dried figs

1½ cups all-purpose flour

¾ teaspoon baking powder

In a bowl, cream the sugar and butter; stir in the eggs and vanilla and lemon extracts. Add the pistachios and figs. In another bowl, combine the flour and baking powder and add to the fig mixture. Divide the dough in thirds. On a well-floured surface, shape into logs. Transfer the logs to a parchment paper–lined or lightly sprayed baking sheet and bake in a preheated 350°F oven for 15 to 20 minutes until firm and lightly browned. Cool on a rack for at least 5 minutes. Cut the logs on the diagonal into ¾-inch slices. Return the slices to the baking sheet, leaving space around each slice, and continue baking for 10 to 15 minutes or until desired crispness. Cool completely on a wire rack.

Biscotti di Arancio e Ciocolatta

(CHOCOLATE-DIPPED ORANGE BISCOTTI)

These biscotti make the most of the ever-popular chocolate and orange flavor combination.

1 cup sugar	1½ teaspoons baking powder
½ cup butter, softened	2 cups coarsely chopped toasted
2 teaspoons orange extract	walnuts
2 tablespoons grated orange peel	1 cup bittersweet chocolate chips,
4 medium eggs	melted
3 cups all-purpose flour	

In a large bowl, cream the sugar and butter. Add the orange extract, orange peel, and eggs. In a medium bowl, combine the flour and baking powder and stir into the orange mixture. Add the nuts. Divide the dough in half or into thirds. On a well-floured surface, shape into logs. Transfer the logs to a parchment paper–lined or lightly sprayed baking sheet and bake in a preheated 350°F oven for 15 minutes or until firm and lightly browned. Cool on a rack for at least 5 minutes. Cut the logs on the diagonal into ¾-inch slices. Return the slices to the baking sheet, leaving space around each slice, and continue baking for 10 to 15 minutes or until desired crispness. Place on a rack and, when completely cooled, dip about one-third of each biscotti into the melted chocolate. Dry on a wire rack.

Biscotti di Ciocolatta e Marmalata
(CHOCOLATE-MARMALADE BISCOTTI)

Seville orange marmalade, which is not too sweet, is best in this recipe.

⅔ cup sugar

⅓ cup butter, softened

2 medium eggs

3 tablespoons Seville orange
    marmalade

2 tablespoons grated orange peel

2⅓ cups all-purpose flour

1½ teaspoons baking powder

Pinch of salt

½ cup toasted walnuts

¾ cup milk chocolate chips

In a large bowl, cream the sugar and butter. Beat in the eggs, marmalade, and orange peel. In a medium bowl, combine the flour, baking powder, and salt and add to the marmalade mixture. Blend in the nuts and chocolate chips. Divide the dough in half or into thirds. On a well-floured surface, shape into logs. Transfer the logs to a parchment paper–lined or lightly sprayed baking sheet and bake in a preheated 325°F oven for 25 minutes or until firm and lightly browned. Cool on a rack for at least 5 minutes. Cut the logs on the diagonal into ¾-inch slices. Return the slices to the baking sheet, leaving space around each slice, and continue baking for 10 minutes or until desired crispness. Cool completely on a wire rack.

Biscotti di Ciocolatta e Miele

(MILK CHOCOLATE AND HONEY BISCOTTI)

These biscotti are especially good with a big glass of milk.

½ cup honey

¼ cup butter, softened

1 teaspoon vanilla extract

2 medium eggs

1½ cups coarsely chopped milk
    chocolate

3 cups all-purpose flour

1 tablespoon baking powder

In a bowl, combine the honey, butter, vanilla, and eggs. Stir in the chocolate. In another bowl, combine the flour and baking powder and add to the chocolate mixture. Divide the dough in half or into thirds. On a well-floured surface, shape into logs. Transfer the logs to a parchment paper–lined or lightly sprayed baking sheet and bake in a preheated 350°F oven for 15 to 20 minutes. Cool on a rack for at least 5 minutes. Cut the logs on the diagonal into ¾-inch slices. Return the slices to the baking sheet, leaving space around each slice, and continue baking for 10 to 15 minutes or until desired crispness. Cool completely on a wire rack.

Biscotti Pieni di Ciocolatta
(CHOCK-FULL-OF-CHOCOLATE BISCOTTI)

Two types of chocolate make these biscotti a delight.

½ cup toasted almonds	1 teaspoon baking soda
2½ cups all-purpose flour	3 large eggs, lightly beaten
¾ cup sugar	½ cup milk chocolate chips
Pinch of salt	½ cup white chocolate chips

In a food processor or blender, grind the almonds finely. In a bowl, combine the almonds, flour, sugar, salt and baking soda. Stir in the eggs. Place the dough on a lightly floured surface. Knead to blend well and work in the chocolate chips. Divide the dough into thirds. On a well-floured surface, shape into logs. Transfer the logs to a parchment paper–lined or lightly sprayed baking sheet and bake in a preheated 375° oven for 20 minutes or until firm and lightly browned. Cool on a rack for at least 5 minutes. Cut the logs on the diagonal into ¾-inch slices. Return the slices to the baking sheet, leaving space around each slice, and continue baking for 20 minutes. Cool completely on a wire rack.

Biscotti con Coco e Ciocolatta
(COCONUT BISCOTTI DIPPED IN CHOCOLATE)

Coconut and chocolate are a well-loved flavor combination.

½ cup sugar

½ cup butter, softened

2 tablespoons vanilla extract

2 medium eggs

1½ cups unsweetened coconut

1½ cups all-purpose flour

¾ teaspoon baking powder

½ cup bittersweet chocolate chips, melted

In a large bowl, cream the sugar and butter. Add the vanilla, eggs, and coconut. In a medium bowl, combine the flour and baking powder and stir into the coconut mixture. Divide the dough in half or into thirds. On a well-floured surface, shape into logs. Transfer the logs to a parchment paper–lined or lightly sprayed baking sheet and bake in a preheated 350°F oven for 15 to 20 minutes or until firm and lightly browned. Cool on a rack for at least 5 minutes. Cut the logs on the diagonal into ¾-inch slices. Return the slices to the baking sheet, leaving space around each slice, and continue baking for 10 to 15 minutes or until desired crispness. Place on a rack and, when completely cooled, dip about one-third of each biscotti into the melted chocolate. Dry on a wire rack.

Biscotti con Varie Ciocolatta

(CHOCOLATY CHOCOLATE BISCOTTI DIPPED IN CHOCOLATE)

This is a biscotti made to order for chocolate lovers.

½ cup sugar	1 cup bittersweet chocolate chips
¼ cup butter, softened	1½ cups all-purpose flour
1 tablespoon chocolate extract	¾ teaspoon baking powder
2 medium eggs	½ cup white chocolate chips, melted

In a large bowl, cream the sugar and butter. Stir in the chocolate extract and eggs. Add the bittersweet chocolate chips. In a medium bowl, combine the flour and baking powder and add to the chocolate mixture. Divide the dough in half or into thirds. On a well-floured surface, shape into logs. Transfer the logs to a parchment paper–lined or lightly sprayed baking sheet and bake in a preheated 350°F oven for 10 to 15 minutes or until firm and lightly browned. Cool on a rack for at least 5 minutes. Cut the logs on the diagonal into ¾-inch slices. Return the slices to the baking sheet, leaving space around each slice, and continue baking for 10 minutes or until desired crispness. Cool completely on a wire rack and, using a pastry brush, paint each biscotti on one side with melted white chocolate.

Biscotti con Lampone e Ciocolatta
(CHOCOLATE RASPBERRY BISCOTTI)

Chocolate and raspberry are a magic flavor combination.

½ cup sugar

¼ cup butter, softened

1 medium egg

2 cups all-purpose flour

⅓ cup unsweetened cocoa powder

¾ teaspoon baking powder

¾ cup raspberry jam

In a medium bowl, cream the sugar and butter. Mix in the egg. In a small bowl, combine the flour and cocoa and baking powders and add to the butter mixture. Stir in the jam. Divide the dough in half or into thirds. On a well-floured surface, shape into logs. Transfer the logs to a parchment paper–lined or lightly sprayed baking sheet and bake in a preheated 325°F oven for 25 minutes or until firm and lightly browned. Cool on a rack for at least 5 minutes. Cut the logs on the diagonal into ¾-inch slices. Return the slices to the baking sheet, leaving space around each slice, and continue baking for 10 to 15 minutes or until desired crispness. Cool completely on a wire rack.

Biscotti con Noci Brasiliani e Caffé

(MOCHA BRAZIL NUT BISCOTTI)

Watch the second baking carefully—these burn easily.

½ cup sugar

¼ cup butter, softened

1 tablespoon chocolate extract

2 medium eggs

1 cup coarsely chopped toasted
   Brazil nuts

1⅓ cups all-purpose flour

1¼ teaspoons baking powder

2 tablespoons unsweetened cocoa
   powder

2 tablespoons instant coffee
   powder

In a bowl, cream the sugar and butter. Add the chocolate extract and eggs and mix well. Add the nuts. Combine the remaining ingredients and add to the egg mixture. Divide the dough in half. On a well-floured surface, shape into logs. Transfer the logs to a parchment paper–lined or lightly sprayed baking sheet and bake in a preheated 350°F oven for 20 minutes or until firm and lightly browned. Cool on a rack for at least 5 minutes. Cut the logs on the diagonal into ¾-inch slices. Return the slices to the baking sheet, leaving space around each slice, and continue baking for 10 to 15 minutes or until desired crispness. Cool completely on a wire rack.

Biscotti Pepati con Noci Arachidi
(PEPPER AND PEANUT BISCOTTI)

These biscotti have a peppery bite and are not very sweet.

¼ cup sugar

1½ tablespoons butter, softened

2 large eggs

1 tablespoon water

1 cup coarsely chopped salted
    peanuts, without skins

2 cups all-purpose flour

2 teaspoons coarsely ground pepper

⅛ teaspoon chili powder

1 teaspoon baking powder

½ teaspoon baking soda

1 teaspoon salt

In a large bowl, cream the sugar and butter. Add the eggs and water and mix well. Stir in the peanuts. In a medium bowl, combine the flour, pepper, chili powder, baking powder, baking soda, and salt; add to the peanut mixture. Divide the dough in half or into thirds. On a well-floured surface, shape into logs. Transfer the logs to a parchment paper–lined or lightly sprayed baking sheet and bake in a preheated 350°F oven for 18 to 20 minutes or until firm and lightly browned. Cool on a rack for at least 5 minutes. Cut the logs on the diagonal into ¾-inch slices. Return the slices to the baking sheet, leaving space around each slice, and continue baking for 15 to 20 minutes or until desired crispness. Cool completely on a wire rack.

Biscotti con Farina di Granoturco e Grana Parmigiana

(CORNMEAL PARMESAN BISCOTTI)

These biscotti are slightly savory, slightly sweet, and filled with good flavor.

⅓ cup sugar	⅔ cup toasted pumpkinseeds
¼ cup butter, softened	1½ cups all-purpose flour
2 tablespoons hot mustard	½ cup cornmeal
2 medium eggs	¾ teaspoon baking powder
1 cup finely grated Parmesan cheese	Pinch of salt

In a large bowl, cream the sugar and butter. Add the mustard and eggs. Stir in the Parmesan cheese and pumpkinseeds. In a medium bowl, combine the flour, cornmeal, baking powder, and salt; add to the mustard mixture. If the dough is too sticky, refrigerate for 1 to 2 hours. Divide the dough in half or into thirds. On a well-floured surface, shape into logs. Transfer the logs to a parchment paper–lined or lightly sprayed baking sheet and bake in a preheated 375°F oven for 20 minutes or until firm and lightly browned. Cool on a rack for at least 5 minutes. Cut the logs on the diagonal into ¾-inch slices. Return the slices to the baking sheet, leaving space around each slice, and continue baking for 10 to 15 minutes or until desired crispness. Cool completely on a wire rack.

Biscotti a L'Anice
(ANISETTE BISCOTTI)

⅓ cup pur olive oil

1 cup granulated sugar

3 large eggs

3 cups all-purpose flour

3 teaspoons baking powder

¹/₂ teaspoon salt

2 tablespoons anisette liqueur

Preheat over to 350 degrees Fahrenheit.

In mixer bowl, cream sugar and oil. Add eggs one at a time, until each is absorbed.

Sift together flour, baking powder, and salt. Add to liquid in mixer bowl and blend with the paddle. Add anisette. Mix well. Shape into 4 loaves. Place the loaves on a parchment paper–lined cookie sheet. Bake for 35 minutes. Lower heat to 300 degrees. Remove from oven and place immediately on a cutting board; with a sharp chef's knife, cut into ¹/₂ inch slices. Place slices cut side up. Place them back on the cookie sheet and replace them in the 300 degree oven to toast. After 10 minutes, turn them over to toast the other sides. Toast for another 10 minutes.

Remove the cookies and place them on a wire rack for 35 minutes. Store in a cookie tin.

These are made to dunk in wine, hot coffee, or tea.

Biscotti Olandesi con Noci di Ghergigli

(DUTCH WALNUT RUSKS)

This a very sticky dough. Use well-floured hands.

2 medium eggs	1 teaspoon baking powder
½ teaspoon vanilla extract	Pinch of salt
¼ teaspoon grated orange peel	¼ cup butter, softened
⅔ cup sugar	1 cup chopped toasted walnuts
1⅔ cups all-purpose flour	

In a bowl, combine the eggs, vanilla, orange peel, and sugar. In a small bowl, combine 1 cup flour, baking powder, and salt; add to the orange mixture. Beat in the butter and remaining flour. Add the walnuts. Divide the dough in half or into thirds. On a well-floured surface, shape into logs. Transfer the logs to a parchment paper–lined or lightly sprayed baking sheet and bake in a preheated 325°F oven for 25 minutes. Cool on a rack for at least 5 minutes. Cut the logs on the diagonal into ¾-inch slices. Return the slices to the baking sheet, leaving space around each slice, and continue baking for 10 to 15 minutes. Cool completely on a wire rack.

Biscotti Greci

(GREEK PAXEMADIA)

This is a Greek version of biscotti that originated as oven-dried slices of anise-flavored country bread.

1 cup sugar	2 tablespoons grated orange peel
¾ cup butter, softened	2 tablespoons grated lemon peel
3 medium eggs	3 cups all-purpose flour
1 tablespoon crushed coriander seeds	1½ teaspoons baking powder
1 tablespoon crushed anise seeds	1½ cups coarsely chopped toasted walnuts

In a large bowl, cream the sugar and butter. Add the eggs. Mix in the coriander and anise seeds and orange and lemon peels. In a medium bowl, combine the flour and baking powder and stir into the seeds mixture. Add the walnuts. Divide the dough in half or into thirds. On a well-floured surface, shape into logs. Transfer the logs to a parchment paper–lined or lightly sprayed baking sheet and bake in a preheated 350°F oven for 25 to 30 minutes or until firm and lightly browned. Cool on a rack for at least 5 minutes. Cut the logs on the diagonal into ¾-inch slices. Return the slices to the baking sheet, leaving space around each slice, and continue baking for 10 minutes or until desired crispness. Cool completely on a wire rack.

Biscotti dei Giudei

(MILK CHOCOLATE WALNUT MANDELBROT)

These Jewish cookies are dry because they are supposed to be for dunking, not as hard as many biscotti.

3½ cups all-purpose flour

2 tablespoons baking powder

Pinch of salt

1 cup canola oil

1 cup sugar

3 medium eggs

1¼ cups coarsely chopped toasted walnuts

⅓ cup milk chocolate chips

Combine the flour, baking powder, and salt. In a large bowl, beat the oil, sugar, and eggs. Gradually stir in half of the flour mixture. Fold in the nuts, the remaining flour, and chocolate chips. Divide the dough in half or into thirds. On a well-floured surface, shape into logs. Transfer the logs to a parchment paper–lined or lightly sprayed baking sheet and bake in a preheated 375°F oven for 20 minutes. Cool on a rack for at least 5 minutes. Cut the logs on the diagonal into ¾-inch slices. Return the slices to the baking sheet, leaving space around each slice, and continue baking for 15 minutes. Cool completely on a wire rack.

Biscotti Ucraini

(ROYAL DUNKERS)

These cakelike Ukrainian-style cookies are baked in a loaf pan.

1½ cups all-purpose flour

½ teaspoon salt

1 teaspoon baking powder

4 medium eggs

1 cup sugar

¼ cup canola oil

¼ cup frozen orange juice
   concentrate

2 teaspoons vanilla extract

1 cup dried sour cherries

In a bowl, combine the flour, salt, and baking powder. In a medium bowl, beat the eggs and sugar until fluffy. In another bowl, combine the oil, orange juice concentrate, and vanilla; stir into the egg mixture alternately with the flour mixture. Add the cherries. Divide the batter between 2 lightly sprayed 6 × 3 × 2-inch loaf pans; bake in a preheated 350°F oven for 30 minutes or until a toothpick inserted in the center comes out clean. Remove from the pans, cool on a rack for 10 minutes, and cut into ¼-inch slices. Arrange on a baking sheet, leaving space around each slice, and continue baking for 10 to 15 minutes. Cool completely on a wire rack.

Biscotti con Due Tipi di Noci

(DOUBLE NUT COOKIES)

Almonds and hazelnuts star in these wonderfully rich treats.

2 cups toasted almonds

2 large egg whites, lightly
   beaten

1 cup sugar

2 tablespoons sherry, dark rum, or
   fruit liqueur

⅓ cup finely chopped toasted
   hazelnuts

In a medium bowl, combine the almonds and egg whites; stir to coat the almonds. With a slotted spoon, remove the nuts and reserve the egg whites. Put the nuts into a blender or food processor and blend to a smooth puree. Transfer to a bowl and stir in the reserved egg whites, sugar, and sherry to form a paste. Pinch off small portions of dough and shape with your hands into disks about 1½ inches in diameter. Press one side of each disk into the hazelnuts and place on a parchment paper–lined baking sheet, nut side up. Allow to stand at room temperature for 2 hours. Bake in a preheated 400°F oven for 5 to 8 minutes or until beginning to brown around the edges.

Biscotti per il Vino
(WINE DUNKERS)

These are delicious on their own, and even better dunked in wine.

½ cup sugar

½ cup butter

3 large eggs

2 tablespoons anise seeds

2 tablespoons anise liqueur (Anisette)

2 tablespoons whiskey

1 cup coarsely chopped toasted
  almonds

2¾ cups all-purpose flour, unsifted

½ teaspoon baking powder

In a large bowl, cream the sugar and butter. Add eggs one at a time until absorbed. Add the anise seeds, liqueur, whiskey, and almonds. In another bowl, mix the flour and baking powder and blend thoroughly into the sugar mixture. Cover and chill for 2 to 3 hours. On lightly sprayed baking sheets, shape the dough into flat loaves ½ inch thick, 2 inches wide, and as long as the sheets. Place no more than 2 loaves parallel and well apart per sheet. Bake in a preheated 375°F oven for 20 minutes. Remove from the oven and cool enough to handle. Cut in diagonal slices ½ to ¾ inch thick. Return to the sheets and bake at 375°F for 15 minutes or until lightly toasted. Cool on a wire rack.

Biscotti Amaretti

(AMARETTI COOKIES)

These are flat rather than the traditional round balls, but otherwise they are the real thing.

2 cups blanched almonds

1 cup sugar

1 teaspoon almond extract

2 egg whites, stiffly beaten

Confectioners' sugar, for sprinkling

With a blender or food processor, finely grind the almonds. Spread on a baking sheet and allow to dry in a slightly warm oven for several hours. In a medium bowl, combine the almonds, sugar, and almond extract. Fold in the egg whites and blend thoroughly but gently. Spray and flour 2 baking sheets and drop the batter by tea-spoonfuls, leaving 2 inches between cookies. Sprinkle with the confectioners' sugar and allow to stand at room temperature for 2 hours. Bake in a preheated 325°F oven for 15 minutes or until golden. Cool on the baking sheets for 2 minutes and remove to a wire rack to cool completely.

Biscotti Veneziani di Granoturco

(VENETIAN CORNMEAL COOKIES)

These unusual cornmeal cookies are delightful with wine.

¾ cup golden raisins

⅔ cup rum

3 large egg yolks, save egg whites for
   next recipe

¾ cup sugar

1 teaspoon vanilla extract

Grated peel of 1 lemon

1 cup butter, melted

1½ cups fine cornmeal

2 cups all-purpose flour

⅓ cup toasted pine nuts

In a bowl, combine the raisins and rum and set aside. In a large bowl, whisk the egg yolks, sugar, and vanilla until smooth and thick. Stir in the lemon peel and butter. In a medium bowl, combine the cornmeal and flour and add to the egg mixture. Drain the raisins and save the rum to use again. Add the pine nuts and raisins. Break off walnut-sized pieces of dough, roll each into a ball, and flatten to a ¼-inch thickness. Place on parchment paper–lined or lightly sprayed baking sheets; bake in a preheated 375°F oven for 20 minutes or until beginning to brown. Cool on a wire rack.

Biscotti della Vedova

(WIDOWS' KISSES)

These light and airy meringue-like kisses are completely delectable.

4 large egg whites
½ cup plus 1 tablespoon
   sugar

1 cup coarsely chopped toasted
   walnuts
¼ cup finely chopped citron

In the top of a double boiler over simmering water, beat the egg whites and sugar until the mixture is quite firm. Remove from the hot water and stir in the nuts and citron. Drop by teaspoonfuls onto a lightly sprayed baking sheet. Bake in a preheated 300°F oven for 25 to 30 minutes or until lightly browned. Cool on a baking sheet before removing to a wire rack.

Biscotti di Regina

(QUEEN'S BISCUITS)

1½ cups all-purpose flour	2 tablespoons grated orange peel
2 cups sugar	Milk, as needed
¾ teaspoon baking powder	¾ cup finely chopped toasted
6 tablespoons butter, melted	walnuts
1 teaspoon vanilla extract	

In a large bowl, combine the flour, sugar, and baking powder. In a small bowl, whisk the butter, egg, vanilla, and orange peel; add to the dry mixture. If the dough is too dry, add milk, a teaspoon at a time, to make a workable dough. Pinch off small pieces of dough and form into cylinders about the size of your little finger. Roll each cylinder in the chopped nuts to coat completely and place on a parchment paper–lined or lightly sprayed baking sheet. Bake in a preheated 350°F oven for 15 minutes or until golden. Cool completely on a wire rack.

Biscotti Siciliani con Mandorle e Cedro

(SICILIAN ALMOND AND CITRON COOKIES)

These simple and unusual cookies are slightly chewy and not too sweet.

¼ cup toasted almonds	1 teaspoon cinnamon
⅓ cup sugar	½ teaspoon ground cloves
2 cups all-purpose flour	½ cup finely chopped citron
1¼ teaspoons baking powder	Warm water, as needed

With a blender or food processor, blend the almonds and sugar to a fine purée. In a bowl, combine the almond purée, flour, baking powder, cinnamon, cloves, and citron. Add enough warm water to make a firm dough and knead until elastic. On a well-floured surface, roll the dough to a ½-inch thickness and cut into ½-inch strips. Place the strips on a parchment paper–lined or lightly sprayed baking sheet and decorate in a crosshatch pattern with the tines of a fork. Bake in a preheated 400°F oven for 15 minutes or until golden around the edges. Cool completely on a wire rack.

Biscotti all' Arancio

(ITALIAN ORANGE COOKIES)

1 cup sugar	2 cups all-purpose flour
4 medium eggs, at room temperature	1 tablespoon grated orange peel
	Sugar, for sprinkling

In a medium bowl, beat ½ cup sugar and 2 eggs. Slowly add the remaining sugar and continue beating. Add another egg and beat. Add the remaining egg and beat until light and foamy. Fold in the flour and orange peel. Drop by teaspoonfuls onto a parchment paper–lined or lightly sprayed baking sheet, making the cookies as round as possible. Lightly sprinkle each cookie with sugar and allow to stand at room temperature for 3 hours. Bake in a preheated 350°F oven for 10 minutes. Cool completely on a wire rack.

Biscotti alla Veneziana

(VENETIAN COOKIES)

These Venetian cookies are similar to flat, little sponge cakes.

5 medium eggs, separated	1 cup all-purpose flour
½ cup sugar	Pinch of salt
½ tablespoon brandy	Confectioners' sugar, for sprinkling

In a large bowl, beat the egg yolks and sugar until creamy. Add the brandy. In a medium bowl, combine the flour and salt and fold into the egg yolk mixture. Beat the egg whites until soft peaks form and stir one-third into the flour mixture. When well combined, fold in the remaining egg whites. Drop by teaspoonfuls onto a parchment paper–lined or lightly sprayed baking sheet and bake in a preheated 350°F oven for 10 minutes or until firm and beginning to brown around the edges. Cool completely on a wire rack and dust with confectioners' sugar when cold.

Biscotti di Sardinia con Miele

(SARDINIAN HONEY CAKES)

Make these little honey-flavored cookies in various shapes.

2 tablespoons honey

1 tablespoon butter

1 cup all-purpose flour

Pinch of salt

1 medium egg, lightly beaten

1 teaspoon baking powder mixed
    with 2 tablespoons milk

In a small saucepan, heat the honey and butter, stirring until the butter is melted and the mixture is well blended. In a medium bowl, combine the flour and salt. Add the honey mixture, egg, and baking powder mixed with milk. Mix to a smooth dough. On a lightly floured surface, roll the dough to a ⅛-inch thickness. Cut with cookie cutters. Place the cookies on a parchment paper–lined or lightly sprayed baking sheet and bake in a preheated 375°F oven for 10 minutes or until brown around the edges. Cool completely on a wire rack.

Zeppoli di San Giuseppe

(ST. JOSEPH'S CREAM PUFFS)

CREAM PUFF PASTE

1 cup hot water

½ cup butter

Pinch of salt

1 cup cake flour

4 medium eggs

FILLING

1 pound ricotta cheese

⅓ cup chopped milk chocolate
   chips

½ cup sugar

1 tablespoon chopped candied
   orange peel

2 tablespoons chopped toasted,
   unsalted pistachio nuts

To make the cream puff paste: In a 2-quart saucepan, heat the water, butter, and salt to boiling. When the butter is melted, lower the heat and add the flour all at once. Stir with a wooden spoon until the mixture leaves the sides of the pan. Remove from the heat and cool to lukewarm. With a wooden spoon, beat in the eggs one at a time. Drop the batter by teaspoonfuls onto a lightly sprayed baking sheet, leaving 2 inches between each puff. Bake in a preheated 450°F oven for 10 minutes. Reduce the heat to 300°F and continue baking for 15 to 20 minutes. Cool completely on a wire rack.

To make the filling: Blend all the ingredients.

Make a slit in the side of the cooled puffs and fill with the cream puff paste. Refrigerate until ready to serve.

Torta di Formaggio Dolce di Evelina

(MY SISTER EVELYN'S CHEESECAKE)

2 cups crushed graham cracker or any crispy cookies, even sugarless	1 stick melted butter or ¾ cup vegetable oil

In a springform cake pan, cover the bottom with the crushed cookies. Pour the melted butter or oil over the crust.

Preheat the oven to 350°F.

Cream together:

20 ounces cream cheese (3 packs), at room temperature	6 large eggs
1 pint sour cream	2 tablespoons all-purpose flour or whole wheat
1½ cups sugar or Splenda	1 teaspoon vanilla extract

With an electric mixer, blend all the ingredients until very smooth. Pour the batter into a 10-inch greased springform pan. Bake for 1½ hours. Turn off the oven and open the door, leave in the oven for 1½ hours. Remove from the oven and let cool at room temperature for 2 hours. Refrigerate until ready to serve. To freeze, cover with plastic wrap and aluminum foil tightly. When ready to use, remove from the freezer and defrost in the refrigerator for 8 hours. Uncover, cut, and serve.

Torta della Nonna

(GRANDMOTHER'S CAKE)

½ cup unsalted butter or ¾ cup olive
  oil or vegetable oil

¾ cup sugar or Splenda

1 envelope Paneangeli vanilla baking
  powder (see page 124)

4 egg yolks (beat egg whites
  separately until stiff, reserve)

Zest from 1 orange or 1 lemon

1 tablespoon rum

Pinch of salt

¾ cup all-purpose flour or whole
  wheat

½ cup cornstarch

¼ cup *pignoli* (pine) nuts

2 tablespoons of powdered sugar to
  sift over cooled cookies

Cream the butter, sugar, vanilla-flavored baking powder, egg yolks, orange or
lemon zest, rum, and salt until fluffy. Sift the flour and cornstarch over the butter
mixture. Beat until smooth. Fold in the stiff egg whites. Grease the bottom of a
springform cake pan. Pour the batter into the pan. Sprinkle with the pine nuts.
Bake at 350°F for 40 minutes. Remove from the oven and let cool. Remove from
the pan and sprinkle with powdered sugar.

Budino di Caffé

(COFFEE CAKE)

1 cup all-purpose flour or whole
  wheat

2 teaspoons baking powder

½ teaspoon salt

⅔ cup granulated sugar or Splenda

⅓ cup and 2 tablespoons cocoa
  powder

½ cup water

2 tablespoons vegetable oil

1 cup roughly chopped nuts

1 cup brown sugar, packed down

1¾ cups hot espresso coffee

Whipped cream, optional

Preheat the oven to 350°F

Combine the flour, baking powder, salt, sugar, and ⅓ cup cocoa. Blend in the water and oil well. Stir in the nuts. Pour into a 23 × 13 × 8-inch Pyrex dish. Sprinkle the brown sugar and 2 tablespoons cocoa over the batter. Slowly pour the coffee over the batter.

Bake for 40 minutes. Remove and let rest for 10 minutes. Scoop into dessert bowls. Serve warm. Garnish with whipped cream, if desired.

Baba Grande con Rhum

(VINCENZO CALDERONE—MASTER ITALIAN PASTRY CHEF, BAYONNE, NEW JERSEY)

½ cup skim milk

4 teaspoons (½ ounce) active dry yeast

2 cups flour, all-purpose unbleached, or self-rising flour

3 jumbo eggs, at room temperature

2 teaspoons granulated sugar or Splenda

⅛ teaspoon salt

1 stick unsalted butter, melted (4 ounces), or ½ cup olive oil

½ cup dark rum

Whipped cream and strawberries

Scald the milk (I microwave it for 30 seconds). Place the yeast and ½ cup of flour in the bowl of my KitchenAid mixer. Cover with the plastic cover that comes with the bowl. Before covering, mix well with a wooden spoon. Let rise covered in a cold oven for 1 hour, until doubled. With the paddle, mix in 1 egg at a time until each is completely absorbed. Add the remaining 1½ cups flour, the sugar, and salt. Slowly beat in the melted butter or oil until the dough is smooth. Cover and let rise covered for 20 minutes. Place the dough (it will be sticky, so I use plastic food handler's gloves) in a well-greased 10-inch springform pan. Cover tightly with plastic wrap, place in a cold oven, and let rise for 40 minutes.

Preheat the oven after you remove the bowl of dough to 375°F.

Place the pan on a cookie sheet and bake in the oven on the middle rack for 30 minutes or until the top of the baba is golden brown and the sides have pulled away from the side of the pan. Unlock the pan and let cool while you prepare the rum sauce.

For the rum sauce: Dissolve 2½ cups granulated sugar or Splenda in 3¾ cups water in a 1-quart saucepan. Add 2 teaspoons pure vanilla extract. Bring to the boil and stir. Remove from the heat, add the rum, and mix well. Allow to cool for 1 hour.

Place the baked baba on a wire rack over a rimmed cookie sheet.

Use a skewer and poke holes all over the top of the baba. Pour the rum syrup over the baba and allow to drain over the cookie sheet for ½ hour. Place the soaked baba in a deep 12-inch rimmed bowl and pour the remaining liquid into the cookie sheet over the top of the baba.

Slice and serve warm. Garnish with whipped cream and sliced seasonal fruit. I use either fresh or thawed frozen strawberries.

Pizzelle

To make these traditional holiday cookies, you must have a well-seasoned pizzelle maker. It looks like an electric waffle iron.

1½ cups granulated sugar or Splenda	2 tablespoons anise or vanilla extract
6 large eggs, at room temperature	3½ cups all-purpose flour or whole
1 cup (2 sticks softened butter) or 1	wheat
cup vegetable oil	4 teaspoons baking powder

Cream the sugar and eggs until pale yellow and add the butter and anise or vanilla. Beat until smooth. Sift in the flour and baking powder. Beat until smooth. Spray cooking oil on the surface of the pizzelle maker. Close and heat for 5 minutes. Open and pour ¼ cup of batter on each bottom iron. Close the iron and cook for 2 minutes. Discard the first two pizzelle. Continue the process until all the batter is used. Place the cooked pizzelle on a flat clean surface—do not stack one on top of another. Allow to cool and crisp. Store in an airtight container.

Brutti ma Buoni Alla Milanese ✿

(HAZELNUT PASTE COOKIES)

MAKES 2 $^{1}/_{2}$ DOZEN COOKIES

The translation of brutti ma buoni *is "ugly but good," and there's no question that these cookies are aptly named. Nothing about their appearance is one bit tempting, but pop one of these chewy, crunchy little hazelnut lumps into your mouth and they're irresistible.*

8 to 9 egg whites, at room temperature	1¾ cups hazelnuts, toasted, skinned, and chopped to the size of fat rice kernels
1 cup plus 3 tablespoons sugar	
¾ teaspoon vanilla extract	

Beat 8 egg whites in a mixer bowl until soft peaks are formed. Beat, gradually adding the sugar, and continue beating until the peaks are stiff and shiny. Stir in the vanilla until blended. Fold in the nuts. Transfer the mixture to a saucepan and cook over low heat for 10 minutes. Initially the mixture will soften and then, as it cooks, it should come together in a single, although not well defined, lump. It is done when it is light brown and pulls away from the side of the pan. If the mixture is dry and crumbly, add the last egg white, a bit at a time, to moisten it. Remove the mixture from the heat. Drop the dough by teaspoonfuls 1½ inches apart onto a well-buttered or parchment-lined baking sheet.

Heat the oven to 300°F. Bake until lightly colored, 25 to 30 minutes. If the cookies seem too soft, you can turn off the oven and leave them there for 10 minutes. Cool on wire racks. These keep well stored in airtight containers.

Variations—Tuscans use half almonds and half hazelnuts in addition to adding about 1½ teaspoons ground coriander to their dough. In Venice, the cookies are sometimes made with the addition of ½ cup unsweetened cocoa powder to the dough.

Amaretti

(MACAROONS)

MAKES 30 COOKIES

Amaretti Lombard style are crisp little almond-flavored cookies that crunch before they dissolve on the tongue.

1 cup plus 2 tablespoons blanched almonds	¾ cup plus 3 tablespoons confectioners' sugar
2½ tablespoons bitter apricot kernels or ¾ teaspoon almond extract	1 teaspoon all-purpose flour
	2 egg whites
	⅓ cup granulated sugar

Grind the almonds and apricot kernels to a fine powder in a nut grinder or food processor fitted with the steel blade. (If using the processor, add ¼ cup of the confectioners' sugar, a bit at a time to keep the almonds from becoming too oily.) Mix the nuts with the confectioners' sugar and flour. Beat, gradually adding the granulated sugar, until stiff and shiny. Fold the nut mixture and the almond extract, if you are using it, until blended.

Spoon the meringue into a pastry bag fitted with a ½-inch plain tip. Pipe 1½-inch-wide mounds 1½ inches apart on parchment-lined or buttered baking sheets. Smooth the top of each cookie with a damp finger. Or simply drop rounded teaspoonfuls on the cookie sheet.

Preheat the oven to 300°F. Bake for 40 to 45 minutes until very lightly brown. Turn off the oven and let the amaretti dry in the oven for an additional 20 to 30 minutes. Cool on wire racks. Store in airtight containers.

Crumiri

(BUTTERY HORSESHOE-SHAPED COOKIES FROM PIEDMONT)

MAKES 2 DOZEN COOKIES (THE RECIPE CAN BE EASILY DOUBLED.)

These delicate, crumbly horseshoe-shaped cookies come from Piedmont where the oldest families of the region traditionally made them every Saturday. They are rich and surprisingly tender and get their special taste from the slightly crunchy cornmeal.

1½ sticks plus 2 tablespoons unsalted butter, at room temperature	1¾ cups all-purpose flour
¾ cup sugar	Pinch of salt
2 large eggs, at room temperature	⅔ cup plus 1 tablespoon fine yellow cornmeal

Cream the butter and sugar in a mixer bowl until very light and fluffy. Add the eggs, one at a time, beating thoroughly after each addition. Sift the flour, salt, and cornmeal together and sift again over the batter; mix well.

You can shape these cookies either with a pastry bag or by hand (I think the latter is easier). If using a pastry bag, spoon the dough into the bag fitted with a ⅜-inch star-shaped tip (the traditional cookies are ribbed). Pipe 4 inches long, ½ inch thick, about 2 inches apart on buttered and floured or parchment-lined baking sheets. Or roll the pieces of dough, each about the size of a walnut, into long thin logs of the same dimension. Place 2 inches apart on the prepared baking sheets. Bend each piped or rolled log into a horseshoe.

Preheat the oven to 325°F. Bake until lightly golden, about 12 minutes. Cool on wire racks.

Variations—To make *Lunette Siciliane*, another polenta cookie of the same dough and shape, brush the tops of the unbaked cookies with beaten egg and coat with sesame seeds. Place seeds side up on the baking sheets and bake as directed for *crumiri*.

Biscotti di Mandorle

(ALMOND COOKIES)

5 cups chopped almonds	½ cup milk
2½ cups granulated sugar	Pinch of salt
Grated zest of 1 lemon	6 egg whites
Pinch of cinnamon	1 egg yolk, beaten

Preheat the oven to 400°F.

Place the almonds, sugar, grated lemon zest, cinnamon, milk, and salt into a bowl and stir well. Whisk the egg whites until stiff and fold gently into the milk mixture. Spoon the dough into a pastry bag. Pipe rounds onto a greased baking tray or parchment paper. Place an almond in the center of each one and bake in a hot oven for 15 minutes. Remove from the oven and brush the biscuits with the beaten egg yolk. Return to the hot oven for another 10 minutes.

Biscotti Pepati
(PEPPER COOKIES)

3½ cups white flour	Pinch of nutmeg
¾ cup granulated sugar	Pinch of cloves
1½ cups chopped almonds	Pinch of cinnamon
4 tablespoons butter or lard	Pinch of black pepper
½ cup honey	Pinch of baking soda

Preheat the oven to 425°F.

Work the flour, sugar, and almonds with the butter, honey (dissolved in a small amount of warm water), spices, and baking soda. Roll into thick fingers and place on greased cookie sheets or parchment paper. Bake in the oven for 15 minutes. Remove from the oven and let rest for 10 minutes. Cut into ½-inch slices. Return to the oven for 5 minutes. Turn off the oven and let the cookies rest in the oven until cool.

Biscotti Regina Calabresi

(SESAME COOKIES)

2 cups white flour	1 large egg
Pinch of salt	1 cup lard or butter
½ cup granulated sugar	6 tablespoons sesame seeds

Preparation time: 30 minutes, plus an hour's rest for the dough

Heap the flour, salt, and sugar on a pastry board. Work in the egg and lard or soft butter (not melted). Knead gently until the flour is completely absorbed. If necessary, add ½ glass of warm water. Shape into a ball, wrap in a tea cloth, and leave to rest in a warm place for about an hour.

Make fat fingers like breadsticks and cut into lengths 2 to 2½ inches. Turn the sesame seeds into a bowl, roll the fingers in them, and place on a greased baking tray. Bake in a hot oven for about 20 minutes.

Biscotti Taralle

(ICED COOKIES)

6 large eggs	1⅔ cups confectioners' sugar
2½ cups granulated sugar	¼ teaspoon vanilla extract
3½ cups white flour	4 tablespoons plain or jasmine-
3½ cups cornstarch	flavored water
4 tablespoons milk	1 tablespoon lard or butter

Preparation time: 40 minutes

Separate the egg whites from the yolks. Beat the egg whites and sugar to a smooth cream. Add 2 tablespoons milk. Sprinkle in the flour and cornstarch and mix well, add the remaining milk.

Either pipe the mixture from a piping bag or spoon it onto a greased baking tray to form fingers or rings and bake in a moderate oven for about 20 minutes.

To make the frosting, dissolve the confectioners' sugar and vanilla in the water and heat to just under the boiling point. Before turning off the oven, brush the biscuits with the icing. Return to the still-warm oven and leave until the cookies are cool.

Biscotti Spagnolette

(RICOTTA COOKIES)

3 large eggs	¾ pound ricotta cheese
1¼ cups granulated sugar	Milk
1¾ cups white flour	2 tablespoons vanilla sugar
Zest of 1 lemon	

Preheat the oven to 400°F.

Cream the yolks with ¾ cup sugar. When you have a smooth foam, add the flour and the grated lemon zest a little at a time. Crush the ricotta in a bowl with ½ cup sugar and work it in with a fork to get a smooth mixture. A little milk may be added to make it creamier. Whisk the egg whites until stiff and add the vanilla sugar. Slowly mix the ricotta into the creamed yolks and fold in the whisked egg whites. When the mixture is well blended, put some into a piping bag and pipe onto an oiled iron or aluminum baking tray in rounds. Repeat, using up all the paste, and bake for 20 minutes in a hot oven. Cool completely on a wire rack.

Buccellato

(DOUGH RING)

¾ cup lard or butter

½ cup granulated sugar

2 cups white flour

8 tablespoons Marsala wine

Pinch of salt

2 cups raisins

2 cups dried figs, cut up

1 cup toasted almonds

½ cup walnuts, shelled

½ cup semisweet chocolate squares, broken up

Pinch of cinnamon

1 egg yolk

½ cup chopped pistachios

Zest of 1 lemon

Preparation time: 3 hours

Work the lard or butter into the sugar and flour on a pastry board, together with half the Marsala and a pinch of salt. When you have obtained a smooth dough, wrap in a tea towel and leave to rest for about 2 hours.

Prepare the filling by placing the cut-up figs, toasted almonds (roughly chopped up with the walnuts), grated lemon zest, chocolate, the remaining Marsala, and a pinch of cinnamon into a saucepan. Simmer on low for 20 minutes, stirring constantly.

With the aid of a rolling pin, roll the dough into a rectangle about ½ inch thick. Pour the cooled filling into the center, roll up the dough, and join the ends to make a ring. Pierce the surface with a fork and place on a greased baking tray. Bake in a 425°F oven for 30 minutes.

Remove the tray from the oven.

Beat an egg yolk energetically and, using a pastry brush, spread it over the dough ring. Sprinkle with the chopped pistachios and bake for 5 more minutes.

Cannoli

(RICOTTA-FILLED SHELLS)

SHELL

1 cup white flour

1 large egg

2 tablespoons lard or butter

2 tablespoons granulated sugar

½ tablespoon bitter cocoa

¼ cup red wine or Marsala

Pinch of salt

12 steel tubes

Oil

FILLING

¾ cup ricotta cheese

2 cups confectioners' sugar

Pinch of cinnamon

1 ounce milk

4 ounces semisweet chocolate, diced

⅜ cup candied citron

2 ounces pistachios, chopped

Candied orange peel

Preparation time: 4 hours.

Heap the flour on a pastry board and carefully work in the egg, lard or butter, sugar, the cocoa dissolved in the red wine or Marsala, and salt. When you have a smooth dough, leave to rest for about 1 hour. With a rolling pin, roll it out into a thin sheet and cut it into 4-inch squares. Roll each one diagonally around a steel tube. Delicately press the edges together with a dampened finger. Heat plenty of oil in a deep saucepan and, when it is boiling, immerse the dough-covered tubes. Remove the shells when they have turned golden and allow to cool.

Meanwhile, work the ricotta with the confectioners' sugar and cinnamon. Mix well with a wooden spoon, adding a few drops of milk. The cream should be smooth and rather thick. Add the diced chocolate and candied citron at this point, then carefully remove the tubes from the "cannoli" and fill them with a teaspoonful of the filling.

Garnish with pieces of candied orange peel, which you will stick into the ends. Dredge the biscuit part with a little confectioners' sugar. Or you can buy cannoli shells almost everywhere.

Caramelle di Carrube

(CAROB SQUARES)

8 ounces carob powder
1 cup honey
Oil

Preparation time: 30 minutes

Heat the carob powder very gently with the honey in a small saucepan. Stir from time to time and when the mixture becomes syrupy and caramelized, pour onto an oiled slab. Spread the caramel out with a spatula to a ½-inch thickness. Cut into little squares to leave to dry. They keep well in glass jars.

Street vendors in Sicily used to sell these sweets to grandmothers who would give them to their grandchildren to suck, especially as a remedy against coughs.

A few decades ago, they disappeared off the market and unfortunately also from the domestic kitchen.

Cassata Casalinga

(SICILIAN CASSATA)

1 pound store-bought sponge cake

4 tablespoons vermouth

2 cups confectioners' sugar

one ounce of milk

1 pound ricotta cheese

¼ cup diced candied fruit

4 ounces semisweet chocolate
   morsels

Pinch of ground cinnamon

¼ teaspoon vanilla extract

½ cup pistachios

Preparation time: 2 hours

Cut the sponge cake into rectangular slices and place half of them side by side on the bottom of a springform baking pan.

Sprinkle with vermouth. Work the confectioners' sugar and a few drops of milk into the ricotta to get a creamy mixture, add the diced candied fruit, chocolate, cinnamon, vanilla, and pistachios.

Cassatine di Carnevale

(CASSATA PASTRIES)

3½ cups white flour

4 tablespoons olive oil

Pinch of salt

1 cup granulated sugar

Pinch of ground cinnamon

1 pound ricotta cheese

½ cup semisweet chocolate, diced

Knead the flour with the oil, salt, and warm water until the dough is even and elastic. Wrap in a tea towel and leave to rest for about 1 hour. Make the filling by working the sugar and cinnamon into the ricotta. When you have a creamy mixture, add the diced chocolate. Roll out the pastry into a thin sheet with a rolling pin. Cut out rounds by pressing an upturned teacup down into the pastry. Put a spoonful of cream in the center of each pastry and close it over, lightly pinching the edges together with a dampened finger.

Arrange the pastries on a greased baking tray and bake for 40 minutes in a 350°F oven.

Variation—The pastries may be fried in hot oil or lard and dredged with powdered sugar while still hot.

Zuppa Inglese

(SICILIAN TRIFLE)

¾ pound store-bought sponge cake

½ cup pastry cream (page 222)

½ cup orange candied fruit

4 tablespoons pomegranate juice

4 tablespoons rum

3 egg whites

3 tablespoons granulated sugar

Slice the sponge cake. Pour the pastry cream into a bowl (reserve 3 to 4 tablespoons) and add the candied fruit. Transfer the reserved cream to a deep oven dish and arrange half the sponge cake slices, sprinkle pomegranate juice on top. Cover with the candied fruit, pastry cream, and the remaining sponge cake slices, sprinkled with the rum. Whisk the egg whites until stiff, add 2 tablespoons of sugar, and pour over the trifle.

Decorate the surface with the candied orange peel, dredge with the remaining sugar, and bake in a 350°F oven until the meringue is dry.

Crema Pasticcera

(PASTRY CREAM)

2 cups milk	½ cup granulated sugar
½ teaspoon vanilla extract	⅓ cup white flour
4 egg yolks	Pinch of salt

Pour the milk into a pan and bring to a boil. You may flavor it by adding the vanilla to the milk. Turn off the heat. Cream the egg yolks with the sugar, sprinkle in the flour, stirring continuously, and add the warmed milk and salt. Thicken the custard over the heat, stirring until it starts to boil. Pour into a bowl and leave to cool. This custard can be used as a filling for cream puffs, short pastry, or flaky pastry pies.

Crema Fritta
(FRIED CUSTARD)

4 large eggs, separated	4 cups milk
1 cup cornstarch	White flour
Confectioners' sugar–2 cups plus 2 tablespoons for dredging	dried bread crumbs
	Oil

Place the egg yolks with the cornstarch and sugar in a saucepan, add the milk, and stir well to dissolve the cornstarch. Put the pan over a medium heat and keep stirring in the same direction until the custard has thickened.

As soon as it starts to boil, take off the heat and pour the custard onto a dampened marble slab or a large moistened ceramic plate. When it has cooled off, cut into small fingers, roll in flour, in the whisked egg whites from the 4 eggs and in the bread crumbs. Fry in hot oil. Dredge with confectioners' sugar and serve.

Frittelle di Carnevale

(CARNIVAL FRITTERS)

3 cups milk	2 large eggs, whisked
1 cup water	⅓ cup white flour
1½ tablespoons fresh brewer's yeast	⅔ cup raisins
or 1 package dry yeast	Freshly grated zest of 1 orange
2 tablespoons olive oil	1 tablespoon honey
¼ cup granulated sugar	Cinnamon

Heat the milk and water for a few minutes and dissolve the yeast in it. Add the oil, sugar, and whisked eggs. Sprinkle in the flour, stirring slowly so that lumps do not form. When you have a nice thick cream, add the raisins and orange zest. Stir well and cover with the lid. Wrap the saucepan in a woolen cloth. When the batter is well risen after about 1 hour, drop teaspoonfuls into plenty of hot oil and fry. Dissolve the honey in a little water in a small pan, dip the fritters into the honeyed water, dust with sugar and cinnamon, and eat hot.

Frittelle di Ricotta

(RICOTTA CHEESE FRITTERS)

1 generous cup ricotta cheese	Grated zest of 1 lemon
1⅓ cups white flour	Oil for frying
2 large eggs	Pinch of salt
Pinch of cinnamon	1 tablespoon honey

Work the ricotta with the flour, eggs, cinnamon, a pinch of salt, and grated lemon zest. Leave to rest for a couple of hours. Put a little of the mixture in the palm of your hand and shape into little rings. Deep fry them in a frying pan with plenty of hot oil. Dissolve the honey in 4 tablespoons water in a small pan and pour over the ricotta fritters. Dust with sugar and cinnamon. The dough used in this recipe is not leavened. The fritters, therefore, will be flat, not puffed up like in the previous recipe.

Iris

(FRIED RICOTTA PUFFS)

3½ cups white flour

4 tablespoons lard, butter, or oil

1 large egg

2 tablespoons fresh brewer's yeast or
    2 packages dry yeast

2 cups milk

1 cup granulated sugar

2⅓ cups ricotta cheese

½ cup plain semisweet chocolate
    morsels

2 large eggs, beaten

Dried bread crumbs

Oil

Knead the flour with the lard, eggs, yeast dissolved in a ¼ cup of warm milk, add 1¾ cups warm milk and one-quarter of the sugar. Knead the dough until soft, cover, and leave to rise for about 2 hours. Meanwhile, prepare the filling by putting the ricotta with the rest of the sugar in a bowl. Mash with a fork until you have a smooth cream. You may add a little milk if the ricotta is rather thick. Add the chocolate. When the dough has risen, roll out with a rolling pin and cut out rounds with the rim of a glass. In the center of the round put a spoonful of cream and seal with another round on top. Let rest 1 hour at room temperature. When the *iris* are nice and puffy, dip them in the beaten eggs and dried bread crumbs and fry in boiling oil in a deep pan until they float to the top and are light brown.

Mostaccioli

(NUT TARTS)

PASTRY

3 cups plain flour   ½ cup lard

¼ cup milk   2 large eggs

¾ cup granulated sugar

FILLING

½ cup honey   ½ orange zest of one orange

1 tablespoon plain flour   Pinch of ground cinnamon

1 cup walnut kernels

1 cup each almonds and hazelnuts,
   toasted

Pile the flour into a heap on a pastry board and work in the milk. Make a smooth dough with the sugar, lard, and eggs. Roll into a ball and allow it to rest for ½ an hour. Dilute the honey in ½ a glass of water and pour into a small pan. Bring to a boil and gradually sprinkle in the flour, 1 cup of walnut kernels and toasted almonds and hazelnuts, grated orange rind, and cinnamon. Roll out the dough into a fairly thin sheet. Cut into 4- by 2-inch rectangles. At the center of each, place a mound of the filling, and wrap the pastry diagonally around itself. Lay the *mostaccioli* in a greased dish and place in a preheated oven at 400°F for ½ an hour. Let cool in dish 10 minutes. Transfer to wire rack to cool completely. Place into a cookie tin with an air-tight cover.

Pan di Spagna

(SPONGE CAKE)

8 large eggs, separated	Grated lemon zest
1¼ cups granulated sugar	¾ cup cornstarch
⅔ cup white flour	1 tablespoon lard or butter, melted
Pinch of salt	

Preheat the oven to 350°F. Cream together the yolks and sugar until soft and frothy. Slowly add the flour, salt, and lemon zest. Whisk the egg whites until stiff. Cook the creamed yolks in a double boiler (the water must be simmering) and gradually fold in the egg whites, sprinkling the cornstarch over, and adding the melted lard or butter in a thin stream. When everything is well blended, pour into a deep baking dish 8 to 10 inches in diameter, which has been oiled and floured. Bake in a 350°F oven for 30 to 40 minutes.

Pasta Fritta con Miele

(FRIED LOAVES WITH HONEY)

This dish has almost disappeared because bread is rarely made at home nowadays.

2 pounds leavened dough (this can be bought from your local pizza shop)	1 tablespoon honey
	1 tablespoon granulated sugar
Olive oil	Pinch of cinnamon

Knead the leavened dough with 1 tablespoon of oil. Make little flat loaves and fry in the hot oil. Place the little loaves on a large serving dish and pour over the honey dissolved in 4 tablespoons of water. Dredge with sugar and cinnamon and eat while hot.

Pignolata
(FRIED PASTRY)

These *are traditionally made for Christmas. In Calabria they are called* pignolata, *in Sicily* pignuccata, *and in Naples* struffoli.

3½ cups flour	1 cup honey
5 egg yolks	¼ cup water or orange water
Pinch of salt	Grated zest of 1 orange or lemon
¼ cup granulated sugar	Confectioners' sugar
Vegetable oil or lard, for frying	Pinch of cinnamon

Heap the flour up on a work surface and pour the yolks, salt, and sugar into a hollow in the middle. Knead to a soft, even dough. Form into fingers the thickness of bread sticks, cut into small lengths, and fry in boiling vegetable oil or lard.

In a small pan, dissolve the honey in the plain or flavored water with the grated orange or lemon zest. Pile the fried pastries into a pyramid pinecone. Place on a serving dish and dust with confectioners' sugar and cinnamon.

In the Messina district, *pignolata* is typically served covered with cocoa and confectioners' sugar.

Ravioli Dolci

(SWEET RAVIOLI)

PASTRY

3 cups plain flour

½ cup granulated sugar

6 tablespoons lard or butter

1 egg yolk, beaten

1 teaspoon vanilla extract

FILLING

8 cups granulated sugar

The zest of 1 lemon

1 teaspoon vanilla extract

Pinch of ground cinnamon

1 tablespoon candied fruit

1 cup plain semisweet chocolate
    chips

4 cups fresh ricotta cheese

Oil, for frying

Confectioners' sugar, for decorating

Mix the flour with 1 cup of water, working in the sugar, lard or butter, the beaten egg yolk, and vanilla. When the dough is smooth and elastic, form it into a ball and leave for ½ hour to rest. To make the filling, use a spatula to combine the sugar, grated lemon rind, vanilla, cinnamon, candied fruit, and chocolate chips with the ricotta. Blend well. Roll out the pastry thinly and cut into 6-inch squares. Pile a little of the filling to one side of each square, fold the other side over, and trim the edges with the tines of a fork. Fry the pastry squares in plenty of boiling oil. When the ravioli have turned golden, drain, and dredge them with confectioners' sugar.

Seni di Vergine

(CANDIED FRUIT CUSTARD TARTS)

Seni di Vergine *translates literally in English to "Wombs of Virgins." The name most probably originates from the fact that these tarts were made exclusively by cloistered virgin nuns.*

3 cups plain flour	2 tablespoons candied fruit
½ cup milk	½ cup plain semisweet chocolate chips
¾ cup granulated sugar	1 egg yolk, beaten, and 1 egg white,
¾ cup lard	whisked stiffly
1 cup pastry cream (page 222)	Confectioners' sugar

Mix the flour into the milk along with the sugar and the lard until you have a smooth, fluid dough. Form a ball and leave for 1 hour to rest. Roll out the dough into 2 differently sized sheets. At regular intervals, place teaspoonfuls of pastry cream, mixed with cubes of candied fruit and chocolate chips, on the smaller sheet. With the beaten egg yolk, brush the pastry all around the mounds of filling. Lay the other sheet of pastry on top and seal the edges. Use a small round, scalloped mold to cut out the tarts. Brush each one with the stiffly whisked egg white and bake in a preheated oven at 400°F for 20 minutes. When the pastries are cooked, dust with confectioners' sugar.

Sfinci di San Giuseppe

(SAINT JOSEPH'S CREAM PUFFS)

¾ cup water	½ teaspoon vanilla extract
4 tablespoons butter	Grated zest of 1 lemon
Salt	3 large eggs, separated
1 tablespoon cognac	Oil
⅔ cup white flour	¾ cup confectioners' sugar

FILLING

2¾ cups ricotta cheese	¼ cup candied fruit
1¼ cups granulated sugar	2 tablespoons candied orange peel
½ cup plain semisweet chocolate chips	2 tablespoons pistachios, chopped

Bring the water to a boil with the butter and salt, add cognac then put in the flour, vanilla extract, and lemon zest, stirring well until thoroughly cooked, about 10 minutes.

Remove the dough and spread it out over a work surface to cool rapidly. When cold, work in 1 egg yolk and 1 stiffly whisked egg white and, with a wooden spoon, continue mixing until incorporated. Repeat the procedure with the other 2 eggs. The end result should be smooth and creamy. Pour plenty of oil into a deep frying pan and, when boiling, spoon in the dough to obtain soft, even-sized fritters. Once fried, allow to cool and slit each one open with a knife.

Meanwhile, for the filling, work the ricotta into the icing sugar in a bowl and, if the mixture is too stiff, add a few drops of milk.

When the mixture is nice and creamy, add the chocolate chips and candied fruit.

Fill the cold *sfinci* and garnish with the candied orange peel and chopped pistachios.

Torroncini

(NOUGAT CANDY)

2½ cups granulated sugar

¼ cup honey

2⅓ cups almonds, toasted and
  chopped

2½ cups pistachios, chopped

Almond or vegetable oil

Dissolve the sugar with the honey in a saucepan and add the almonds and pistachios. Cook for 5 to 10 minutes over a low heat to allow the flavors to blend. Pour onto a slab of oiled marble (preferably with almond oil), spread it out with a spatula, and cut into short lengths. When the nougat is cold, wrap each piece in greaseproof waxed paper and store in glass jars.

In Sicily, nougat is not only made with almonds and pistachios but there are also versions with peanuts or sesame seeds.

Torta di Riso

(SWEET RICE CAKE)

1 cup rice	⅓ cup raisins
2 cups milk	2 large eggs, separated
½ cup granulated sugar	Oil
Grated zest of 1 lemon	Dried bread crumbs
½ teaspoon vanilla extract	½ cup flour

Boil the rice for 5 to 6 minutes in salted water. Drain and continue cooking in another saucepan with the milk and 1 glass of water brought to the boil.

Add the sugar, grated lemon zest, and vanilla. When the rice is cooked, mix in the raisins tossed in flour, take off the heat, and allow to cool.

One at a time, incorporate the egg yolks into the mixture, stirring well. Whisk the egg whites until stiff and fold into the mixture. Pour into an oiled baking dish with bread crumbs and bake in a 350°F preheated oven for 30 minutes.

Terry Weiner's Mother's Biscotti

(MARTHA'S BISCOTTI)

The Weiner family traces its origin to Bolzano, close to the Austrian border, but it is still Italy. Northern Italy was once part of the Austrian Empire. Austria has always had a reputation of excellent baking. This recipe was adopted and used by northern Italians for centuries. We were fortunate enough to obtain this from my niece Carmel Orsini Ferrante who received it from her dear friend Terry Weiner.

2 cups unbleached flour

1 teaspoon baking powder

Pinch of salt

2 tablespoons cinnamon

Then use:

2 whole eggs

¾ cup sugar

2 tablespoons unsalted butter

½ cup oil

¾ teaspoon almond extract

1 teaspoon vanilla extract

1 cup chopped walnuts

½ cup softened raisins

Cover ½ cup raisins with hot water until they soften.

Sift and set aside the dry ingredients.

Combine the eggs, sugar, butter, and oil in a food processor until well mixed. Add the almond and vanilla extracts and add the mixture to the dry ingredients and mix well. Add the nuts and softened raisins.

With a floured hand, divide the dough into 3 logs. Place on a greased cookie sheet (Pam works well). Bake for 20 minutes at 350°F, watching carefully so that the dough does not burn. When done, remove the logs from the oven and cut into diagonal slices. Return the slices to the cookie sheet and bake an additional 5 to 8 minutes.

Easter in Italy

The greatest event in the history of mankind is the Resurrection of Jesus Christ that is celebrated each year on Easter Sunday. The reason the Passion, Death, and Resurrection of Jesus were the greatest events in Christian's history is because through the paschal mystery humans were freed from the bonds of sin and death and were enabled to become once again the children of God and heirs of heaven.

I have had the privilege of spending one Easter season in Rome. Although it would be ludicrous to declare Easter an exclusively Roman holiday, Easter and Rome do have a special relationship. Few will dispute the fact that watching the Pope officiate at Easter Sunday mass, amid the divinely inspired glory that is Saint Peter's Basilica, can make the mortal spirit feel as if it has gotten a genuine glimpse of heaven.

Easter in Rome is a series of splendid images and gripping emotions that can humble the mighty and uplift the lowly. From the happiness of Palm Sunday, when the Pope leads an impressive procession before throngs waving plaited fronds and olive branches sprayed with silver and gold; through the solemnity of Holy Thursday, when the Pope reenacts Christ's washing of His Apostles' feet beneath Bernini's magnificent baldachin; it is the sadness of Good Friday and the relief and anticipation felt on Holy Saturday, when each church prepares for the feast to follow by blessing the holy water and paschal candle, and it is the unbridled joy of Easter itself, when the Pope celebrates morning mass and delivers his traditional *Urbi et Orbi* (*To the City and to the World*) message to the crowds embraced by Bernini's massive colonnade. The atmosphere that pervades Rome at Easter is as vibrant as the colors of the azaleas that adorn the Spanish Steps at this festive time of year.

As with most holidays, food plays an integral part in a true Roman Easter celebration. After the abstinence from meat and days of individual fasting that marked
Lent, Easter is a time to rejoice and enjoy the fruits of a renewed earth.

Lamb, which in the Christian tradition is a symbol of Christ and which was used
during the first Passover to save the Jews from the wrath of the Almighty, is a popular main course throughout the world at Easter. For the Romans, lamb is especially appropriate, for the Latins were a sheep-herding people even before the days
of the Empire. Surprisingly, the Romans can boast that even Easter eggs have a Roman connection. According to Russian tradition, Mary Magdalene gave an egg that
had turned red in her hand to the Roman Emperor Tiberius as proof of the Resurrection. In Estonian lore, she is said to have offered it to Pilate, begging him not to
have Christ put to death.

The main ingredient of the Easter pie recipe that follows is wheat. Jesus himself
told us the parable about the grain of wheat that must die and be buried in order
for it to burst into new life. The grain of wheat was the symbol of His love and sacrifice. The Lord's Supper, or Eucharist, is a representation of Jesus' death, burial,
and resurrection. The following recipes are fitting symbols for Easter.

Pastiera di Grano

(EASTER COOKED-WHEAT PIE)

CRUST

2 cups all-purpose flour

¾ cup granulated sugar

¼ pound unsalted butter

One 16-gram pack of Paneangeli vanilla-

flavored baking powder or

1 teaspoon baking powder and

1 teaspoon vanilla extract, blended

in ¼ cup milk

Mix all the ingredients well. Knead for 5 minutes on a lightly floured surface. Shape into a round disk ¼ inch thick, wrap in plastic wrap, and refrigerate for ½ hour. Roll out the dough to fit into a 12½-inch wide 2-inch-deep pie tin.

PASTRY CREAM

½ cup sugar

¼ cup cornstarch

1 teaspoon vanilla extract

2 egg yolks

1 quart milk

Beat the sugar, cornstarch, vanilla, and egg yolks with a wire whisk in a large saucepan. Place on medium heat, add the milk, and whisk well. Whisk until the mixture comes to a boil and thickens. Remove from the heat and refrigerate. Meanwhile, make the filling:

FILLING

1 pound ricotta

½ cup sugar

1 can cooked wheat berries (found in
    Italian specialty shops)

Dilute the wheat berries with:

    1 tablespoon milk

1 teaspoon orange flour water or
    orange juice

2 egg yolks

1 teaspoon vanilla extract

½ cup candied citron, diced

¼ cup brandy

Beat all the ingredients well. Fold into the pastry cream. Pour into a greased large springform pan. Bake for 2 hours at 350°F. Allow to cool. This can be frozen and thawed to room temperature before serving.

Pizza Rustica

(RUSTIC PIE)

This pie is traditional for Easter and has its origins in Naples, where it is called Pizza Ghena or Full Pie; in northern Italy it is called Pizza Piena Alla Napolitana.

1 piecrust (packaged refrigerated crust works very well) or follow the recipe for Pasta Frolla Semplice, page 124

4 to 5 slices Genoa salami

¼ pound ham, cut into small chunks

1 small pepperoni, sliced or in chunks

¼ pound soppresate or cooked salami, sliced or in chunks

5 eggs, beaten

2 pounds ricotta

One 8-ounce package mozzarella, shredded or in chunks

¼ cup grated Romano cheese

¼ cup fresh chopped Italian flat-leaf parsley

Place the piecrust by pushing with your fingers to cover bottom completely in a springform pan. Mix all the ingredients and pour into the pan. Bake for 1 hour or until the top is brown. Allow the pie to cool in the oven with the door open for 1 hour. Serve warm or at room temperature.

Cannoli

(RICOTTA-FILLED PASTRIES)

These famous Sicilian favorites get their name from the Sicilian imagination. Cannoli means curls, the attractive curls on the hairstyles of beautiful Sicilian girls and women.

To make the pastry shells by hand is a long and tedious process; I suggest you do what I do; buy boxes of already made cannoli shells. These can be purchased by mail order or if you have an Italian import store near you, you can get them there. (Ferrara is the brand I use the most.)

FILLING

1 pound (500 grams) ricotta cheese with ¼ cup milk	4 ounces (100 grams) semisweet chocolate morsels
2 cups (250 grams) powdered sugar	3 ounces (80 grams) finely diced citrus
Pinch of ground cinnamon	24 pieces candied orange peel

In a standing heavy-duty mixer (I use my KitchenAid mixer), with whisk, cream the ricotta, sugar, and cinnamon. The cream should be thick and creamy; if not creamy enough, add another ½ pound ricotta and whip well.

Stir in the chocolate morsels and diced citron. Fill the shells from each side with a teaspoon or a wide-tipped pastry bag. Garnish each end with candied orange peel. Using a fine strainer or powdered sugar cup, dust the cannoli with the powdered sugar.

These are better than the already filled cannoli you can purchase at an Italian bakery shop.

You and your family will love these Sicilian specialties. Have napkins ready to wipe off the white moustaches created by the powdered sugar.

Do not refrigerate your filled cannoli! Refrigeration will make the cannoli soggy. Serve immediately after cooling.

Italian Family Christmas Memories

The season of Advent is the season of preparation for Christmas, when people all around the world anticipate and commemorate what they believe is the pivotal event in the history of humankind, the birth of Jesus of Nazareth through the Virgin Mary. Christmas, in the language of the church, is called the Feast of the Incarnation, when the second person of the Blessed Trinity, the Savior and Redeemer of the human race, took on the burden of human flesh. Incarnation, in simple terms, means "to become flesh."

Curiously, the Christian church prepares us for the celebration of Christ's first coming to earth with a reference to Christ's second coming in the gospel reading for the first Sunday of Advent. The point made in the reading is the unpredictability of the second coming, "No one knows the day nor the hour" (Mark 13:33–37). That being so, it makes sense to be ready at every moment of our lives. This is God's will, and as Dante stated: "In His will is our peace."

The mass for the Monday after the first Sunday of Advent sounds the theme of the Advent season: The second coming of the Lord will take place in the last day of the history of humankind when the peoples "from the east and the west shall assemble . . . at the banquet in the kingdom of God." The bread and wine that become the body and blood of Jesus at every mass is a foretaste of the banquet which we eagerly await after human history as we know it comes to an end and we enter the "new heavens and the new earth" planned for us by our loving father, God, through his Son Jesus Christ. Please take note of the word "banquet" and the elemental foodstuffs "bread and wine."

There is one Advent season that I shall never forget. The year was 1943. I still lived in the house where I was born, in Bayonne, New Jersey. World War II was raging in Europe and in the Pacific. My brother John, a soldier, was in the midst of fierce battles in Belgium. My mother and father listened daily to the Italian language newscasts on the radio and heard how their beloved Reggio Calabria was suffering death and destruction from the constant bombing by the allied forces. Their hearts were torn with worry about my brother John and the relatives they had left behind in Reggio Calabria nineteen years earlier.

I was only six years old and didn't quite understand all that was happening. I remember that Papa and Mamma spent every evening baking Italian Christmas cookies and allowing my brothers, Oreste, Anthony, and Dominick and my sister Evelyn and me to roll out the dough. My father, Giuseppe, worked as a longshoreman at the Pennsylvania railroad terminal in nearby Jersey City, New Jersey. In the early morning of November 17, 1943, I remember hearing Papa and Mamma in the kitchen as she pleaded with him not to go to work that day. She had a premonition that something terrible would happen to him. Papa said "Carmela, I must go to work or the kids won't eat."

Mamma kept me home from school that day because she didn't want to be alone. At precisely 3:00 P.M. a kindly Bayonne police officer knocked on our door. I clung to her apron as he told my mother that her husband had been in a serious accident at work. Mamma knew immediately that Papa was dead. She screamed, *É morto, mio marito é morto* ("He's dead, my husband is dead"). She collapsed. A few minutes later our small rented apartment was filled with our Italian neighbors. The policeman came back and gave the details to my oldest brother, Leo. Indeed, Giuseppe Orsini was crushed to death in an accident at work.

My very strong and courageous mamma decided to make the coming Christmas very special for her children, even though my papa would be missing. We all went to midnight mass, and then Mamma began to deep-fry the traditional Christmas Eve *zeppole,* a treat enjoyed by Calabrian families from Reggio. Our entire family assembled in the kitchen, hovering close to Mamma, impatiently waiting for the first batch to be done, and hardly allowing them to cool before we gobbled one up. Mamma's eyes were brimming with tears as she served her children the *zeppole* that Papa had taught her to make when they were first married. Here is Papa and Mamma Orsini's recipe for *zeppole,* which I have modernized a bit.

Zeppole 🦎

1 package active dry yeast, or
   2½ teaspoons Red Star or
   Fleischmann's dry yeast
1¼ cups lukewarm water

3 cups all-purpose flour
¼ teaspoon salt
1 cup vegetable oil, for frying

In a large measuring cup, dissolve the yeast with ¼ cup lukewarm water. Measure the flour and salt onto a large wooden pastry board. Make a well in the center of the flour and gradually add the dissolved yeast and the remaining water. Pull the flour with your fingers into the liquid. Knead for 8 minutes until the dough is smooth and elastic. Put the dough into a lightly oiled bowl. Turn to coat with oil, and cover with a thick towel. Let the dough rise in a warm place for 2 hours; it will double in size. Pinch off a piece of the dough the size of a golf ball, stretch it with your fingers into a 2- × 5-inch rectangle, and place it on wax or parchment paper. Repeat the process until all the dough is used. Then simply fold each rectangle to make plain zeppole.

Fry briskly in very hot oil at 500°F, a few at a time without crowding. Turn until all sides are golden and crisp, 3 to 4 minutes. Remove with a slotted spoon and drain on paper towels. Keep fried zeppole warm in a 170°F oven until all are cooked. For plain zeppole, sprinkle with powdered sugar while they are still hot. Serve them to your family and guests as you celebrate a southern Italian Christmas Eve antipasto.

Variation—If you wish you may place 1 or 2 drained anchovies in the center of each zeppola, fold over, twist, and pinch all edges tightly.

Gifts from the Heart—Homemade Italian Christmas Cookies

If your home is like my residence, then at this time of year your mailbox overflows with mail-order catalogs, department store flyers, and local shop notices that presuppose you never learned basic arithmetic and can't do addition. "Less than two weeks left for Christmas shopping!" they say. Radio and television newscasts join in the chorus: "You'd better get to the stores now; don't be a last-minute Christmas shopper!"

Wise shoppers bought their gifts at last year's sales at the end of January and saved tons of money. Even wiser shoppers will buy their friends and relatives my books, and save them as gifts for next Christmas.

The best gifts that one can give are family love and loyalty as expressed in the southern Italian manner—with food. It serves as something that holds families together. At Christmastime that means baking dozens and dozens of Italian cookies, a sweetness that is an expression of family love and makes life together very special.

We southern Italians begin our relationships as friends, and they soon become members of our extended families. At Christmastime we like to demonstrate to our dear ones that they are truly appreciated, so we spend hours in our kitchen preparing special cookies (biscotti) that take a great deal of time and effort. We then give tins or trays of biscotti that we made with care and love to our relatives and friends, and this says more about our feelings for one another than simply buying gifts from a store or catalog.

As soon as Thanksgiving Day was over, my papa and mamma spent every evening together making Italian Christmas cookies for all our *comari* and *compari*—either the godparents of their seven children or simply close friends of our family. The variety of biscotti was dazzling: almond cookies, anise cookies, *mostaccioli* (Calabrian chocolate cookies), *crispelle* (fluffy fried pastry chips), *amaretti* (macaroons), and *biscotti della Regina* (crispy sesame seed cookies). Papa stored these biscotti in brown paper shopping bags, carefully folding the tops of the bags several times to make them airtight, and hid them in the coolest and darkest places in our home. He always warned us kids not to open the bags because these biscotti were Christmas gifts for our friends. The week before Christmas he would call us all to the kitchen and show us the biggest bags of cookies. This bag, he would tell us, was the most special one because it was for our landlord's family, the Amatos. With a broad smile on his face, he would fold the top of this bag only once and hide in the pantry outside the kitchen door. He would warn us with a serious look, "Don't you dare touch these biscotti or you'll be sorry!"

When we thought that Mamma and Papa weren't looking, my brothers, my sister, and I would borrow a few biscotti every day from that forbidden bag. When Papa got home from work on the day before Christmas Eve, he loudly announced that he was going to get the Amato family's bag of biscotti and deliver it to Sam and Santuzza. We watched with trepidation as he entered the pantry to retrieve the huge paper sack of cookies. *"Marrona Mia!* The bag is empty. Someone ate all the biscotti. Who could have eaten them all?" We were practically wetting ourselves with fear. He then returned to the kitchen with one empty bag and one full one.

He sweetly smiled at each one of his kids and said, "Santa Closi came early this year and ate his whole bag of biscotti, but he left another full bag for the Amatos, *Grazie a Dio!"*

We were so relieved that we confessed to Papa that we ate all the biscotti. Papa said, *Sugno contento. Voi siti bravi e onesti fighioli e to papa e mamma vi vogghiuno tanto beni.* (I'm happy. You are good and honest kids, and your papa and mamma love you very much.)

Sta sera facimo I pretrali! (Tonight we'll make *petrali* [fig, raisin, *and nut-filled cookies*]. These were our favorite Christmas cookies.

Petrali

PASTRY

4½ cups all-purpose flour

3 teaspoons baking powder

⅔ cup granulated sugar

¾ teaspoon salt

1 tablespoon freshly grated orange
zest (peel)—wash the orange well,
and grate only the skin, being

careful not to get any of the
white bitter pith beneath the
skin

1¼ stick softened unsalted butter or
¾ cup plus 3 tablespoons light
olive oil

1⅓ cups cold water

FILLING

1¼ cups dried figs, stems removed

1¼ cups seedless raisins

¾ cup almonds, shelled

¾ cup walnuts, shelled

½ cup semisweet chocolate bits

¼ cup honey

2 tablespoons freshly grated orange
zest (peel) and the juice of the
orange

1 tablespoon cinnamon

Powdered sugar, for sprinkling

Preheat the oven to 400°F.

In a large mixing bowl, add most of the flour, baking powder, sugar, salt, and orange zest. With a pastry blender, cut in the butter or olive oil. Add the water gradually and mix with your fingers until the dough holds together. If sticky, add the remaining flour. Put on a lightly floured surface and knead for 4 to 5 minutes. (I use my KitchenAid mixer. I pour all the ingredients in the bowl and mix with the paddle until the dough is formed. Then I change to a dough hook and knead on number 2 speed for 5 minutes.) Put the dough in a lightly greased bowl, turn to coat, cover, and refrigerate while making the filling.

Fit the food processor with the metal blade. Add the figs, raisins, almonds, walnuts, and chocolate bits. Pulse until the contents are chopped into ¼-inch pieces. Add the honey, orange juice, orange zest, and cinnamon. Pulse for 1 second 4 times.

Pull the dough to stretch it. Roll it into 2 long rectangles, about ⅛ inch thick and 9 inches wide. Divide the filling between each rectangle and spoon the filling down the center of each one. Fold the dough over the filing. Seal tightly with the tines of a fork. Bake each one on a greased cookie sheet for 30 minutes. When cool, cut into 1-inch slices. Store in tightly covered cookie tins. Sprinkle with powdered sugar before serving.

The Christmas Tree and the Nativity Scene in the Italian Manner

The tradition of the Christmas tree began in the dark misty forests of the Germanic pre-Christian Druids and was part of their pagan celebration of the Winter Solstice. When the early missionaries were sent by Rome to convert these Germanic and Celtic pagans, the wise missionaries transformed the pagan practice of decorating an evergreen tree into a Christian symbol. The evergreen tree now represented the eternal life won for us by the first coming of Jesus, the Son of God, into our world to bring us the good news of universal salvation through His sacrificial execution on the tree of the Holy Cross. The decorations of lights and garlands became symbols of the resurrection of Jesus and our own resurrection that is to come at the end of time.

The Christmas tree tradition eventually spread all over Christian Europe and eventually into Italy. But one Italian, Francesco Bernadone whom we know as Saint Francis of Assisi, was uncomfortable with the pagan origin of the Christmas tree and invented an Italian Catholic symbol of the birth of Jesus Christ. He planned and organized a living tableaux dramatizing St. Luke's story—that of Christ's birth in an animal stable in a cave on the outskirts of Bethlehem. In the woods near Assisi, he gathered people and live animals to depict the Nativity. He constructed an altar and asked a priest to celebrate midnight mass right in front of the first Presepio, crèche, or nativity scene, to help the mostly illiterate peasants understand the tremendous significance of the birth of Christ through the Blessed Virgin Mary.

The event was so dramatic and moving that the members of his order, the Friars Minor (Franciscans), spread its use throughout Italy, then France, and eventually throughout the world wherever Franciscan missionaries were sent.

In later centuries, the Nativity scenes became beautiful works of art in wooden sculptures and ceramic figures. The most remarkable ones were created in southern Italy, especially in Naples, Calabria, and Sicily. Today, in most Christian homes, the Presepio, crèche, or nativity scene is in a special place of honor reserved for it beneath the Christmas tree.

In both Italy and in Italian parishes in our own country, the nativity scene is placed right in front of the main altar of the church, and Christmas trees adorn the spaces behind or on the side of the altar.

The manger is usually empty until the beginning of midnight mass on Christmas Eve. The churches are muted and darkened. Then, to the Christmas hymn *Tu scendi dalle stele* ("You come down from the stars"), written by the founder of the Redemptionist Order, Saint Alfonso Liguori, the pastor carries the figure of the baby Jesus in a solemn procession down the center aisle of the church and places the statue of the infant Jesus in the manger. Now all the lights of the church are switched on to signify that the Light of the World, the Savior Jesus, dispels all darkness, and the beautiful mass begins.

When I was a young priest in the many parishes I served, there were literally dozens of phone calls from parishioners every Christmas Eve afternoon until right before midnight mass with the same question: "What time does midnight mass begin?" We in the rectory knew that the phone calls came from what we called "C and E Catholics," that is, Christmas and Easter Catholics whose only contacts with the church were on these two great feasts. I would thank God that these twice-a-year church-attending Catholics were at least coming to midnight mass and that perhaps they would now become weekly members of mass every Sunday.

Please remember that back then Christmas Eve was a day of abstinence from eating meat. This tradition of abstaining from meat on Christmas Eve reflected the fact that the Son of God, Jesus, became incarnate (that means he took on flesh), and it was only proper and respectful not to eat animal flesh (meat) on that special day.

One year, when I was a parish priest, at a predominately Sicilian-Italian-American parish, I was introduced to a delicious Sicilian custom. I was invited to a wonderfully warm Sicilian-American's home after midnight mass to partake of their post-midnight mass feast.

The matriarch of the family, Nonna Carmelina Girgenti, served her platters of homemade sweet and hot grilled sausages surrounded by a medley of roasted green, red, and yellow bell peppers mixed with crisp roasted potatoes. Huge loaves of homemade Sicilian semolina bread artistically twisted and covered with crunchy sesame seeds were on the table. Gallons of her husband Carmelo's ruby red wine, made in his basement in October, were gathered on the floor right next to his chair at the table.

What a feast! What joy! What family love! Even today, many years later, my post-midnight mass feast is a huge sandwich of good grilled sausage smothered with al dente bell peppers and crisp roasted potatoes washed down with Sicilian red wine. By the way, my grandfather, Don Letterio Amore, was a Sicilian from

Messina. I'm proud to say I am part Sicilian, and am, therefore, entitled to celebrate Christmas Sicilian style.

A Calabrian Christmas Eve

In most southern Italian homes, both here and in Italy, Christmas Eve demands observing two absolute rules; the first requires the family to gather around the dining room table for a feast of fish; the second was attendance as a family at midnight mass.

An old Calabrian proverb *U pisci nata sempri: nta lacqua, nto; l'ogghiu, e nto vino* ("The fish swims always in water, in oil, and in wine") is truest on Christmas Eve.

For innumerable centuries the ruggedly beautiful coastline along the Tyrrhenian and Ionian seas of Calabria has provided Calabrians with a wealth of seafood. Almost 20 percent of all the world's swordfish are still harpooned off the coast of Bagnara Calabria and in Scilla, both of which are in the province of Reggio Calabria. The same techniques that were used by the Greek colonists who came to this enchanting land as far back as 12,000 B.C. are still used today to harvest these great fish. Each morning, as the mists of dawn slowly rise, small fishing boats can be seen bringing in their daily catch from the previous night's hunt for swordfish.

The ancient Romans had access to a large variety of fish, but because of the impossibility of transporting freshly caught fish inland to the city or Rome, the fish were dried in the sun and/or salted to preserve them for later use. This tradition continues today with baccalà, dried, salted cod.

Today, most fish in Italy are only hours out of the water when bought at the *pescevendoli* (fresh fish stands) and cooked both in the home and in restaurants. Very recently, the Italian government has cracked down on restaurants that try to pass off frozen fish as fresh. A law was passed that caused restaurants to list their fish in prominent print to indicate whether the fish they serve is fresh or frozen. This would be a good law in our country also, because frozen fish and seafood do not taste the same as fresh, and once defrosted, become very soggy. It is your right as a consumer in a restaurant to ask your waiter if the seafood or fish you are about to order is fresh or frozen. In some authentic Italian restaurants, both in Italy and in the United States, live selections can be made from a clear glass water tank; in others, the preparation and cooking of your choice of fish can be viewed from start to finish. If both of these opportunities are available, know that when your meal is set before you there will be no fish smell at all.

Traditionally, southern Italians who live on the coasts of the regions of Molise, Campania, Puglia, Basilicata, Calabria, Sicilia, and Sardegna may consume on Christmas Eve either seven different dishes (symbolizing the seven sacraments), or nine (to symbolize the Trinity multiplied by three), or finally, thirteen (to symbolize the twelve Apostles and Christ).

Many varieties of fresh Italian fish are available in the United States: swordfish, fresh tuna, anchovies, sea trout, clams, sardines, mussels, red mullet, squid, octopus, prawns, crab, eel, sole, whiting, and either fresh or dried, salted cod.

Each region that I named has its own recipes for preparing fish. Most of them are simple preparations that allow the fresh, subtle flavor of the fish to remain intact. Only fish that are not fresh are smothered with sauces or overpowered with too many flavors to mask its age.

It is best to purchase fish the day you plan to serve it. The flesh beneath the shiny skin should be white and firm and have absolutely no odor. The eyes should be clear and bright. Rinse immediately in cold water, pat dry with paper towels, place on a platter, and cover loosely with paper towels, not plastic wrap. Have your fish seller scale and gut the fish when you buy it. If you want it skinned and filleted, your fish seller can do that, too.

When baking fish, remember that your oven's heat will sap most of the fish's natural moisture. To prevent that, brush lightly with olive oil and coat with bread crumbs seasoned with minced fresh garlic and freshly grated Parmesan or pecorino cheese. Bake fish if it's thick at 350°F; if thin, bake quickly at 425°F.

Do not overcook!

If you would like to make the traditional Calabrian Christmas Eve baked cod with potatoes and tomatoes (Baccalà Agghiota), then purchase your dried/salted cod three days before cooking. Try to get pieces in a large pan, cover with cold water, and refrigerate. (Cover the pan tightly with plastic and aluminum foil, or your refrigerator will be filled with a very strong fishy smell. Soak for three days to remove the salt. Turn the pieces periodically and change the water every six hours. On the third day, the cod will be plump, soft, fleshy, and well hydrated. Rinse under cold running water, drain, and pat dry, then try the following recipe.

1 pound dried cod, processed according to directions above

2 tablespoons olive oil

3 medium potatoes, peeled and diced

2 medium onions, peeled and diced

one 16-ounce can Italian peeled plum tomatoes with their juice, coarsely chopped

½ cup crushed and chopped Italian flat-leaf parsley

½ cup seedless raisins, plumped in warm water, drained

¼ cup *pignoli* (pine nuts), lightly toasted in a dry skillet on the stove

2 tablespoons capers, rinsed and drained

¼ cup green olives, brine-cured, pitted, and sliced

1 teaspoon salt

1½ teaspoons freshly ground black pepper

Preheat the oven to 325°.

Remove any skin and bones from the fish, dry with paper towels, and cut into 6 pieces.

Grease a 9- × 12-inch-deep ovenproof dish with 1 tablespoon olive oil. Layer ⅓ of the potatoes, ½ of the onions, ½ of the cod, and ½ of the tomatoes. Sprinkle with ½ of the parsley. Add the raisins, pine nuts, capers, olives, and the rest of the potatoes, onions, and cod. Pour in the rest of the tomatoes, season with salt, pepper, and the remaining parsley. Drizzle the remaining 1 tablespoon olive oil over the top and bake uncovered for 45 minutes. Remove from the oven and let rest for 10 minutes. Serve in soup bowls and have plenty of crusty Italian bread available to scoop up the sauce.

Remember, at least 7, 9, or 13 more fish or seafood dishes are going to follow in this same meal. Enjoy and *buono natale*! (A blessed Christmas to you all!)

Panettone

(CHRISTMAS BREAD)

Panettone *is a porous rich egg bread studded with candied fruit. Its origins are found in the city of Milan. No bread has so many stories of its origins. Some say it means a big fancy bread. In Italy today the most popular* panettones *are manufactured by the Motta and Allemagna companies. These two companies produce 55 million pounds of* panettones *a year. It goes very well with espresso coffee, cappuccino, or tea.*

SPONGE

2½ teaspoons dry yeast

⅓ cup warm water (105°)

½ cup unbleached white flour or whole wheat

Stir the yeast into the water in a small bowl; let stand for 10 minutes covered with plastic wrap. Stir in the flour well. Cover tightly and let rise for 30 minutes.

FIRST DOUGH

2½ teaspoons dry yeast

3 tablespoons warm water (105°)

2 large eggs, at room temperature (This recipe calls for 7 large eggs. To bring them to room temperature, place them in a bowl and cover with hot tap water.)

1¼ cups white flour or whole wheat

¼ cup sugar or Splenda, for baking

½ stick unsalted butter, at room temperature

Use a stand-up electric mixer (I use a KitchenAid Pro-Line).

Stir the yeast in the bowl of your mixer with the warm water. Let stand covered for 10 minutes. Add the sponge, eggs, flour, and sugar and mix with the paddle attachment. Add the butter and mix on medium until absorbed. This will take about 6 minutes. Cover with plastic wrap and let rise until doubled, 1¼ hours. I put mine in my cold oven.

SECOND DOUGH

1 pound candied fruit (available at supermarkets for baking fruit cake)	2 tablespoons honey
	2 teaspoons pure vanilla extract
	1 teaspoon salt
2 large eggs	2 sticks unsalted butter, at room temperature
3 egg yolks	
¾ cup sugar or Splenda, for baking	3 cups of all-purpose flour, sifted

Add the eggs, egg yolks, sugar, honey, vanilla, salt, and flour to the first dough and mix well with the paddle (spray paddle and dough hook with vegetable spray; they will be easier to clean) for 6 minutes at medium speed. Add the butter and mix until smooth. Add the 3 cups sifted flour and mix until smooth. Change to the dough hook (invert the bottom of the springform pan; it will make it easier to remove the bread with a large spatula. You may freeze it and thaw overnight in the refrigerator before serving and knead for 5 minutes. Add 1 pound candied fruit to the cake mix and knead for 5 more minutes.

First Rise—Place the dough in a lightly oiled bowl, cover with plastic wrap, and let rise for 4 hours.

Shaping and Second Rise—The dough will be very sticky. Spoon into a well-greased 10-inch springform pan and smooth it with a wet spoon. Cover tightly with plastic wrap and a towel. Let rise for 2 hours.

Baking—Heat the oven to 400°F. Bake for 10 minutes. Reduce the heat to 375°F and bake for 50 minutes. Cool completely in the pan, about 1 hour. Unlock the springform pan and unmold on a wire rack. Cut and serve hefty slices.

The Tradition of Christmas Gifts

Many years ago, Italian children didn't receive Christmas season gifts until the eve of the Catholic Feast of the Epiphany, which takes place on January 6, according to the Church's calendar. In the Italian language the Epiphany is also called the Feast of the Holy Magi.

Epiphany comes from a Greek word that means disclosure or manifestation. In this case it refers to the disclosure that the child born of the Virgin Mary in Bethlehem was indeed the Messiah, the long awaited king of the Jews, the Savior who would free the Jewish people from oppression, bondage, and slavery imposed upon them by the Gentile invaders of the Holy Land.

This disclosure or manifestation could have been done in many ways: through a vision, an angelic messenger, or a divine proclamation. But God chose a star, and three Wise Men to understand it. The star of Bethlehem heralded the greatest event of all ages—the birth of Jesus Christ. It was not uncommon in ancient countries of the East to seek knowledge through the position and brilliance of the stars. God wanted to tell the Wise Men of the birth of his son, and He did so in a way they would understand, a new star in the heavens.

They followed the star to Bethlehem and each brought a significant gift. The gift of gold signified the Christ child's kingship; the incense proclaimed His divinity; and the myrrh, a rare perfume used in embalming the dead represented His humanity and acceptance of His sacrificial death. This is the origin of giving gifts to children during the Christmas season.

The Magi, as non-Jews, represented the gentile world which would also be saved and redeemed by the King of the Jews, the Savior of all who would come to believe in Him.

Many centuries later, when Italy was invaded and dominated by pagan Germanic and Celtic barbarian tribes, these tribes brought their kindly witches. After these tribes were converted to Christianity, most of the pagan beliefs were retained and "Christianized." Bad witches became those who gave their souls to Satan. Good witches became saintly creatures whom God used to help His people.

In northern Italy, which was peopled by these former Pagan Teutonic and Celtic tribes, one of their good witches was transformed into La Befana, a kindly old witch whom God used to bring gifts to children on the eve of the Feast of the Epiphany in remembrance of the gifts brought to the Christ child by the three Wise Men from the East.

Today in Italy, the tradition of La Befana has almost disappeared, and now Italian children receive their Christmas gifts through the personage of Saint Nicholas of Myra on Christmas Eve.

Saint Nicholas of Myra (a town in present-day Turkey) was a bishop and is undoubtedly one of the most popular saints to be honored in the Western world. In English-speaking countries, his memory has survived in the unique personality of Santa Claus, the rotund, white-bearded gentleman whose laughter captivates children the world over with promises of gifts on Christmas Eve. His legend as the jolly red-suited Father Christmas who lives at the North Pole and travels the skies of the world in a gift-laden sleigh pulled by flying reindeer, and who climbs down chimneys and deposits Christmas gifts to sleeping children, is celebrated even in non-Christian Japan.

In actuality, Saint Nicholas was a bishop in Myra. The most famous legend is that of a man of Patra, a town in Nicholas's diocese, who lost his fortune, and because he was unable to support his three unmarried daughters, planned to let them become prostitutes to support themselves and him. Nicholas heard of this man's intentions and secretly threw three bags of gold through a window into their home, thus providing dowries for the girls who could now marry honorably.

Nicholas died in A.D. 345 and his body was buried in the Cathedral of Myra. There it remained until 1087, when seamen of Bari, Italy, seized his bones and took them to their town. From that time, Saint Nicholas was known as San Nicola di Bari (Saint Nicholas of Bari).

Our present-day version of Saint Nicholas came to America in a distorted fashion. The Dutch Protestants carried a popularized version of the saint's life to New Amsterdam (now New York City), which portrayed Nicholas as nothing more than a Nordic magician and wonder worker. Our modern conception of Santa Claus grew from this version. Saint Nicholas, the real one, was a holy bishop and should be admired as a Saint of the Catholic Church, not the jolly old saint Nick from the long poem *A Visit from St. Nicholas.* The only food I can think of that is connected to this story are the proverbial milk and cookies that children leave for Santa to strengthen him for his hard work every Christmas Eve.

Christmas is a special season for the world, Christian and non-Christian, because it inspires the dream of peace for all of us who inhabit this planet and believe in the essential goodness of humankind.

Healthy Baking

I am a diabetic and must follow a special diet. You can still enjoy all these wonderful breads and sweet baked goods as I do.

Simply substitute stone-ground whole wheat flour for white flour.

Instead of sugar use pourable artificial sweetener. Dietetic sugarless jams, jellies, and marmalades are available in most supermarkets and health food shops.

If you are being careful about cholesterol, substitute olive or canola oils for butter, margarine, or lard.

Here is a conversion chart for using monounsaturated and polyunsaturated oils instead of saturated fats.

BAKING WITH OLIVE OIL

Butter or Margarine	Olive Oil
1 teaspoon	¾ teaspoon
1 tablespoon	2¼ teaspoons
2 tablespoons	1½ tablespoons
¼ cup	3 tablespoons
⅓ cup	¼ cup
½ cup	¼ cup and 2 tablespoons
⅔ cup	½ cup
¾ cup	½ cup and 1 tablespoon
1 cup	¾ cup

When you use olive oil instead of butter or margarine, your cookies and pastries will be lighter and crisper and your cakes fluffier and much moister.

Now get into your kitchen and bake guiltless breads, mouthwatering tarts and pies, and all the goodies you crave.

I wish you . . .

Good Food

Warm Friends

Long Life!

May God Bless You!

Father Giuseppe Orsini

Tips for the Baker in Your Family

Freezing Temperature
32 Degrees Fahrenheit (32°F) = 0 Degrees Celsius (0°C)

Boiling Temperature
212 Degrees Fahrenheit (212°F) = 85 Degrees Celsius (85°C)

USA Liquid Ingredients
¼ cup = 2 fluid ounces = 12 teaspoons
½ cup = 4 fluid ounces = 8 tablespoons
1 cup = 8 fluid ounces = ½ pint
2 cups = 16 fluid ounces = 1 pint
4 cups = 42 fluid ounces = 1 quart
½ gallon = 64 fluid ounces = 2 quarts
1 gallon = 128 fluid ounces = 4 quarts

Cooking Conversion Table
Dry Ingredients (USA to Metric)
1 teaspoon = 5 ml
3 teaspoons = 15 ml
6 teaspoons = 30 ml
¼ cup = 60 ml

$\frac{1}{3}$ cup = 90 ml

$\frac{1}{2}$ cup = 120 ml

$\frac{2}{3}$ cup = 160 ml

$\frac{3}{4}$ cup = 175 ml

1 cup = 250 ml

1 ounce = 25 grams

2 ounces = 50 grams

4 ounces = 100 grams

8 ounces = 200 grams

$\frac{3}{4}$ pound = 300 grams

1 pound = 500 grams

Cooking Measurement Equivalents

16 tablespoons = 1 cup

12 tablespoons = $\frac{3}{4}$ cup

8 tablespoons = $\frac{1}{2}$ cup

6 tablespoons = $\frac{3}{8}$ cup

5 tablespoons plus 1 teaspoon = $\frac{1}{3}$ cup

4 tablespoons = $\frac{1}{4}$ cup

2 tablespoons = $\frac{1}{8}$ cup

2 tablespoons plus 2 teaspoons = $\frac{1}{6}$ cup

1 tablespoon = $\frac{1}{16}$ cup

2 cups = 1 pint

2 pints = 1 quart

3 teaspoons = 1 tablespoon

48 teaspoons = 1 cup

Oven Temperatures

	FAHRENHEIT	CELSIUS
Very slow	250–275 degrees	120–135 degrees
Slow	300–325 degrees	150–165 degrees
Moderate	350–375 degrees	180–190 degrees
Hot	400–425 degrees	200–220 degrees
Very hot	450–475 degrees	230–245 degrees
Extremely hot	500–525 degrees	260–275 degrees

Emergency Substitutions

1 cup cake flour = 1 cup minus 2 tablespoons all-purpose flour

1 cup all-purpose flour = 1 cup plus 2 tablespoons cake flour

1 cup self-rising flour = 1 cup all-purpose flour plus ½ teaspoon baking powder and ½ teaspoon salt

1 cup granulated sugar = 1 cup brown sugar or 2 cups confectioners' sugar

½ cup brown sugar = ½ cup granulated sugar plus 2 tablespoons molasses

1 package active dry yeast = 1 cake compressed fresh yeast

1 square unsweetened chocolate = 3 tablespoons unsweetened cocoa powder plus 1 tablespoon vegetable oil or butter

1 cup buttermilk = 1 cup whole milk plus 1 tablespoon white vinegar or lemon juice. Stir and let stand 2 minutes or use 1 cup plain yogurt or sour cream.

1 cup plain yogurt = 1 cup sour cream

1 cup whole milk = ½ cup evaporated milk plus ½ cup water. Or use dry milk and follow the package instructions to reconstitute the amount you need.

1 cup raisins = 1 cup currants or other dried fruits such as cranberries, blueberries, and cherries

1 tablespoon cornstarch = 2 tablespoons flour (for thickening purposes)

1 cup corn syrup = 1 cup sugar plus ¼ cup water

1 cup honey = 1¼ cups granulated sugar plus ¼ cup liquid

Pan Size Substitutions

Sometimes you just don't have the right size pan on hand. If you substitute pan sizes, be sure to closely monitor the baking time of your items. It will most likely change. If you substitute glass for metal pans, be sure to lower the baking temperature by 25 degrees.

Rectangular 12 × 7½	8 cups	None
Rectangular 13 × 9	15 cups	Two 9-inch rounds or three 8-inch rounds
Rectangular 11 × 7	8 cups	None
Square 8 × 8	8 cups	11 × 7, 12 × 7½, 9 × 5 loaf, or two 8-inch rounds
Square 9 × 9	10 cups	None
Round 8 inch	5 cups	10 × 6 or 8½ × 4½ loaf
Round 9 inch	6 cups	None

Eggs

Always use large unless otherwise indicated. Eggs should also always be at room temperature. If you take them cold from the refrigerator, place them in a bowl of very hot water for 10 minutes.

Index